Wiley Study Guide for Level I CFA Exam

Volume 4: Corporate Finance, Portfolio Management, & Equity

Thousands of candidates from more than 100 countries have relied on these Study Guides to pass the CFA® Exam. Covering every Learning Outcome Statement (LOS) on the exam, these review materials are an invaluable tool for anyone who wants a deep-dive review of all the concepts, formulas, and topics required to pass.

Wiley study materials are produced by expert CFA charterholders, CFA Institute members, and investment professionals from around the globe. For more information, contact us at info@efficientlearning.com.

Wiley Study Guide for 2019 Level I CFA Exam

Volume 4: Corporate Finance, Portfolio Management, & Equity

WILEY

Contents

ABOUT THE AUTHORS

Wiley's Study Guides are written by a team of highly qualified CFA charterholders and leading CFA instructors from around the globe. Our team of CFA experts work collaboratively to produce the best study materials for CFA candidates available today.

Wiley's expert team of contributing authors and instructors is led by Content Director Basit Shajani, CFA. Basit founded online education start-up Élan Guides in 2009 to help address CFA candidates' need for better study materials. As lead writer, lecturer, and curriculum developer, Basit's unique ability to break down complex topics helped the company grow organically to be a leading global provider of CFA Exam prep materials. In January 2014, Élan Guides was acquired by John Wiley & Sons, Inc., where Basit continues his work as Director of CFA Content. Basit graduated magna cum laude from the Wharton School of Business at the University of Pennsylvania with majors in finance and legal studies. He went on to obtain his CFA charter in 2006, passing all three levels on the first attempt. Prior to Élan Guides, Basit ran his own private wealth management business. He is a past president of the Pakistani CFA Society.

There are many more expert CFA charterholders who contribute to the creation of Wiley materials. We are thankful for their invaluable expertise and diligent work. To learn more about Wiley's team of subject matter experts, please visit: www.efficientlearning.com/cfa/why-wiley/.

READING 33: CORPORATE GOVERNANCE AND ESG: AN INTRODUCTION

LESSON 1: CORPORATE GOVERNANCE AND ESG: AN INTRODUCTION

LOS 33a: Describe corporate governance. Vol 4, pp 6–8

Corporate governance is increasing in its significance with investment professionals and investors. Due to various high-profile accounting scandals and corporate bankruptcies, the importance of understanding the framework that is used to define the rights, roles, and responsibilities of stakeholders continues to grow.

Corporate governance is defined as the system of internal controls and procedures through which individual companies are managed. It aims to minimize and manage conflicts of interest between those within the company and stakeholder. In the 1990s, a couple of different reports helped to shape the landscape of corporate governance. One report, which was the genesis of corporate governance, was the Cadbury Report (named after its chairman). It defined corporate governance as simply "the system by which companies are directed and controlled."

Governance varies by jurisdiction, and reflects influences in either shareholder or stakeholder theory. Shareholder theory leans more toward maximizing shareholder return, while stakeholder theory has a much broader company focus. In stakeholder theory, emphasis is placed on the various stakeholders when taken together, although they have separate interests in the company.

Various reports have been issued in the recent past that continue to place emphasis on corporate governance. There is a global movement toward convergence between jurisdictions of regulations that have similar principles.

LOS 33b: Describe a company's stakeholder groups and compare interests of stakeholder groups. Vol 4, pp 8–11

A stakeholder is any person or group that has an interest in the company. Not all stakeholders' interests are aligned in the same manner, and they often are in conflict with one another. There are approximately seven primary stakeholder groups within a corporation:

1. Shareholders
2. Creditors
3. Employees (managers, executives, other)
4. Board of directors
5. Customers
6. Suppliers
7. Governments/regulators

Shareholders provide capital to the company and are entitled to the company's net value. They are typically focused on those efforts that support growing the profitability of the company and maximizing the value of it. Even though they have little involvement in the company's activities, they elect the board of directors and vote on important resolutions.

Creditors have little influence on the company, other than covenants and restrictions they can put in place as its banks or bondholders. They receive interest and principal payments, and have a primary goal of being repaid through the company's ability to generate cash flow. Creditors look for stability, in contrast to shareholders, who may desire and are willing to tolerate higher risks to obtain higher returns.

Employees have a significant stake in the company's operation, as they are paid salaries as well as other incentives and perquisites for their work. It is in their best interest to protect their position, and to increase their compensation in different time frames through incentives, even though it may not be in the best interest of the company in the short or long term.

The **board of directors** acts in the best interest of the shareholders who elect them. They oversee the operations through monitoring the company and management performance while providing strategic direction.

Customers would like a product that is a good value for the price and is safe to operate. In addition, they desire ongoing support. If done properly, this will increase the future value of the company through greater name recognition, safety records, and sales, but it requires potentially greater cost, which may harm profitability.

Company **suppliers** have a goal of being paid for their services and materials. They are viewed alongside creditors as they see financial stability as an important attribute toward achieving their objective.

The **government and regulators** wish to protect the economy and the interests of the general public. Implementing procedures or guidelines that increase costs or additional burdens on the company can be at odds with other stakeholders. In addition, regulators have an interest in having corporations act within the guidelines of the law on a consistent basis.

Nonprofit organizations tend to differ from those that are for-profit as they do not have shareholders. Stakeholders generally are focused on serving the intended cause while utilizing funds as agreed. These stakeholders include volunteers, donors, organizations, patrons, trustees, employees, board of directors, and others.

LOS 33c: Describe principal–agent and other relationships in corporate governance and the conflicts that may arise in these relationships. Vol 4, pp 11–13

Key Relationships in Corporate Governance

When a principal hires an agent to act on its behalf, a principal–agent relationship is created. Embedded in the relationship are characteristics involving trust, an expectation of loyalty, and other obligations to act in the best interest of the principal. However, conflicts can occur due to the inherent interests of both parties. Five key relationships to consider for potential conflicts are the following:

1. Shareholder and manager/director relationships
2. Controlling and minority shareholders
3. Manager and board relationships
4. Shareholder versus creditor interests
5. Other stakeholder conflicts

Shareholder and Manager/Director Relationships

Directors and managers are agents of the shareholders. They are given the power to transact business on the shareholders' behalf, with the intent of serving the shareholders' best interest. However, these employees may take on more risk than is warranted to maximize their personal benefits for remuneration and perquisites. They have "information asymmetry" due to their proximity to the business. This situation may weaken the shareholders' control over them, while allowing the employees to make the principals' best interest a lower priority.

Controlling and Minority Shareholders

Another relationship that may lead to conflicts is between a **controlling** and a **minority** shareholder group that adopts a **straight voting** structure (one vote for each share owned). This framework would clearly allow the controlling group significant power, as they hold enough shares to exercise control. Voting on takeover offers that benefit the controlling group and create no value for the minority group has been documented in several high-profile cases. In addition, related-party transactions also become a concern when a controlling group has the power to vote on items that are in their best interest, but not in the minority group's interest.

An equity structure that has multiple share classes in which one class is nonvoting (or limited) will create a divergence between ownership and control rights. This has traditionally been called a dual-class structure whereby the founders, executives, and other key insiders control the company by holding the superior voting power.

Manager and Board Relationships

Conflicts between the board of directors and management can arise when limited information is provided to the board. This will reduce the directors' ability to perform their monitoring function. It is particularly pronounced for those who are not involved in day-to-day operations, specifically a nonexecutive director.

Shareholder versus Creditor Interests

The relationship between shareholders and creditors has the basis for differences due to the risk tolerance and expected return of each side. A shareholder takes additional risk for greater return; however, a creditor looks for stability and lower risk. Increasing leverage creates risk and is at odds with a creditor's desire.

Other Stakeholder Conflicts

Other stakeholder conflicts can arise between various groups. The following are three examples, to name a few:

1. If a company decides to reduce product safety, this can cause a conflict between customers and shareholders, as customers want a safe product, but shareholders want to reduce costs and increase profits.
2. Customers and suppliers may be at conflict when the company extends lenient credit terms to customers. This will affect the ability of the company to repay suppliers on time.
3. If a government reduces the tax burden on a company, that is beneficial for the shareholders but detrimental to the tax base of the government, thereby causing a conflict.

LOS 33d: Describe stakeholder management. Vol 4, pg 14

Stakeholder Management

Identifying the various stakeholder positions and relationships is the basis for managing the potential conflicts that arise. It then requires understanding and prioritizing these positions, and dealing with them in a methodical and logical manner.

The two most important aspects of stakeholder management are effective communication and active engagement. In order to balance the various positions and reduce conflict, a framework is built. The foundation is constructed from the various legal, contractual, organizational, and governmental components that define the rights, responsibilities, and powers of each group.

- The legal infrastructure lays out the framework of rights established by law as well as the ease or availability of legal recourse.
- The contractual infrastructure is the means used to secure the rights of both parties through contractual agreements between the company and its stakeholders.
- The manner in which the company manages its stakeholder relationships through its governance procedures, internal systems, and practices is the organizational structure.
- The regulations imposed on the company are considered the governmental infrastructure.

LOS 33e: Describe mechanisms to manage stakeholder relationships and mitigate associated risks. Vol 4, pp 15–20

There is no standard approach to managing stakeholders, and it will vary across companies and cultures. However, there are 10 common elements that are seen among various companies:

1. General meetings
2. Board of directors
3. Audit function
4. Reporting and transparency
5. Remuneration policies
6. Say on pay
7. Contractual agreements with creditors
8. Employee laws and contracts
9. Contractual agreements with customers and suppliers
10. Laws and regulations

General Meetings

One of the most widely adopted practices in mitigating agency problems is the general meeting. Shareholders have the right to participate in these meetings and exercise their voting rights. When they are unable to attend a meeting, they have the ability to have their shares voted by another person they authorize. This is called proxy voting. With a cumulative voting structure (compared to straight voting), shareholders have the ability to accumulate and vote all their shares for a single candidate in an election involving more than one director.

At general annual meetings, shareholders will be presented with the annual audited financial statements as well as an overview of the company's performance and activities. Shareholders are able to better monitor the company through a direct exchange of information. Extraordinary general meetings may be called and could include special resolutions that will require larger voting margins to pass, typically including amendments to bylaws, mergers, and so on.

Board of Directors

The board of directors acts as the link between shareholders and managers, as it is impractical in a complex ownership structure for shareholders to be involved in the direct running of the company. Shareholders will then monitor board activities and exercise their voting power to elect members to the board (or remove them). The main responsibilities of the board include evaluating management performance and assisting in strategy, as well as supervising the audit, control, and risk management functions.

Audit Function

The audit function not only helps to provide assurances that financial statements are properly reported, but also provides a service that evaluates the control environment within a company. It reviews and analyzes the various systems, controls, and policies/procedures that are in place to examine the operations and the manner in which financial information is accumulated. External auditors are independent from the company and elected by the shareholders (though recommended by the audit committee).

Reporting and Transparency

Due to additional transparency of reported information, shareholders can acquire a great deal of information from various sources. These sources include, but aren't limited to, required filings such as quarterly and yearly reporting, as well as information from social media. This reduces information asymmetry and allows the shareholders to better assess performance of the company and the board.

The handling of related-party transactions has become a point of focus because it may benefit an insider to the detriment of the company due to a related-party relationship, and thus it is increasingly common that policies in this area are implemented among companies. These procedures require disclosure of any potential or actual situations, whether direct or indirect. The policies are put in place to reduce issues related to transparency, risk, and management of potential issues.

Remuneration Policies

Another important area requiring management is executive remuneration. Aligning pay with shareholder interests helps to ensure that long-term strategies are implemented that will benefit the overall value of the company. The most common potential issues arise when executives act in the short term ("short-termism") to increase their own pay or take on excessive risk. Some companies have even implemented clawback provisions whereby they will recover previous remuneration if certain events or misconduct occurs.

Say on Pay

Say on pay is a concept that helps to decrease potential conflicts and issues with shareholders by gaining their insights on the company's remuneration policy. It was first introduced in the United Kingdom in the early 2000s. The implementation varies by country. Some have nonmandatory and nonbinding say on pay systems (e.g., Canada), which means that the company is required to ask for feedback on renumeration policies, but is not required to act upon it. Those systems that have less force draw criticism because of the limited impact they may have. By contrast, in the Netherlands, the United Kingdom, and China, the system is mandatory and binding. Other systems are found somewhere between the two extremes.

Contractual Agreements with Creditors

Another management tool is the contractual agreement with creditors. The **indenture** is a legal contract that outlines the obligations and rights of the issuer and the bondholder. Normally, there will be **covenants** within the indenture that identify actions that are both required (e.g., providing periodic financials) and prohibited (e.g., additional or excessive debt). **Collaterals** are another way to further increase the likelihood of repayment through the offering of assets or financial guarantees.

Employee Laws and Contracts

The framework that outlines employee rights is based on labor law. This will vary by geographic area, but will include such items as working hours, hiring and firing, pensions, and other employee benefits. Employment contracts are for the individual and outline the employee's rights and responsibilities; they are not all-encompassing, leaving some discretion within the relationship. Other items such as the code of ethics and human resources documents are intended to outline the relationship in order to manage and mitigate any legal or reputational risks.

Contractual Agreements with Customers and Suppliers

Customers and suppliers have contractual agreements that explain the relationship with the company, including the financial relationship (e.g., price, terms, support, and any guarantee provisions).

Laws and Regulations

The government and regulators seek to protect the public through developing laws and monitoring compliance. Regulations vary by industry and increase with the level of risk that the public is exposed to.

LOS 33f: Describe functions and responsibilities of a company's board of directors and its committees. Vol 4, pp 21–25

The Board of Directors

The board of directors monitors the management and strategic direction of the company, while reporting to shareholders. The makeup of the board depends primarily on the size, structure, and complexity of the company. Diversity of experience, knowledge, and skill sets gives the board strength. Having business insights in regard to key areas of responsibility, including the following, is key to performing their positions properly:

- Strategy
- Finance
- Audit
- Risk management
- Human resources

A one-tier structure is made of executive (internal) directors and nonexecutive (external) directors who offer objective insight. A two-tier system has a supervisory board and a management board that are independent of each other. There is a trend to separate the CEO from the chairperson role, which is called the "CEO duality."

The general practice is to elect the entire board simultaneously for a specified term (three years, for example). However, other companies have **staggered boards**, which will break the board into three classes, and have separate elections in consecutive years. This will require several years for shareholders to elect the entire board, thereby limiting their ability to effect major change of control at the company quickly.

The board plays an active role in managing the company through managers, who are given the responsibility for the day-to-day operations of the company. The board will establish milestones for the company based on the strategic direction it oversees. In monitoring progress, the board will select, appoint, and terminate the employment of senior management. They thereby play a key role in ensuring leadership continuity.

The board will establish committees to aid in the oversight of key functions. These committees will provide feedback and recommendations. Committees vary by organization; however, six common committees are:

1. Audit committee
2. Governance committee
3. Remuneration committee
4. Nomination committee
5. Risk committee
6. Investment committee

Audit Committee

Given the importance of ensuring the integrity of the financial statements, the board plays a key role in the audit and control systems within the company. This would include setting the overall structure and making certain it is properly implemented. The audit committee can be crucial in this role, as it helps to evaluate the effectiveness of the control system. The audit committee will:

- Review information technology.
- Evaluate policies and procedures.
- Supervise the internal audit group.
- Appoint and evaluate the findings from the external auditors.
- Perform other necessary processes and procedures.

Governance Committee

The governance committee will monitor the adoption and implementation of good corporate governance practices. The committee will determine if the implementation is occurring and will review whether the policies and standards are in compliance with applicable laws and regulations.

Remuneration Committee

Given the role the board plays in its oversight of management, it plays a crucial role in remuneration. The remuneration committee will develop and propose policies and present them for approval. It will also deal with other aspects, including setting performance criteria, establishing human resource policies, and setting and overseeing the implementation of various employee benefits.

Nomination Committee

The nomination committee will create the nomination policies and procedures for new board members and executive management. It will recruit new board members who have the needed qualities and experience for the company. In addition, the committee will regularly examine various aspects of the existing board members to determine if their skills, expertise, and performance meet the current and future needs of the company and the board.

Risk Committee

The risk committee plays a critical role in establishing, implementing, and monitoring the appropriate level of risk within the company. The committee seeks to systematically manage existing and potential issues by identifying, assessing, and mitigating risk throughout the enterprise.

Investment Committee

The board is responsible for the strategic direction of the company, and will be involved in large investments. The investment committee will establish and regularly review and update the investment policies. The committee will review and reach conclusions on material investment opportunities, including expansion projects, acquisitions, and major divestitures.

LOS 33g: Describe market and nonmarket factors that can affect stakeholder relationships and corporate governance. Vol 4, pp 25–28

Stakeholder Relationships and Corporate Governance

There are three **market** factors that affect the stakeholder relationship and corporate governance. They are:

1. Shareholder engagement
2. Shareholder activism
3. Competition and takeover

Shareholder Engagement

The first is **shareholder engagement**. It is a growing trend that companies engage with shareholders on a more frequent basis throughout the year. The additional transparency and information sharing tend to increase management support and reduce the potential for efforts by shareholders to more actively pursue other means to influence outcomes.

Shareholder Activism

Shareholder activism is the second market factor that seeks to modify the behavior within a company. The ultimate goal is to increase shareholder value. It is a more forceful path that seeks to compel the company to act in a particular manner. There are several ways to accomplish this, but they are not available in all countries. Lawsuits can be brought against various groups, including the board of directors, management, and/or controlling shareholders. Raising public awareness to exert pressure on the company is another way, or a proxy battle. Hedge funds tend to draw the largest amount of activism due to their loosely regulated nature.

Competition and Takeover

When shareholders believe the company's performance is not acceptable, they may pursue a more aggressive stance, which leads to the third market factor: competition and takeover. If the company is underperforming a competitor, senior managers may lose their positions and directors can be voted out by shareholders. It is in the best interest of board members and management to maximize the value of the company. However, if not viewed in this manner, a corporate takeover may ensue, which could be a **proxy contest**, a **tender offer**, or a **hostile takeover**.

- In a proxy contest (or proxy fight), shareholders are persuaded to vote for a group seeking to take positions that will control the company's board of directors.
- A tender offer is one that attempts to persuade shareholders to sell their shares to the group seeking to gain control.
- A hostile takeover results when an entity acquires a company without the consent of company management.

In addition, staggering board member terms can dilute shareholder rights, as the entire board cannot be removed immediately.

Nonmarket factors present an environment that can change governance and its relationship with stakeholders. There are generally three factors:

1. The legal environment
2. Media
3. The corporate governance industry

The Legal Environment

The legal environment varies around the world and offers different protections to the shareholder or creditor. Creditors generally have a better protected position due to the contractual nature of their relationship.

Media

The media have played an important role in bringing attention to various topics to raise the awareness of stakeholders over the years. More recently, social media has become a powerful tool that has leveled the playing field between the company and stakeholders. It has the ability to influence stakeholder relationships instantly and at little cost.

The Corporate Governance Industry

The corporate governance industry has arisen out of the demand for information surrounding the subject. Information wasn't available previously, until the industry was required to change. The reporting services are concentrated and exert significant influence, as corporations must pay attention to their ratings and thus change their behavior if necessary.

LOS 33h: Identify potential risks of poor corporate governance and stakeholder management and identify benefits from effective corporate governance and stakeholder management. Vol 4, pp 28–31

Risks of Poor Corporate Governance and Stakeholder Management

When a company has poor corporate governance, it opens itself up to various risks. In a weak control environment, four potential issues are:

1. Weak control systems
2. Ineffective decision making
3. Legal, regulatory, and reputational risks
4. Default and bankruptcy risks

Weak Control Systems

Poor financial information can lead to many issues, including lack of confidence in financial information, an inability to obtain financing, as well as producing poor information internally. These are some of the issues related to a poor control environment due to weak control systems. In addition, the company's ability to catch fraudulent activity or erroneous accounting records is another. Audit deficiencies due to a weak control environment at Enron Corporation led to one of the largest bankruptcies in history.

Ineffective Decision Making

In the absence of sufficient monitoring, there may be information asymmetry, leading to ineffective decision making. This situation would give one stakeholder group an advantage over another group. In particular, if managers have better information, they would have the ability to make decisions for their benefit. This would undermine the board that monitors them, as the board would be unable to act on behalf of the shareholders to maximize corporate value.

Legal, Regulatory, and Reputational Risk

If the company has weaknesses in its implementation of regulatory requirements, it could be exposed to various legal, regulatory, and reputational risks. Legally, the company could be held responsible for noncompliance, which would also bring regulatory risks. In addition, its reputation would be at stake when the information is disseminated almost instantly on one of the various news outlets, including social media.

Default and Bankruptcy Risks

When corporate governance is poor and there is weak management of the creditors' interest, this can lead to poor decision making from management. These decisions can easily affect the company's financial position, which can lead to default and bankruptcy.

Benefits of Effective Governance

Effective governance can lead to four benefits:

1. Operational efficiency
2. Improved control
3. Better operating and financial performance
4. Lower default risk and cost of debt

Operational Efficiency

When a company clarifies the organizational structure that outlines responsibilities, reporting lines, and the internal control environment, employees will have a clear understanding of their perspective duties. This will increase the likelihood that the company will experience operational efficiencies.

Improved Control

Improved control can also be realized, which helps to minimize various risks, including regulatory, legal, and financial risks. This ultimately reduces costs as well.

Better Operating and Financial Performance

With a strong control system, the company can see better operating performance and better information gathering. This leads to improved decision making and can decrease the response time to changes in the market.

Lower Default Risk and Cost of Debt

With a strong governance structure, business and investment risk is reduced. This will help to protect creditors' interests and will ultimately reduce the company's cost of debt and default risk.

LOS 33i: Describe factors relevant to the analysis of corporate governance and stakeholder management. Vol 4, pp 31–36

Analysis of Corporate Governance and Stakeholder Management

Analyzing a company's corporate governance structure is a subjective endeavor. However, there are several potential items that should be considered, as a good structure leads to several benefits in the long-term success of a company. Six key areas of interest are:

1. Economic ownership and voting control
2. Board of directors representation

3. Remuneration and company performance
4. Investors in the company
5. Strength of shareholders' rights
6. Managing long-term risks

Economic Ownership and Voting Control

Evaluating the economic ownership and voting control helps to understand how decisions are made by shareholders. Generally, there is a structure that gives one vote for each share owned. However, there are dual-class systems that split voting rights by different classes. The differences in each setup will have implications, potentially on valuations, as dual-class companies tend to trade at a discount to their peers.

Board of Directors Representation

Evaluating the makeup of the board is another important aspect that should be reviewed. Do the directors have the proper backgrounds and skills to guide the company in the current environment and the future? Having a long-tenured board may have a negative impact on the future success of the company, if it limits the board's diversity and adaptability.

Remuneration and Company Performance

Remuneration is one way to incentivize management to act in the long-term interests of the company. Reviewing compensation programs and ensuring they align with shareholder interests are important. Various warning signs could present themselves, including:

- The lack of equity incentives to align with shareholders
- Little variation in results over multiple years due to inadequate hurdles
- Excessive payouts relative to comparable companies with comparable results
- Strategic implications of incentives that may not be appropriate
- Plans that have not changed with the company's life cycle change

Investors in the Company

Understanding the investor composition gives insights into control and directionality of decisions. If there is a concentrated holding that controls voting, this can dictate how the company is run for the immediate future, and potentially longer. In addition, if the shareholder group has a significant number of experienced activists, this can lean toward a short-term-oriented investor mentality, which can create substantial turnover in a very short period of time.

Strength of Shareholders' Rights

The strength of shareholders' rights is another aspect to consider. The framework of the rights will help determine whether there could be structural obstacles to certain transactions in the company's charter or bylaws. Can shareholders remove board members? Can they convene special stockholder meetings? These and other questions should be answered. Some rights vary by country.

Managing Long-Term Risks

It is important to investigate stakeholder relations and the ability of management to manage long-term risks. When poor, these have had an enormous impact on share value. One way to assess management quality is by examining patterns of fines, accidents, regulatory issues, and so on. If they are persistent, it is a good indicator there may be an issue.

The analysis of these additional areas that are nonfinancial in basis is a subjective exercise. However, it provides a basic framework for uncovering incremental insights about a company.

LOS 33j: Describe environmental and social considerations in investment analysis. Vol 4, pp 36–37

Social and environmental considerations are beginning to be thought of more frequently, but have been slower to take hold compared to corporate governance as a factor impacting investing. However, there are many issues that exist in these two realms. Identifying factors that will have a substantial effect on the performance of a company is difficult. Global trends in resource scarcity, and societal and environmental changes, as well as other related concerns, are beginning to take a more dominant place in the investment process.

Incorporating these social and environmental considerations, together with corporate governance in the investment process, is called ESG (environmental, social, governance) integration. Even though it was once thought of as being nonfinancial in nature, as more information becomes available, it is increasingly quantifiable and can be used in the investment process.

The terminology is sometimes confusing, as sustainable investing (SI) and responsible investing (RI) are used interchangeably with ESG integration. However, SI and RI utilize ESG in their investment process. Historically, there has been an exclusionary process called socially responsible investing (SRI) that limits investments in companies whose products are contrary to the ethical and moral values of an investor, such as weapons and tobacco. With impact investing (sometimes used as the "I" in SRI), investors seek to meet their specific social and environmental goals with identifiable financial returns.

LOS 33k: Describe how environmental, social, and governance factors may be used in investment analysis. Vol 4, pp 38–40

ESG Market Overview

ESG considerations can be widely defined, but clearly can have a significant impact on the financial outcomes within a company. The 2010 explosion of the *Deepwater Horizon* oil rig in the Gulf of Mexico caused a massive oil spill with various financial costs, as well as the loss of human life, marine and wildlife habitat, tourism, and more. Investors are becoming more aware of the various situations that have a negative impact not only on the environment but also on society. In the recent past, Walmart has had several strikes and lawsuits that have cost hundreds of millions of dollars to settle.

Therefore, there is a growing emphasis on investing that utilizes ESG criteria. Some large institutional asset owners embrace the concept of being a **universal owner**. This is a long-term investor with a diversified global portfolio that is linked to economic growth while being exposed to costs resulting from environmental damage. It is thus important to consider various factors while performing investment analysis.

ESG Factors in Investment Analysis

Environmental issues have various financial risks for companies. One of the primary risks is associated with stranded assets. Also referred to as carbon assets, these items are at risk of no longer being economically viable because of changes in regulations or investor sentiment. It is difficult to assess the full impact of such assets. For an energy company, the potential financial risks can be significant but difficult to quantify, as these companies do not provide sufficient information on the existence of these assets.

Material events that impact the environment can be costly in terms of legal and regulatory issues, generating fines and litigation. They very well may include clean-up costs as well as reputational costs. Therefore, in any analysis, it is important to factor in both the risk and the potential costs if an error occurs.

Societal issues can be very broad, including issues within the workplace, human rights, and welfare. They can also include the impact on the community. Companies that incorporate social factors into their business can potentially benefit from a sustainable competitive advantage, as workforce training, safety, turnover, and morale (to name a few) positively impact a company. This can lead to higher productivity and lower costs.

Governance factors have long been recognized in investment analysis. Performance indicators that may be used to evaluate risks arising from governance issues include ownership structure, board independence and composition, and compensation. Note that although several governance factors apply across industries and geographic regions, other factors are unique to certain industries (such as systemic risk management for financial services companies).

One area of debate is whether the consideration of ESG factors is consistent with fiduciary duty. For example, in the past, when managing pension fund assets, portfolio managers had a fiduciary duty to act solely in the interest of pension plan participants and beneficiaries. Accepting lower returns or assuming greater risk in a private pension plan to promote environmental, social, or public policy causes would therefore violate fiduciary duty. Recently, however, the U.S. Department of Labor (DOL) determined that certain ESG-related investment considerations do not violate fiduciary duty. These considerations include the addition of ESG factors in investment policy statements, the integration of ESG factors in the evaluation of an investment's risk or return, and using ESG considerations as determining factors when choosing among investments that are otherwise financially or economically equivalent.

ESG Implementation Methods

ESG implementation approaches range from value-based to values-based.

- A value-based approach aims to mitigate risks and identify opportunities by analyzing ESG considerations in addition to traditional financial metrics.
- A values-based approach simply expresses the moral or ethical beliefs of an investor.

Between the value-based and values-based approaches lie a continuum of approaches that strives for value creation through values investing.

The implementation of ESG mandates can include the following five methods:

1. Negative screening
2. Positive screening and best-in-class
3. ESG integration/incorporation
4. Thematic investing
5. Impact investing

Negative Screening

Also referred to as exclusionary screening, **negative screening** is used to exclude certain sectors as defined by the investor, such as fossil fuels, companies with human rights or environmental concerns, or companies that do not align with religious or personal beliefs. This is the most common form of ESG-related investing.

Positive Screening and Best-in-Class

In contrast to negative screening, **positive screening** or **best-in-class** approaches focus on including investments with favorable ESG aspects. This could include companies that promote human dignity, workplace well-being, respect for the environment, and so forth. Best-in-class approaches will evaluate and score companies on ESG criteria and choose those with the highest rating in each industry.

ESG Integration/Incorporation

This implementation approach uses ESG factors alongside traditional analysis, looking for opportunities and risks. It seeks to evaluate a company's ability to manage its ESG resources within a sustainable business model and make investment decisions based on its findings.

Thematic Investing

Thematic investing is utilized when a strategy is implemented utilizing only one factor to evaluate companies relative to ESG criteria. For example, a thematic approach could include clean water technologies, climate change, energy efficiencies, or a myriad of other specific focuses.

Impact Investing

This investing model seeks to achieve social or environmental objectives while meeting identified financial returns. It focuses on doing this through engagement with the company or by direct investments in companies or projects. Two examples are venture capital investing directly in a company and purchasing "climate bonds," which finance environmental projects related to climate change.

Another example of impact investing relates to green finance, which relates to achieving economic growth while reducing pollution and improving efficiency in the use of natural resources. The primary investment vehicles used in green finance are green bonds, in which issuers earmark the proceeds toward environmental-related projects.

READING 34: CAPITAL BUDGETING

LESSON 1: CAPITAL BUDGETING

Capital budgeting is the process that companies use for making long-term investment decisions (e.g., acquiring new machinery, replacing current machinery, launching new products, and spending on research and development). Capital budgeting is very important because:

- A significant amount of capital is usually tied up in long-term projects. The success of these investments has a significant influence on the future prospects of the company.
- The principles of capital budgeting can also be used in making other operating decisions (e.g., investments in working capital and acquisitions of other companies).
- The valuation principles used in capital budgeting are also applied in security analysis and portfolio management.
- Sound capital budgeting decisions maximize shareholder wealth.

LOS 34a: Describe the capital budgeting process and distinguish among the various categories of capital projects. Vol 4, pp 48–49

The steps typically involved in the capital budgeting process are as follows:

1. Generating ideas: Generating good investment ideas is the most important step in the process. These ideas can be generated from any part of the organization or even from sources outside the company.

2. Analyzing individual proposals: This step involves collecting information to forecast the cash flows of a particular project as accurately as possible. Cash flows are then used to evaluate the feasibility of the project.

3. Planning the capital budget: Projects that are undertaken should fit into the company's overall strategy. Further considerations include the timing of the project's cash flows and availability of company resources.

4. Monitoring and post-auditing: In this step, actual performance is compared to forecasts and the reasons behind any differences are sought. Post-auditing helps monitor the forecasts to improve their accuracy going forward *and* to improve operations to make them more efficient. Concrete ideas for future investments may also abound from this step.

Capital budgeting projects can usually be classified into the following categories:

1. Replacement projects: These projects help in maintaining the normal course of business and do not usually require very thorough analysis. For example, if a piece of equipment becomes obsolete, the decision whether to replace it usually does not require detailed analysis. Replacement decisions that involve replacing existing equipment with more efficient equipment, or with newer technology, usually require more detailed analysis.

2. Expansion projects: These are projects that increase the size of the business. Expansion decisions require more careful consideration compared to simple replacement projects because there are more uncertainties involved.

3. **New products and services:** Venturing into new products and services brings added uncertainties to the firm's overall operations. These decisions require extremely detailed analysis along with the participation of a lot more people in the decision-making process.

4. **Regulatory, safety, and environmental projects:** These projects are sometimes made mandatory by a governmental agency or some external party. They might not generate any revenues themselves, but may accompany other revenue-generating projects undertaken by the company. Sometimes, however, the cost of these obligatory projects is so high that the company may be better off shutting down operations altogether or just closing the part of the business that is related to the project.

5. **Other projects:** Some projects cannot be analyzed through capital budgeting techniques. They could be pet projects of senior management and so needless or so risky that they are difficult to evaluate and justify using the typical assessment methods. An example of such a decision is the acquisition of a new private jet by the CEO of a company.

LOS 34b: Describe the basic principles of capital budgeting. Vol 4, pp 50–52

Let's go over some important capital budgeting concepts before moving on to the basic principles of capital budgeting.

Sunk costs are those costs that cannot be recovered once they have been incurred. Capital budgeting ignores sunk costs because it is based only on current and future cash flows. An example of a sunk cost is the market research costs incurred by the company to evaluate whether a new product should be launched.

Opportunity cost is the value of the next best alternative that is *foregone* in making the decision to pursue a particular project. For example, if we invest $1 million in a piece of equipment, the opportunity cost of investing in that piece of equipment is the amount that $1 million would have earned in its next-most-profitable use. Opportunity costs should be *included* in project costs.

An **incremental cash flow** is the additional cash flow realized as a result of a decision. Incremental cash flow equals cash flow with a decision minus the cash flow without the decision.

An **externality** is the effect of an investment decision on things other than the investment itself. Externalities can be positive or negative and, if possible, externalities should be considered in investment decision-making. An example of a negative externality is *cannibalization*, as a new product reduces sales of existing products of the company.

A **conventional cash flow stream** is a cash flow stream that consists of an initial outflow followed by a series of inflows. The sign of the cash flows changes only once. For a **nonconventional cash flow stream**, however, the initial outflow is not followed by inflows only, but the direction of the flows change from positive to negative again. There is more than one sign change in a nonconventional cash flow stream.

The basic principles (assumptions) of capital budgeting are:

1. **Decisions are based on actual cash flows:** Only incremental cash flows are relevant to the capital budgeting process, while sunk costs are completely ignored. Analysts must also attempt to incorporate the effects of both positive and negative externalities into their analysis.
2. **Timing of cash flows is crucial:** Analysts try to predict exactly when cash flows will occur, as cash flows received earlier in the life of the project are worth more than cash flows received later.
3. **Cash flows are based on opportunity costs:** Projects are evaluated on the incremental cash flows they bring in, over and above the amount they would generate in their next best alternative use (opportunity cost).
4. **Cash flows are analyzed on an after-tax basis:** The impact of taxes on cash flows is always considered before making decisions.
5. **Financing costs are excluded from calculations of operating cash flows:** Financing costs are reflected in the required rate of return from an investment project, so cash flows are not adjusted for these costs. If financing costs were also included in the calculation of net cash flows, analysts would be counting them twice. Therefore, they focus on forecasting operating cash flows and capture costs of capital in the discount rate.
6. **Accounting net income is not used as cash flows for capital budgeting** because accounting net income is subject to noncash charges (e.g., depreciation) and financing charges (e.g., interest expense).

LOS 34c: Explain how the evaluation and selection of capital projects is affected by mutually exclusive projects, project sequencing, and capital rationing. Vol 4, pp 52–53

1. **Independent versus mutually exclusive projects.** Independent projects are those whose cash flows are unrelated. Mutually exclusive projects compete directly with each other for acceptance. If Project A and B are mutually exclusive, the firm may only accept one of them, not both.
2. **Project sequencing.** Many projects can only be undertaken in a certain order, so investing in one project creates the opportunity to invest in other projects in the future. For example, a company might invest in a project today and then invest in a second project after three years if the first project is successful and the economic scenario has not been adversely affected. However, if the initial project does not do so well, or if the economic environment is no longer favorable, the company will not invest in the second project.
3. **Unlimited funds versus capital rationing.** When the company has no constraints on the amount of capital it can raise, it will invest in all profitable projects to maximize shareholder wealth. The need for capital rationing arises when the company has limited funds to invest. If the capital required to invest in all profitable projects exceeds the resources available to the company, it must allocate funds to only the most lucrative projects to ensure that shareholder wealth is maximized.

LOS 34d: Calculate and interpret net present value (NPV), internal rate of return (IRR), payback period, discounted payback period, and profitability index (PI) of a single capital project. Vol 4, pp 52–60

The two most popular measures used to evaluate a single capital project are net present value (NPV) and internal rate of return (IRR).

Net Present Value (NPV)

For a project with one investment outflow, which occurs at the *beginning* of the project, the net present value is the present value of the future after-tax cash flows minus the investment outlay. NPV measures the amount in monetary units that a project is expected to add to shareholder wealth.

$$NPV = \sum_{t=1}^{n} \frac{CF_t}{(1+r)^t} - Outlay$$

where:

CF_t = after-tax cash flow at time, t.

r = required rate of return for the investment. This is the firm's cost of capital adjusted for the risk inherent in the project.

Outlay = investment cash outflow at $t = 0$.

Decision Rules for NPV

- A project should be undertaken if its NPV is greater than zero. Positive NPV projects increase shareholder wealth.
- Projects with a negative NPV decrease shareholder wealth and should not be undertaken.
- A project with an NPV of zero has no impact on shareholder wealth.

Example 1-1: Calculating NPV

Calculate the NPV of a capital project with an initial investment of $30 million. The project generates after-tax cash flows of $10 million at the end of Year 1, $14 million at the end of Year 2, and $18 million at the end of Year 3. The required rate of return is 10%.

Solution:

$$NPV = -\$30m + \frac{\$10m}{(1.10)^1} + \frac{\$14m}{(1.10)^2} + \frac{\$18m}{(1.10)^3}$$

$$NPV = -\$30m + \$9.09m + \$11.57m + \$13.52m$$

$$NPV = \$4.184 \text{ million}$$

TI BAII Plus® calculator keystrokes:

Keystrokes	Explanation	Display
[CF][2nd][CE|C]	Clear CF Memory registers	CF0 = 0.0000
30 [+/−][ENTER]	Initial Cash Outlay	CF0 = −30.0000
[↓] 10 [ENTER]	Period 1 cash flow	C01 = 10.0000
[↓] [↓] 14 [ENTER]	Period 2 cash flow	C02 = 14.0000
[↓] [↓] 18 [ENTER]	Period 3 cash flow	C03 = 18.0000
[NPV] 10 [ENTER]	10% discount rate	I = 10
[↓] [CPT]	Calculate NPV	NPV = 4.184

The NPV rule for independent projects recommends investing in a project if the NPV is greater than zero. This project generates a positive NPV of $4.184 million, so it should be undertaken.

Internal Rate of Return (IRR)

For an investment project with only one investment outlay that is made at inception, IRR is the discount rate that makes the sum of present values of the future after-tax cash flows equal to the initial investment outlay. Alternatively, IRR is the discount rate that equates the sum of the present values of all after-tax cash flows for a project (inflows and outflows) to zero. Therefore, IRR is the discount rate at which NPV equals zero.

$$\sum_{t=1}^{n} \frac{CF_t}{(1+IRR)^t} = Outlay \qquad \sum_{t=1}^{n} \frac{CF_t}{(1+IRR)^t} - Outlay = 0$$

Decision Rules for IRR
- A company should invest in a project if its IRR is *greater* than the required rate of return. When the IRR is greater than the required return, NPV is positive.
- A company should not invest in a project if its IRR is *less* than the required rate of return. When the IRR is lower than the required return, NPV is negative.

Example 1-2: Calculating IRR

Calculate the IRR of a capital project with an initial cost of $30 million. The project generates positive after-tax cash flows of $10 million at the end of Year 1, $14 million at the end of Year 2, and $18 million at the end of Year 3. Determine whether the project should be undertaken given that the required rate of return is 10%.

Solution:

$$0 = -\$30m + \frac{\$10m}{(1+IRR)^1} + \frac{\$14m}{(1+IRR)^2} + \frac{\$18m}{(1+IRR)^3}$$

IRR = **17.02%**

TI BAII Plus® calculator keystrokes:

Keystrokes	Explanation	Display
[CF][2nd][CE|C]	Clear CF Memory registers	CF0 = 0.0000
30 [+/−][ENTER]	Initial Cash Outlay	CF0 = −30.0000
[↓] 10 [ENTER]	Period 1 cash flow	C01 = 10.0000
[↓] [↓] 14 [ENTER]	Period 2 cash flow	C02 = 14.0000
[↓] [↓] 18 [ENTER]	Period 3 cash flow	C03 = 18.0000
[IRR] [CPT]	Calculate IRR	**IRR = 17.02%**

Decision: The project should be undertaken because its IRR (17.02%) is greater than the required return (10%).

Payback Period

> Note that if two projects have the same payback period and identical cash flows after the payback period, the project for which cash flows within the payback period occur earlier would be preferred, as it would have a higher NPV.

A project's payback period equals the time it takes for the initial investment for the project to be recovered through after-tax cash flows from the project. All other things being equal, the best investment is the one with the shortest payback period.

Example 1-3: Calculation of Payback Period

Calculate the payback period for a project that has the following cash flows:

Year	0	1	2	3	4	5
	$	$	$	$	$	$
Cash flow	−1,000	250	300	300	400	500

Solution

> The Professional model of the TI calculator allows you to calculate the payback period and discounted payback period directly. When NPV is displayed on the screen, repeatedly press the down arrow [↓] key until PB (payback) is displayed and then press CPT (compute).

First we calculate cumulative cash flows received till the end of each year:

Year	0	1	2	3	4	5
	$	$	$	$	$	$
Cumulative cash flow	−1,000	−750	−450	−150	250	750

> Also note that if net annual cash flows are equal, the payback period can be easily calculated by dividing project cost by the annual cash flow.

The payback for this investment occurs somewhere between the Year 3 and Year 4, where the sign of the cumulative cash flows changes from negative to positive. As of the end of Year 3, the project still needs to recover $150 of the initial outlay. This amount is recovered from the $400 earned over Year 4. The payback period for this investment equals 3 full years plus a fraction of the fourth year. This fraction equals $150 (the amount still not recovered at the end of Year 3) divided by $400 (total amount earned during Year 4). Therefore, the payback period equals 3.375 years.

Advantages
- It is simple to calculate and explain.
- It can also be used as an indicator of *liquidity*. A project with a shorter payback period may be more liquid than one that has a longer payback period.

Drawbacks
- It ignores the risk of the project. Cash flows are *not* discounted at the project's required rate of return.
- It ignores cash flows that occur after the payback period is reached.
- It is not a measure of profitability, so it cannot be used in isolation to evaluate capital investment projects. The payback period should be used along with the NPV or IRR to ensure that decisions reflect the overall profitability of the project being considered.

Discounted Payback Period

The discounted payback period equals the number of years it takes for cumulative *discounted* cash flows from the project to equal the project's initial investment outlay. A project's discounted payback period will always be *greater* than its payback period because the payback period does not discount the cash flows.

Example 1-4: Calculating the Discounted Payback Period

Assuming a discount rate of 10%, calculate the discounted payback period for a project that has the following cash flows:

Year	0 $	1 $	2 $	3 $	4 $	5 $
Cash flow	−1,000	250	300	300	400	500
Cumulative cash flow	−1,000	−750	−450	−150	250	750
Discounted cash flows	−1,000	227.27	247.93	225.39	273.21	310.46
Cumulative discounted cash flows	−1,000	−772.73	−524.80	−299.41	−26.20	284.26

Solution:

$$\text{Discounted payback period} = 4\,\text{full years} + \frac{26.20}{310.46} = 4.08\,\text{years}$$

Advantage
- It accounts for the time value of money and risks associated with the project's cash flows.

Drawback
- It ignores cash flows that occur after the payback period is reached. Therefore, it does not consider the overall profitability of the project.

Average Accounting Rate of Return (AAR)

The AAR is the ratio of the project's average net income to its average book value.

$$AAR = \frac{Average\ net\ income}{Average\ book\ value}$$

Example 1-5: Calculating the Average Accounting Rate of Return

ABC Company invests $150,000 in a piece of equipment that is depreciated straight line over a 5-year period and has zero salvage value. Depreciation expense and net income for the 5 years are given in the table below. Calculate the AAR of the project.

Year	1 $	2 $	3 $	4 $	5 $
Depreciation	30,000	30,000	30,000	30,000	30,000
Net income	25,000	27,000	28,000	26,000	26,500

Solution:

For the 5-year period, the **average net income** equals:

$(25,000 + 27,000 + 28,000 + 26,000 + 26,500)/5 = \$26,500$

The initial book value of the investment is $150,000. The book value declines (as it is depreciated) by $30,000 every year until it equals zero at the end of 5 years. The **average book value** of the asset equals the average of the beginning-of-project and the end-of-project book values:

$(150,000 + 0)/2 = \$75,000$

$$AAR = \frac{Average\ net\ income}{Average\ book\ value} = \frac{\$26,500}{\$75,000} = \mathbf{35.33\%}$$

Advantage
- It is easy to understand and easy to calculate.

Drawbacks
- It is based on accounting numbers and not cash flows. Accounting numbers are more susceptible to manipulation than cash flows.
- It does not account for time value of money.
- It does not differentiate between profitable and unprofitable investments accurately as there are no benchmarks for acceptable AARs.

Profitability Index

The profitability index (PI) of an investment equals the present value (PV) of a project's future cash flows divided by the initial investment.

$$PI = \frac{PV \text{ of future cash flows}}{Initial \text{ investment}} = 1 + \frac{NPV}{Initial \text{ investment}}$$

The PI equals the *ratio* of discounted future cash flows to the initial investment. NPV equals the *difference* between discounted future cash flows and the initial investment. The PI indicates the value we receive in exchange for one unit of currency invested. It is also known as the "benefit-cost" ratio.

Decision Rules for PI

- A company should invest in a project if its PI is *greater* than 1. The PI is greater than 1 when NPV is positive.
- A company should not invest in a project if its PI is *less* than 1. The PI is less than 1 when NPV is negative.

Example 1-6: Calculating the Profitability Index

Calculate the profitability index of a capital project with an initial cost of $30 million. The project generates after-tax cash flows of $10 million at the end of Year 1, $14 million at the end of Year 2, and $18 million at the end of Year 3. The required rate of return is 10%.

Solution:

$$PV \text{ of future cash flows} = \frac{\$10m}{(1.10)^1} + \frac{\$14m}{(1.10)^2} + \frac{\$18m}{(1.10)^3} = \$34.18m$$

Initial cost = **$30m**

$$PI = \frac{PV \text{ of future cash flows}}{Initial \text{ investment}} = \frac{\$34.18m}{\$30m} = 1.14$$

The project's PI is greater than 1, so the company should invest in the project.

LOS 34e: Explain the NPV profile, compare the NPV and IRR methods when evaluating independent and mutually exclusive projects, and describe the problems associated with each of the evaluation methods. Vol 4, pp 60–66

NPV Profiles

An NPV profile is a graphical illustration of a project's NPV at different discount rates. NPV profiles are downward sloping because as the cost of capital increases, the NPV of an investment falls.

Let's consider two projects, Project A and Project B. The cash flow streams for both projects are given below. For both projects, the required rate of return equals 7%.

Year	0	1	2	3	NPV	IRR
Project A	−$350,000	$425,000	$0	$0	$47,196	21.43%
Project B	−$350,000	$16,000	$16,000	$466,000	$59,323	12.96%

The NPVs of the projects at the various discount rates are listed in Table 1-1.

Table 1-1: Project NPVs

Discount Rate	NPV-Project A	NPV-Project B
%	$	$
0.000	75,000	148,000
5.000	54,762	82,299
7.000	47,196	59,323
8.715	**40,930**	**40,930**
10.000	36,364	27,881
12.960	26,239	0
20.000	4,167	−55,880
21.43	0	−65,712
25.000	−10,000	−88,368

The NPV profiles for the projects are illustrated in Figure 1-1. Discount rates are plotted on the x-axis and NPVs are plotted on the y-axis.

Figure 1-1: NPV Profiles

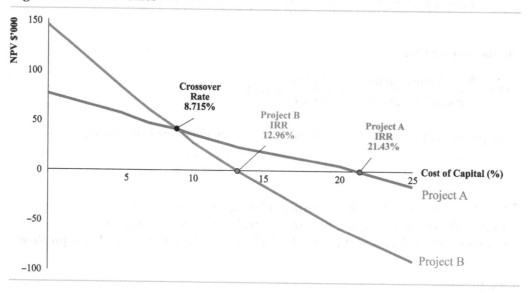

Analysis of the NPV Profiles

- The NPVs of the projects are equal at a cost of capital of 8.715%. This rate, where the NPVs of the two projects are the same and their NPV profiles intersect, is called the **crossover rate**.
- At discount rates above 8.715% (to the right of the crossover point), the NPV of Project A is greater than the NPV of Project B.
- At discount rates below 8.715% (to the left of the crossover rate), the NPV of Project B is greater than Project A.
- The NPV of Project A at a discount rate of 7% (the company's required rate of return) equals $47,196. The NPV of Project B at 7% equals $59,323.
- A project's IRR equals the discount rate at which its NPV equals 0. This means that a project's IRR is the point where its NPV profile *intersects the x-axis*. Therefore, the IRR of Project A equals 21.43% and that of Project B equals 12.96%.
- Project B has higher total cash flows over its entire life. This is why it has a higher NPV at a discount rate of 0% ($148,000 versus $75,000).
- More of Project B's cash flows come later in its life. This is the reason why the NPV profile for Project B falls faster as the cost of capital increases. At a cost of capital above 8.715%, the effect of Project B's total cash flows being higher is more than offset by the effect of its cash flows coming later.

> The crossover rate can be calculated by subtracting the cash flows of one project from the other and then calculating the IRR of the differences.

NPV and IRR Applied to Independent Projects

If Project A and Project B were independent projects and the cost of capital were 7%, the company would accept both projects, as they both have positive NPVs and their IRRs exceed the cost of capital (7%).

NPV and IRR Applied to Mutually Exclusive Projects

If the projects are mutually exclusive, the company can only choose one of them. Project A has a higher IRR (21.43% vs. 12.96%), but Project B has a higher NPV ($59,323 vs. $47,196). The conflict in recommendations is due to the *different pattern of cash flows*. Project A receives a lump sum amount of $425,000 in the first year while Project B receives equal cash flows in the first two years and then a lump sum amount of $466,000 in the third year.

When NPV and IRR rank two mutually exclusive projects differently, *the project with the higher NPV must be chosen*. NPV is a better criterion because of its more realistic reinvestment rate assumption.

IRR assumes that interim cash flows received during the project are reinvested at the IRR. This assumption is sometimes rather inappropriate, especially for projects with high IRRs. NPV, on the other hand, makes a more realistic assumption that interim cash flows are reinvested at the required rate of return.

Aside from cash flow timing differences, NPV and IRR may also give conflicting project rankings because of *differences in project size*.

Consider two mutually exclusive projects, Project C and Project D, whose cash flows are given below. For both projects, the required rate of return equals 5%. The NPVs and IRRs of the projects are also included in the table below.

Project Cash Flows

Year	0	1	2	3	4	5	NPV	IRR
Project C	−1,000	500	500	500	500	500	$1,164.7	41.04%
Project D	−100,000	32,000	32,000	32,000	32,000	32,000	$38,543.3	18.03%

> Note that while the NPV is theoretically the best method (as it is a direct measure of the expected increase in shareholder wealth) it has a shortcoming in that it does not account for differences in project size.

Project C has a higher IRR (41% vs. 18%) but Project D has a higher NPV ($38,543 vs. $1,165). Once again, NPV is the *better* criterion for making the investment decision. NPV represents the absolute increase in shareholder wealth attributable to a particular project. In this case, Project D should be chosen.

Problems with the IRR

The Multiple IRR Problem

A project has a nonconventional cash flow pattern when the initial outflow is not followed by inflows only. The direction of cash flows changes from positive to negative over the project's life (i.e., there is *more than one sign change* in the cash flow stream). Figure 1-2 illustrates the NPV profile of a nonconventional cash flow stream that suffers from the multiple IRR problem. Notice that the NPV profile intersects the x-axis at two different points.

Figure 1-2: NPV Profile for a Project with Multiple IRRs

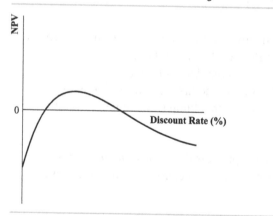

No IRR Problem

Sometimes cash flow streams have no IRR (i.e., there is no discount rate that results in a zero NPV). Figure 1-3 illustrates the NPV profile of a nonconventional cash flow stream that suffers from the "no IRR" problem. The figure also illustrates that projects with no IRRs may have positive NPVs.

Figure 1-3: NPV Profile for a Project with No IRR

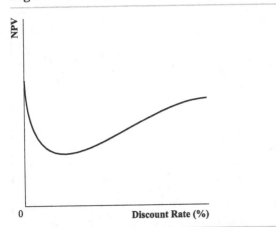

Surveys have studied the relative popularity of various capital budgeting techniques and have found that:

- The payback method is very popular in European countries.
- Larger companies prefer the NPV and IRR methods over the payback method.
- Private corporations use the payback period more often than public companies.
- Companies headed by MBAs have a preference for discounted cash flow techniques.

LOS 34f: Describe expected relations among an investment's NPV, company value, and share price. Vol 4, pp 66–68

If a company invests in a positive NPV project, the expected addition to shareholder wealth should lead to an increase in the stock price. The following example illustrates this.

Example 1-7: NPV and its Effect on Stock Price

Freeman Corp. is planning to invest $50 million in a new project. The present value of the future after-tax cash flows from the project is estimated to be $75 million. This is new information and is independent of other expectations regarding the company. The company has 5 million shares outstanding and the market price of the company's stock is $100.

Describe the effect of the new project on:

1. The value of the company.
2. The company's stock price.

Solution:

NPV of the new project
= $75 million − $50 million = $25 million

Company value before the new project
= 5 million shares × $100 = $500 million

Company value after the new project
= $500 million + $25 million = $525 million

Price/share after the new project
= $525 million/5 million shares = $105

1. The new project will have a positive effect of $25 million on the value of the company (shareholder wealth).
2. The stock price should increase to $105. The positive NPV of the new project should have a positive direct impact on its stock price.

However, the effect of a project's NPV on share prices is not as simple as shown in Example 1-7. The value of a company is determined by valuing its existing investments and adding the expected NPV of its future investments. The impact of the decision to undertake a particular project on a company's stock price will depend on how the actual profitability of the investment differs from the expected profitability of a company's investments. Expected profitability is usually already factored into current market prices.

If the profitability of a positive NPV project that the company is about to undertake is below expectations, stock prices may fall. On the other hand, certain capital projects undertaken by the company may signal that there are other potentially lucrative projects to follow. Taking on a project that brings with it the expectation of even greater future profits from subsequent opportunities may increase stock prices beyond the actual addition to the company value from said project alone.

Capital budgeting processes tell us two things about company management:

1. The extent to which management pursues the goal of shareholder wealth maximization.
2. Management's effectiveness in pursuit of this goal.

READING 35: COST OF CAPITAL

LESSON 1: COST OF CAPITAL

Cost of capital refers to the rate of return that the suppliers or providers of capital require to contribute their capital to the firm. We can also think of the cost of capital as the opportunity cost of funds for the providers of capital. Unless the return offered by a company meets or exceeds the rate that could be earned elsewhere from an investment of similar risk, a potential supplier of capital will not provide capital to the company.

LOS 35a: Calculate and interpret the weighted average cost of capital (WACC) of a company. Vol 4, pg 79

To raise capital, a company can issue either equity or debt (some instruments may have features of both debt and equity). An instrument that is used to obtain financing is called a **component**, and each component has a different required rate of return, which is known as the **component cost of capital**. The weighted average of the costs of the various components used by the company to finance its operations is known as the **weighted average cost of capital (WACC)** or the **marginal cost of capital (MCC)**. The WACC is the expected rate of return that investors demand for financing an average risk investment of the company. A company's WACC is calculated using the following formula (see Example 1-1):

$$WACC = (w_d)(r_d)(1-t) + (w_p)(r_p) + (w_e)(r_e)$$

where:
w_d = Proportion of debt that the company uses when it raises new funds
r_d = Before-tax marginal cost of debt
t = Company's marginal tax rate
w_p = Proportion of preferred stock that the company uses when it raises new funds
r_p = Marginal cost of preferred stock
w_e = Proportion of equity that the company uses when it raises new funds
r_e = Marginal cost of equity

Example 1-1: Calculating WACC

Axen Company's capital structure is composed of 40% debt, 5% preferred stock, and 55% common equity. Axen's before-tax cost of debt is 7%, cost of preferred equity is 8%, and cost of common equity is 10%. The company's marginal tax rate is 30%. Calculate Axen's WACC.

Solution:

$$WACC = (w_d)(r_d)(1-t) + (w_p)(r_p) + (w_e)(r_e)$$

$$WACC = (0.4)(0.07)(1-0.3) + (0.05)(0.08) + (0.55)(0.10) = \textbf{7.86\%}$$

LOS 35b: Describe how taxes affect the cost of capital from different capital sources. Vol 4, pp 79–80

Let's assume that a company pays $50,000 in interest for a given year. The $50,000 is an expense that the company is allowed to recognize for tax purposes to reduce taxable income. Interest expense reduces the company's profits before tax by $50,000, and assuming a 30% tax rate, reduces profits after tax by only $35,000. This is because interest expense provides a tax shield of $15,000. This tax shield is calculated as the interest expense multiplied by the tax rate ($50,000 × 30% = 15,000).

Adjusting for the interest tax shield, the real after-tax cost of debt for the company is not really $50,000, but only $35,000. Tax savings are only realized on payments to holders of debt instruments. Payments to preferred and common stock holders are not expensed on the income statement and do not result in tax savings. Notice that only the cost of debt is adjusted for tax savings in the WACC formula.

LOS 35c: Describe the use of target capital structure in estimating WACC and how target capital structure weights may be determined. Vol 4, pp 80–82

In determining the cost of capital (WACC) for a project, we would ideally want to use the weights of the various components in proportion to their employment in financing the new project. If we assume that the company has a target capital structure and will raise capital in line with its target structure, we should use the target capital structure in calculating WACC.

The target capital structure is the capital structure that the company aims to maintain. The weights used in the calculation of the WACC are the proportions of debt, preferred stock, and equity that the firm hopes to achieve and maintain in its capital structure over time. A simple way to transform a debt-to-equity ratio (D/E) into a weight is to simply divide the ratio by (1 + D/E):

$$\frac{D/E}{1 + D/E} = \frac{D}{D + E} = w_d$$

$$w_d + w_e = 1$$

If information about the target capital structure is not easily available, we can use the weights in the company's current capital structure. The weights of the various components should be based on *market values*.

Another option is to examine trends in the company's capital structure over time or statements by management regarding the company's capital structure policy to estimate the target capital structure.

An analyst may also use the average weights of comparable companies' capital structures as the target capital structure for the company. See Example 1-2 and Example 1-3.

Example 1-2: Calculating Capital Structure Weights

The market values of a company's sources of capital are as follows:

Bonds outstanding	$10 million
Preferred stock	$2 million
Common stock	$38 million
Total capital	**$50 million**

Based on the firm's existing capital structure, what weights should be used to determine the company's WACC?

Solution:

Weight of debt = w_d = $10 million/$50 million = 20%
Weight of preferred stock = w_p = $2 million/$50 million = 4%
Weight of common stock = w_e = $38 million/$50 million = 76%

Always check that the weights add up to 1:

$$w_d + w_e + w_p = 0.2 + 0.04 + 0.76 = 1$$

Example 1-3: Estimating Proportions of Capital

The market value of Becker Inc.'s debt is $25 million and the market value of its equity is $35 million.

1. What is the weight of debt and equity in the company's current capital structure?
2. If the company announces that a debt-to-equity ratio of 0.6 reflects its target capital structure, what weights should be assigned to debt and equity in calculating the company's WACC?

Solutions:

1. Using the current capital structure:

    Weight of debt = w_d = $25 million / ($25 million + $35 million) = 0.417
    Weight of equity = w_e = $35 million / ($25 million + $35 million) = 0.583

2. The weight of debt in the target capital structure is calculated by dividing the target D/E ratio by (1 + D/E):

$$w_d = \frac{D}{D+E} = \frac{D/E}{1 + D/E}$$

$$w_d = 0.6/(1+0.6)$$
$$w_d = 0.375$$

$$w_e = 1 - w_d$$
$$w_e = 1 - 0.375 = 0.625$$

LOS 35d: Explain how the marginal cost of capital and the investment opportunity schedule are used to determine the optimal capital budget. Vol 4, pp 82–84

A company's marginal cost of capital (MCC) *increases* as it raises additional capital. This is because most firms must pay a higher cost to obtain increasing amounts of capital. For example, the more a company borrows, the *greater* the risk that it will be unable to repay its lenders, and therefore, the *higher* the return required by investors.

The profitability of a company's investment opportunities *decreases* as the company makes additional investments. The company prioritizes investments in projects with the highest IRRs. As more resources are invested in the most rewarding projects, remaining opportunities offer lower and lower IRRs. This fact is represented by an **investment opportunity schedule (IOS)** that is downward-sloping.

The **optimal capital budget** occurs at the point where the marginal cost of capital intersects the investment opportunity schedule (see Figure 1-1).

Figure 1-1: Optimal Investment Decision

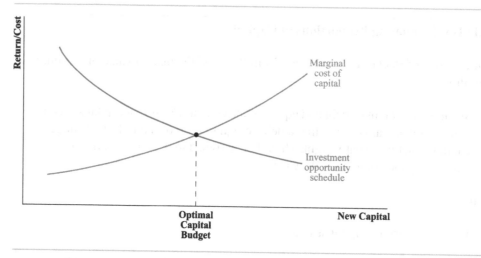

- The company should raise capital (at the given MCC) and undertake all projects (to earn the given IRR) to the left of the intersection point because these projects enhance shareholder wealth given the cost of financing them.
- To raise capital in excess of the optimal capital budget (to the right of the intersection point) the firm will be required to incur a cost of capital that is greater than the return on available investments. Undertaking these projects, given the MCC, will erode the firm's value.

LOS 35e: Explain the marginal cost of capital's role in determining the net present value of a project. Vol 4, pp 82–84

The WACC is the discount rate that reflects the average risk of the company. When we choose WACC as the discount rate to evaluate a particular project, we assume that:

- The project under consideration is an average risk project.
- The project will have a constant capital structure (which equals the company's target capital structure) throughout its life.

The cost of capital for a particular project should reflect the risk inherent in that particular project, which will not necessarily be the same as the risk of the company's average project. If the risk of the project under consideration is above or below the average risk of the company's current portfolio of projects, an adjustment is made to the WACC. Specifically:

- If a project has *greater* risk than the firm's existing projects, the WACC is adjusted *upward*.
- If the project has *less* risk than the firm's exiting projects, the WACC is adjusted *downward*.

The WACC or MCC adjusted for the project's level of risk plays an important role in capital budgeting because it is used to calculate the project's NPV.

LESSON 2: COSTS OF THE DIFFERENT SOURCES OF CAPITAL

LOS 35f: Calculate and interpret the cost of debt capital using the yield-to-maturity approach and the debt-rating approach. Vol 4, pp 84–86

The cost of fixed rate capital is the cost of debt financing when a company issues a bond or takes a bank loan. We will discuss two approaches to estimate the before-tax cost of debt (r_d).

1. Yield-to-Maturity Approach

The bond's yield to maturity (YTM) is a measure of the return on the bond, assuming that it is purchased at the current market price and held till maturity. It is the yield that equates the present value of the bond's expected future cash flows to its current market price. See Example 2-1.

$$P_0 = \left[\sum_{t=1}^{n} \frac{PMT}{\left(1+\frac{r_d}{2}\right)^t} \right] + \frac{FV}{\left(1+\frac{r_d}{2}\right)^n}$$

where:
P_0 = Current market price of the bond.
PMT_t = Interest payment in period t.
r_d = Yield to maturity on a BEY basis.
n = Number of periods remaining to maturity.
FV = Par or maturity value of the bond.

> This equation assumes that we are considering a semiannual-pay coupon bond, so the interim cash flows are discounted at $r_d/2$.

Example 2-1: Calculating the Cost of Debt Using the YTM Approach

Fordova Inc. issues a semiannual-pay bond to finance a new project. The bond has a 10-year term, a par value of $1,000, and offers a 6% coupon rate. Assuming that the bond is issued at $1,010.30 and that the tax rate for the company is 40%, calculate the before-tax and after-tax cost of debt.

Solution:

Present value = $1,010.30
Future value = Par = $1,000
Periodic payment = 6%/2 × 1,000 = $30
Number of discounting periods = 10 × 2 = 20

$$P_0 = \left[\sum_{t=1}^{20} \frac{\$30}{\left(1 + \frac{r_d}{2}\right)^t} \right] + \frac{1,000}{\left(1 + \frac{r_d}{2}\right)^n}$$

Or using our calculator:

N = 20; PV = −$1,010.30; FV = $1,000; PMT = $30; CPT I/Y; I/Y = 2.931

The semiannual yield is multiplied by 2 to calculate the bond's YTM on a BEY basis.

The yield to maturity on the bond equals 2.931 × 2 = 5.862%. This is the before-tax cost of debt (r_d).

After-tax cost of debt = $r_d (1 - t)$ = 5.862 (1 − 0.4) = 3.52%

2. Debt-Rating Approach

When a reliable current market price for the company's debt is not available, the before-tax cost of debt can be estimated using the yield on similarly rated bonds that also have similar terms to maturity as the company's existing debt. See Example 2-2.

Example 2-2: Debt-Rating Approach:

Alextar Inc. has a capital structure that includes AAA-rated bonds with 10 years to maturity. The yield to maturity on a comparable AAA-rated bond with a similar term to maturity is 6%. Using a tax rate of 40%, calculate Alextar's after-tax cost of debt.

Solution:

Alextar's after-tax cost of debt = $r_d (1 - t)$ = 0.06(1 − 0.4) = 3.6%

When using the debt-rating approach, adjustments might have to be made to the before-tax cost of debt of the comparable company. The relative seniority and security of different issues affect ratings and yields, and these factors should be considered when selecting a comparable bond and using its before-tax cost of debt as a proxy for the cost of debt of the company being studied.

Issues in Estimating Cost of Debt

- Fixed-rate versus floating-rate debt: The cost of floating-rate debt is reset periodically based on a reference rate (usually LIBOR) and is, therefore, more difficult to estimate than the cost of fixed-rate debt. For floating-rate bonds, analysts may use the current term structure of interest rates and term structure theory to estimate the cost of debt.
- Debt with option-like features: If currently outstanding bonds contain embedded options, an analyst can only use the yield to maturity on these bonds to estimate the cost of debt if she expects similar bonds (with embedded options) to be issued going forward. If, however, option-like features are expected to be removed from future debt issues, she should adjust the yield to maturity on existing bonds for their option features and use the adjusted rate as the company's cost of debt.
- Nonrated debt: If a company does not have any debt outstanding (to be rated) or yields on existing debt are not available (due to lack of relevant current prices), an analyst may not be able to use the YTM or the debt-rating approach to estimate the company's cost of debt.
- Leases: If a company uses leases as a source of finance, the cost of these leases should be included in its cost of capital.

LOS 35g: Calculate and interpret the cost of noncallable, nonconvertible preferred stock. Vol 4, pp 86–88

A company promises to pay dividends at a specified rate to its preferred stock holders. When preferred stock is noncallable and nonconvertible, has no maturity date, and pays dividends at a fixed rate, the value of the preferred stock can be calculated using the perpetuity formula.

$$V_p = \frac{D_p}{r_p}$$

where:
V_p = Current value (price) of preferred stock.
D_p = Preferred stock dividend per share.
r_p = Cost of preferred stock.

Rearranging this equation gives us the formula to calculate the cost of preferred stock (see Example 2-3):

$$r_p = \frac{D_p}{V_p}$$

Example 2-3: Determining the Cost of Preferred Stock

Shirley Inc. has outstanding preferred stock on which it pays a dividend of $10 per share. If the current price of Shirley's preference shares is $100 per share, what is its cost of preferred stock?

Solution:

$$r_p = \frac{\$10}{\$100} = 10\%$$

LOS 35h: Calculate and interpret the cost of equity capital using the capital asset pricing model approach, the dividend discount model approach, and the bond-yield-plus risk-premium approach. Vol 4, pp 88–93

The cost of equity is the rate of return required by the holders of a company's common stock. Estimating the cost of equity is difficult due to the uncertainty of future cash flows that common stock holders will receive in terms of their amount and timing.

Three approaches are commonly used to determine the cost of common equity.

1. Capital Asset Pricing Model (CAPM)

The capital asset pricing model (CAPM) states that the expected rate of return from a stock equals the risk-free interest rate plus a premium for bearing risk. See Example 2-4.

> We will learn more about the CAPM in a later reading.

$$r_e = R_F + \beta_i [E(R_M) - R_F]$$

where:

$[E(R_M) - R_F]$ = Equity risk premium.

R_M = Expected return on the market.

β_i = Beta of stock. Beta measures the sensitivity of the stock's returns to changes in market returns.

R_F = Risk-free rate.

r_e = Expected return on stock (cost of equity)

Example 2-4: Using CAPM to Estimate the Cost of Equity

Becker Inc.'s equity beta is 1.3. The risk-free rate is 6% and the equity risk premium stands at 10%. What is Becker's cost of equity using the CAPM approach?

Solution:

$$r_e = R_F + \beta_i [E(R_M) - R_F]$$
$$r_e = 0.06 + 1.3 \, (0.10) = 0.19 \text{ or } 19\%$$

The equity market risk premium, $(R_M - R_F)$ can be estimated using a **survey approach**, where the average of the forecasts of financial experts is adjusted for the specific stock's systematic (nondiversifiable) risk. We will learn about systematic and unsystematic risks in the Portfolio Management section.

2. Dividend Discount Model Approach

The dividend discount model asserts that the value of a stock equals the present value of its expected future dividends. We will use the constant-growth dividend discount model (also known as a Gordon growth model), in which dividends grow at a constant rate, to determine the cost of equity. While this model is studied in greater detail in Fixed Income, at this stage we just need to know the following equation, which is used to calculate the price of a stock, assuming a constant growth rate in dividends:

$$P_0 = \frac{D_1}{r_e - g}$$

where:
P_0 = current market value of the security.
D_1 = next year's dividend.
r_e = required rate of return on common equity.
g = the firm's expected constant growth rate of dividends.

Rearranging the above equation gives us a formula to calculate the required return on equity:

$$r_e = \frac{D_1}{P_0} + g$$

The growth rate, g, is a very important variable in this model. There are two ways to determine the growth rate. See Example 2-5.

1. Use the forecasted growth rate from a published source or vendor.
2. Calculate a company's sustainable growth rate using the following formula:

$$g = \left(1 - \frac{D}{EPS}\right) \times (ROE)$$

where:
$(1 - (D/EPS))$ = Earnings retention rate

We will discuss the calculation of the retention rate in the Equity section.

Example 2-5: Dividend Discount Model Approach

Diamond Inc. has an earnings retention rate of 60% and a return on equity of 20%. Its next year's dividend is forecasted to be $2 per share and the current stock price is $40. What is the company's cost of equity?

Solution:

$$g = (\text{Earnings retention rate}) \times (\text{ROE}) = 60\% \times 20\% = 12\%$$

$$\text{Cost of equity} = r_e = \frac{D_1}{P_0} + g$$

$$r_e = \frac{2}{40} + 0.12 = 17\%$$

3. Bond Yield Plus Risk Premium Approach

The bond yield plus risk premium approach is based on the assumption that the cost of capital for riskier cash flows is higher than that of less risky cash flows. Therefore, we calculate the return on equity by adding a risk premium to the before-tax cost of debt. See Example 2-6.

$$r_e = r_d + \text{risk premium}$$

Example 2-6: Cost of Equity Using the Bond Yield Plus Risk Premium Approach

The yield to maturity on Graf Inc.'s long-term debt is 9%. The risk premium is estimated to be 6%. Calculate Graf's cost of equity.

Solution:

$$r_e = r_d + \text{risk premium}$$

$$r_e = 9\% + 6\% = 15\%$$

Each of the three approaches to determine a company's cost of equity usually gives a different value. Analysts must use their judgment to decide which model is appropriate to compute a particular company's cost of equity.

LESSON 3: TOPICS IN COST OF CAPITAL ESTIMATION

LOS 35i: Calculate and interpret the beta and cost of capital for a project. Vol 4, pp 93–100

An analyst must estimate a stock's beta when using the CAPM approach to estimate a company's cost of equity. Beta can be calculated by regressing the company's stock's returns against market returns over a given period. The results of the regression will be in the following format:

$$R_i = a + bR_{mt}$$

where:
  a = Estimate of the intercept.
  b = Estimated slope of the regression (beta).
  R_i = The company's stock's returns.
  R_{mt} = Market returns over the given period.

Beta estimates are sensitive to many factors and the following issues should be considered when determining beta:

- Beta estimates are based on historical returns and are therefore sensitive to the length of the estimation period.
- Smaller standard errors are found when betas are estimated using small return intervals (such as daily returns).
- Betas are sensitive to the choice of the market index against which stock returns are regressed.
- Betas are believed to revert toward 1 over time, which implies that the risk of an individual project or firm equals market risk over the long run. Due to mean reversion, smoothing techniques may be required to adjust calculated betas.
- Small-cap stocks generally have greater risks and returns compared to large-cap stocks. Some experts argue that the betas of small companies should be adjusted upward to reflect greater risk.

While it is fairly simple to use regression to estimate betas for publicly listed companies (given the ease of access to stock and market return data), determining betas for nonlisted companies or individual projects is quite difficult.

A company's or project's beta is exposed to the following systematic (nondiversifiable) risks:

- **Business risk** is comprised of sales risk and operating risk. Sales risk refers to the unpredictability of revenues and operating risk refers to the company's operating cost structure.
- **Financial risk** refers to the uncertainty of profits and cash flows because of the use of fixed-cost financing sources such as debt and leases. The greater the use of debt financing, the greater the financial risk of the firm.

Analysts use the **pure-play** method to estimate the beta of a particular project or of a company that is not publicly traded. This method requires adjusting a comparable publicly-listed company's beta for differences in financial leverage.

- First we find a comparable company that faces similar business risks as the company or project under study and estimate the equity beta of that company. Betas vary with the level of financial risk in a company. Highly leveraged companies have higher financial risk, which is reflected in their high equity betas.
- To remove all elements of financial risk from the comparable's beta, we "unlever" the beta. This unlevered beta reflects only the business risk of the comparable and is known as *asset beta*.
- Finally, we adjust the unlevered beta of the comparable for the level of financial risk (leverage) in the project or company under study.

We use the following formula to estimate the asset beta for the comparable publicly traded firm:

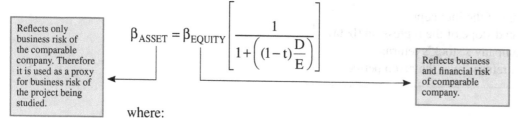

Reflects only business risk of the comparable company. Therefore it is used as a proxy for business risk of the project being studied.

Reflects business and financial risk of comparable company.

where:

D/E = Debt-to-equity ratio of the comparable company.

t = Marginal tax rate of the comparable company.

To adjust the asset beta of the comparable for the capital structure (financial risk) of the project or company being evaluated, we use the following formula (see Example 3-1):

Reflects business and financial risk of the project.

Reflects business risk of project.

where:

D/E = Debt-to-equity ratio of the subject company.

t = Marginal tax rate of the subject company.

Example 3-1: Calculation of a Project's Beta and WACC

Rukaiya Inc. is considering an investment in the confectionaries business. Rukaiya has a D/E ratio of 1.5, a before-tax cost of debt of 6%, and a marginal tax rate of 35%. Tastelicious Foods is a publicly traded company that operates only in the confectionaries industry and has a D/E ratio of 2, an equity beta of 0.7, and a marginal tax rate of 40%. The risk-free rate is 4.5% and the expected return on the market is 11%. Calculate the appropriate WACC that Rukaiya should use to evaluate the risk of entering the confectionaries business.

Solution:

First we calculate Tastelicious Foods' (the reference company's) unlevered (asset) beta, which eliminates the impact of financial risk and only reflects the business risk of the confectionaries industry.

$$\beta_{ASSET} = \beta_{EQUITY} \left[\frac{1}{1 + \left((1-t)\frac{D}{E} \right)} \right]$$

$$\beta_{ASSET} = 0.7 \left[\frac{1}{1 + ((1-0.4)2)} \right] = 0.318$$

Then we "relever" the reference company's beta to reflect Rukaiya's financial risk:

$$\beta_{PROJECT} = \beta_{ASSET}\left[1+\left((1-t)\frac{D}{E}\right)\right]$$

$$\beta_{PROJECT} = 0.318\{1+[(1-0.35)1.5]\} = 0.628$$

Finally, we use the project's cost of equity and the component weights to calculate the WACC of Rukaiya's confectionaries project:

Cost of equity $= r_e = 4.5\% + 0.628\,(11\% - 4.5\%) = 8.582\%$

Rukaiya's D/E ratio is given as 1.5. It has 1.5 units of debt for every unit of equity (the denominator of the D/E ratio is 1). The ratio of debt to equity is 1.5 to 1, or 3:2. The weight for debt in the capital structure is therefore 3/(3 + 2) or 0.6 [(D/D + E)] and that of equity is 2/(3 + 2) or 0.4 [E/(D + E)].

$$WACC = (w_d)(r_d)(1-t)+(w_p)(r_p)+(w_e)(r_e)$$
$$WACC = 0.6(0.06)(1 - 0.35) + 0.4(0.08582) = 5.77\%$$

LOS 35j: Describe uses of country risk premiums in estimating the cost of equity. Vol 4, pp 100–101

Studies have shown that a stock's beta captures the country risk of a stock accurately only in developed markets. Beta does not effectively capture country risk in developing nations. To deal with this problem, the CAPM equation for stocks in developing countries is modified to add a country spread (also called the country equity premium) to the market risk premium.

$$r_e = R_F + \beta\,[E(R_M) - R_F + CRP]$$

The country risk premium (CRP) is calculated as the product of sovereign yield spread and the ratio of the volatility of the developing country's equity market to the volatility of the sovereign bond market denominated in terms of the currency of a developed country. The sovereign yield spread is the difference between the developing country's government bond yield (denominated in the currency of a developed country) and the yield of a similar maturity bond issued by the developed country.

Country risk premium	=	Sovereign yield spread	×	Annualized standard deviation of equity index
				Annualized standard deviation of sovereign bond market in terms of the developed market currency

The sovereign yield spread captures the general risk of an investment in a particular country. This spread is then adjusted for the volatility of the stock market relative to the bond market. See Example 3-2.

Example 3-2: Using Country Risk Premium to Estimate the Cost of Equity

An analyst wants to calculate the cost of equity for a project in Malaysia. She has the following information:

- The yield on Malaysia's dollar-denominated 10-year government bond is 10%.
- The yield on a 10-year U.S. Treasury bond is 4.2%.
- The annualized standard deviation of Malaysia's stock market is 29%.
- The annualized standard deviation of Malaysia's dollar-denominated 10-year government bond is 20%.
- The project's beta equals 1.1.
- The expected return on the Malaysian equity market is 9%.
- The risk-free rate equals 5%.

Calculate the country risk premium and the cost of equity for this project in Malaysia.

Solution:

$$CRP = (0.10 - 0.042)\left(\frac{0.29}{0.20}\right) = 8.41\%$$

$$r_e = R_F + \beta \ [E(R_M) - R_F + CRP]$$

$$r_e = 0.05 + 1.1 \ [0.09 - 0.05 + 0.0841] = \mathbf{18.65\%}$$

Malaysia's country risk premium equals 8.41% and the cost of equity for this project equals 18.65%.

LOS 35k: Describe the marginal cost of capital schedule, explain why it may be upward-sloping with respect to additional capital, and calculate and interpret its break-points. Vol 4, pp 102–105

A company's marginal cost of capital (MCC) increases as additional capital is raised. This is because of the following reasons:

> The marginal cost of capital is the cost of the last additional dollar of capital raised by a firm.

1. The company may have existing *debt covenants* that restrict it from issuing debt with similar seniority. Subsequent rounds of debt will be subordinated to the senior issue so they will obviously carry more risk, and therefore entail a higher cost.
2. Due to economies of scale in raising a significant amount of a component (debt or equity) of capital in one go, firms may deviate from their target (optimal) capital structure over the short term. These deviations may cause the marginal cost of capital to rise.

The marginal cost of capital schedule shows the WACC at different amounts of total capital. Figure 3-1 illustrates the fact that it is upward sloping. The amount of capital at which the WACC changes is referred to as a **break point**. A break point is calculated using the following formula (see Example 3-3):

$$\text{Break point} = \frac{\text{Amount of capital at which a component's cost of capital changes}}{\text{Proportion of new capital raised from the component}}$$

Example 3-3: Determining Break Points

Charlton Inc. has a target capital structure of 70% equity and 30% debt. The schedule of costs for components of capital for the company is contained in the table below. Calculate the break points and illustrate the marginal cost of capital schedule for Charlton.

Amount of New Debt ($ millions)	After-Tax Cost of Debt	Amount of New Equity ($ millions)	Cost of Equity
0 to 150	3.90%	0 to 300	6.00%
150 to 300	4.40%	300 to 600	7.80%
300 to 450	4.80%	600 to 900	10.00%

Solution:

Charlton Inc. will have a break point each time the cost of a component of capital changes. Specifically, its MCC schedule will have four break points.

Break Point	Calculation	Amount
When debt exceeds $150 million	$150 million/0.3	$500 million
When debt exceeds $300 million	$300 million/0.3	$1,000 million
When equity exceeds $300 million	$300 million/0.7	$428.57 million
When equity exceeds $600 million	$600 million/0.7	$857.14 million

The following table shows the company's WACC at the different levels of total capital:

Capital	Equity (70%)	Cost of Equity	Debt (30%)	After-Tax Cost of Debt	WACC
$100.00	70	6%	30	3.90%	5.37%
$428.57	300	7.80%	128.57	3.90%	6.63%
$500.00	350	7.80%	150	4.40%	6.78%
$857.14	600	10.00%	257.14	4.40%	8.32%
$1,000.00	700	10.00%	300	4.80%	8.44%

Figure 3-1: Marginal Cost of Capital Schedule

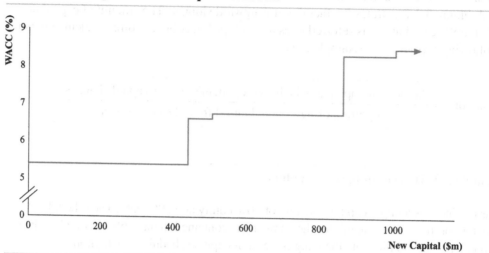

LOS 35l: Explain and demonstrate the correct treatment of flotation costs. Vol 4, pp 105–108

Flotation costs refer to the fee charged by investment bankers to assist a company in raising new capital. In the case of debt and preferred stock , we do not usually incorporate flotation costs in the estimated cost of capital because the amount of these costs is quite small, often less than 1%. However, for equity issues, flotation costs are usually quite significant.

There are two ways of accounting for flotation costs. The first approach, which is often found in finance textbooks, incorporates flotation costs into the cost of capital. When this approach is applied, the cost of capital is calculated in the following manner (see Example 3-4):

$$r_e = \left[\frac{D_1}{P_0(1-f)} \right] + g$$

where:
f = flotation costs as a percentage of the issue price.

> **Example 3-4: Accounting for Flotation Costs Directly into the Cost of Equity**
>
> Ben Company currently pays a dividend of $1 per share, has a current stock price of $20, and has an expected growth rate of 4%. The company wants to raise equity capital and flotation costs will be 5% of the total issue. Calculate the company's cost of equity:
>
> 1. Before it issues new capital.
> 2. After it issues new capital, including flotation costs in the cost of equity.
>
> **Solution**
>
> 1. Cost of equity before Ben raises new capital:
>
> $$r_e = \frac{D_1}{P_0} + g$$
>
> $$r_e = [\$1(1+0.04)/\$20] + 0.04 = \mathbf{9.2\%}$$
>
> 2. Cost of equity after issuance:
>
> $$r_e = \left[\frac{D_1}{P_0(1-f)}\right] + g$$
>
> $$r_e = [\$1(1+0.04)/\$20(1-0.05)] + 0.04 = 9.47\%$$
>
> Ben's cost of equity was 9.2% before it issued new equity. After issuance, when flotation costs are included in cost of equity, the cost rises by 27 basis points to 9.47%.

However, adjusting the cost of capital for flotation costs is incorrect. Flotation costs are a part of the initial cash outlay for a project. Adjusting the cost of capital to account for flotation costs adjusts the present value of all future cash flows by a fixed percentage (27 basis points in Example 3-4). This adjustment will not necessarily equal the present value of flotation costs.

Correct Treatment of Flotation Costs

The correct way to account for flotation costs is to adjust the cash flows used in the valuation. We add the estimated dollar amount of flotation costs to the initial cost of the project (see Example 3-5).

Example 3-5: Correct Treatment of Flotation Costs

Alex Company is planning to invest in a project. The following information is provided:

- Initial cash outflow = $75,000
- Expected future cash flows = $20,000 every year for the next five years
- Alex's before-tax cost of debt = 5%
- Tax rate = 30%
- Next year's expected dividend = $1 per share
- The current price of the stock = $25.
- Expected growth rate = 4%
- The target capital structure = 70% equity and 30% debt
- Flotation costs for equity = 4%

Calculate the NPV of the project after adjusting cash flows to account for flotation costs.

Solution:

First, we determine the after-tax cost of debt and equity to calculate the WACC of the project:

Source of Capital	Weight	Formula	After-Tax Cost
Debt	30%	$r_d(1 - \text{tax rate})$	$0.05(1 - 0.3) = 3.5\%$
Equity	70%	$r_e = \dfrac{D_1}{P_0} + g$	$(1/25) + 0.04 = 8\%$

$$\text{WACC} = 0.3(3.5\%) + 0.70(8\%) = \mathbf{6.65\%}$$

Next, we calculate the dollar amount of flotation costs:

Dollar amount of flotation costs = $52,500 × 4% = $2,100

Finally, we calculate the **NPV** of the project:

Initial cash outflow = Initial outlay for project + Flotation costs = $77,100
Cash inflows = $20,000 for the next five years
WACC (discount rate) = 6.65%

$$\text{NPV} = -\$77,100 + \frac{\$20,000}{(1.0665)^1} + \frac{\$20,000}{(1.0665)^2} + \frac{\$20,000}{(1.0665)^3} + \frac{\$20,000}{(1.0665)^4} + \frac{\$20,000}{(1.0665)^5}$$

NPV = $5,678.20

READING 36: MEASURES OF LEVERAGE

LESSON 1: MEASURES OF LEVERAGE

LOS 36a: Define and explain leverage, business risk, sales risk, operating risk, and financial risk, and classify a risk. Vol 4, pp 126–143

LOS 36b: Calculate and interpret the degree of operating leverage, the degree of financial leverage, and the degree of total leverage. Vol 4, pp 126–143

LOS 36c: Analyze the effect of financial leverage on a company's net income and return on equity. Vol 4, pp 138–140

Leverage refers to a company's use of fixed costs in conducting business. Fixed costs include:

- Operating costs (e.g., rent and depreciation).
- Financial costs (e.g., interest expense).

Fixed costs are referred to as leverage because they support the company's activities and earnings. It is important for analysts to understand a company's use of leverage for the following reasons:

- Leverage increases the volatility of a company's earnings and cash flows, thereby increasing the risk borne by investors in the company.
- The more significant the use of leverage by the company, the more risky it is and therefore the higher the discount rate that must be used to value the company.
- A company that is highly leveraged risks significant losses during economic downturns.

Leverage is affected by a company's cost structure. Generally, companies incur two types of costs.

- Variable costs vary with the level of production and sales (e.g., raw materials costs and sales commissions).
- Fixed costs remain the same irrespective of the level of production and sales (e.g., depreciation and interest expense).

Let's work with two companies, Blue Horizons and Red Electronics, to illustrate the effects of leverage on company value. See Tables 1-1 and 1-2.

Table 1-1: Sales and Cost Information

	Blue Horizons ($)	Red Electronics ($)
Number of units produced and sold	200,000	200,000
Sales price per unit	20	20
Variable cost per unit	7	14
Fixed operating cost	1,000,000	200,000
Fixed financing expense	800,000	200,000

> For simplicity, we are ignoring the effects of taxes. However, the general conclusions remain the same even if taxes are included in our analysis.

Table 1-2: Calculation of Net Income

	Blue Horizons $	Red Electronics $
Revenue	4,000,000	4,000,000
Operating costs (fixed + variable)	2,400,000	3,000,000
Operating income	1,600,000	1,000,000
Financing expense	800,000	200,000
Net income	**800,000**	**800,000**

Both companies earned a net income of $800,000. However, it is important to observe that Blue Horizons has a higher proportion of fixed costs (higher leverage) in its cost structure, while Red Electronics has a higher proportion of variable costs.

In Table 1-3, we vary the number of units produced and sold by the companies to evaluate the impact of their differing cost structures on net income.

Table 1-3: Net Income in Different Sales Scenarios

	If 150,000 Units are Produced and Sold		If 200,000 Units are Produced and Sold		If 250,000 Units are Produced and Sold	
	Blue Horizons	Red Electronics	Blue Horizons	Red Electronics	Blue Horizons	Red Electronics
Revenue	3,000,000	3,000,000	4,000,000	4,000,000	5,000,000	5,000,000
Operating costs	2,050,000	2,300,000	2,400,000	3,000,000	2,750,000	3,700,000
Operating income	950,000	700,000	1,600,000	1,000,000	2,250,000	1,300,000
Financing expense	800,000	200,000	800,000	200,000	800,000	200,000
Net income	**150,000**	**500,000**	**800,000**	**800,000**	**1,450,000**	**1,100,000**
Percentage change in net income	**−81%**	**−38%**			**81%**	**38%**

Takeaway: The dominance of fixed costs (both operating and financial) in Blue Horizons' cost structure (higher leverage) results in higher earnings volatility. A 25% fluctuation in sales results in an 81% fluctuation in Blue Horizons' net income, but only a 38% fluctuation in Red Electronics' net income. See Figure 1-1.

Figure 1-1: Net Income for Different Numbers of Units Produced and Sold

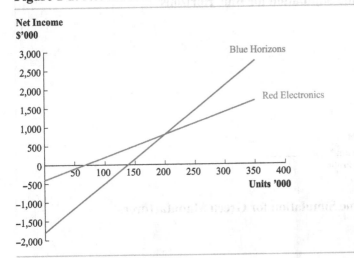

The greater the degree of leverage for a company, the steeper the slope of the line representing net income. For a given change in the number of units produced and sold, the net income of Blue Horizons will change by a greater amount than that of Red Electronics.

Business Risk and Financial Risk

Business Risk

Business risk refers to the risk associated with a company's operating earnings. Operating earnings are risky because total revenues and costs of sales are both uncertain. Therefore, business risk can be broken down into sales risk and operating risk.

> Companies in the same line of business have similar business risk.

Sales risk: The uncertainty associated with total revenue is referred to as sales risk. Revenue is affected by economic conditions, industry dynamics, government regulation, and demographics. See Exhibit 1-1.

Exhibit 1-1: Sales Risk

Blue Horizons expects to produce and sell 200,000 units over the coming year, and the standard deviation of units sold is 10,000 units. Further, assume that the selling price per unit is $20 with a standard deviation of $2.

Green Manufacturers has the same cost structure as Blue Horizons and expects to sell the same number of units at the same price as Blue Horizons. However, its standard deviation of units sold is 20,000 units and its price standard deviation is $4.

> For simplicity, we have assumed that the fixed operating costs are known with certainty and that units sold follow a normal distribution. Figures 1-2 and 1-3 show the distributions of operating income for the two companies.

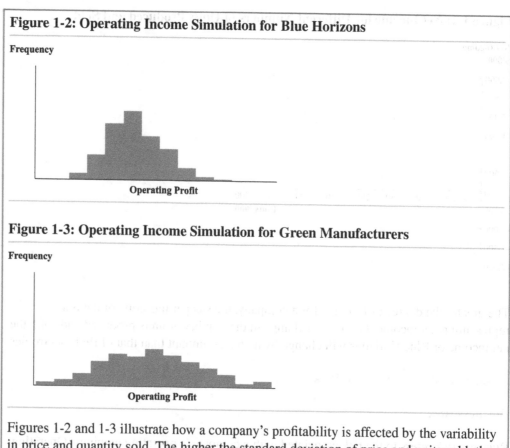

Figure 1-2: Operating Income Simulation for Blue Horizons

Frequency

Operating Profit

Figure 1-3: Operating Income Simulation for Green Manufacturers

Frequency

Operating Profit

Figures 1-2 and 1-3 illustrate how a company's profitability is affected by the variability in price and quantity sold. The higher the standard deviation of price and units sold, the wider the distribution of operating profit. The greater volatility in earnings shows that Green Manufacturers has more sales risk than Blue Horizons.

Operating risk: The risk associated with a company's operating cost structure is referred to as operating risk. As shown earlier, a company that has a greater proportion of fixed costs in its cost structure has greater operating risk.

The cost structure of a company generally depends on the type of industry that it operates in. However, companies within the same industry may vary their cost structures by employing different production methods. A company that has a greater proportion of fixed costs relative to variable costs in its cost structure will find it more difficult to adjust its operating costs to changes in sales and is therefore more risky. In order to examine a company's sensitivity of operating income to changes in unit sales, we use the **degree of operating leverage (DOL)**. DOL is the ratio of the percentage change in operating income to the percentage change in units sold.

> We assume that the company sells everything that it produces in the same period.

$$DOL = \frac{\text{Percentage change in operating income}}{\text{Percentage change in units sold}}$$

Table 1-4 illustrates the effects of a 10% increase in the number of units sold on Blue Horizon's operating income:

Table 1-4: Sensitivity of Operating Income to Unit Sales

| | Number of Units Produced and Sold | | Percentage Change |
	200,000	220,000	
Revenues	$4,000,000	$4,400,000	10.00%
Less variable costs	1,400,000	1,540,000	10.00%
Less fixed costs	1,000,000	1,000,000	0.00%
Operating income	$1,600,000	$1,860,000	16.25%

For a 10% increase in revenues, Blue Horizons' operating income increases by 16.25%.

The DOL can also be expressed in terms of its basic elements:

$$DOL = \frac{Q \times (P - V)}{Q \times (P - V) - F}$$

where:

Q = Number of units sold
P = Price per unit
V = Variable operating cost per unit
F = Fixed operating cost
Q × (P − V) = Contribution margin (the amount that units sold contribute to covering fixed costs)
(P − V) = Contribution margin per unit

You are not required to derive this formula, but make sure you commit it to memory.

Looking at the formula for DOL you should realize that if there are no fixed costs, DOL would equal one. This implies that if there are no fixed costs, there would be no operating leverage.

Using the equation above, the DOL for Blue Horizons can be calculated as:

$$DOL \ (at \ 200,000 \ units) = \frac{200,000 \times (20 - 7)}{200,000 \times (20 - 7) - 1,000,000} = 1.625$$

Interpretation: At 200,000 units, a 1% change in units sold will result in a 1.625% change in Blue Horizons' operating income.

Next, let's calculate Blue Horizons' DOL at a sales volume of 400,000 units.

$$DOL \ (at \ 400,000 \ units) = \frac{400,000 \times (20 - 7)}{400,000 \times (20 - 7) - 1,000,000} = 1.238$$

Interpretation: At 400,000 units, a 1% change in units sold will result in a 1.238% change in Blue Horizons' operating income. See Figure 1-4.

Conclusion: DOL is different at different levels of sales. If the company is making operating profits, the sensitivity of operating income to changes in units sold decreases at higher sales volumes (in units).

Figure 1-4: Blue Horizons' DOL for Different Number of Units Produced and Sold

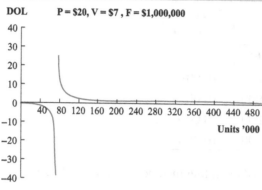

Takeaways:

- DOL is negative when operating income (the denominator in the DOL equation) is negative, and is positive when the company earns operating profits.
- Operating income is most sensitive to changes in sales around the point where the company makes zero operating income.
- DOL is undefined when operating income is zero.

The degree of operating leverage is also affected by a company's cost structure. Let's work with Red Electronics, which has a lower proportion of fixed costs in its cost structure relative to Blue Horizons. The DOL of Red Electronics at 200,000 units is calculated as:

$$\text{DOL (at 200,000 units)} = \frac{200,000 \times (20 - 14)}{200,000 \times (20 - 14) - 200,000} = 1.2$$

At 200,000 units, a 1% change in units sold will change Red Electronics' operating income by 1.2%.

The point to recognize here is that at 200,000 units, Red Electronics has a lower DOL (1.2) than Blue Horizons (1.625), which implies that its operating income is less sensitive to changes in units sold compared to Blue Horizons. The lower the proportion of fixed costs in a company's cost structure, the less sensitive its operating income is to changes in units sold and therefore the lower the company's operating risk. The degrees of operating leverage are similar for the two companies at higher quantities sold.

Business risk is composed of operating and sales risk, both of which are largely determined by the industry in which the company operates. It is important to note, however, that a company has more control over operating risk than sales risk. This is because it cannot control the number of units it will sell and the price per unit (sales risk), but it does choose the production method it wants to employ (which determines operating risk).

Industries that require a significant initial investment but less expenditure to make and distribute the product (e.g., pharmaceuticals) have a higher proportion of fixed costs and therefore higher operating leverage. On the other hand, companies that have a significant portion of variable costs in cost of goods sold (e.g., retailers) have relatively low operating leverage.

Most companies produce more than one product, which makes it difficult to obtain a breakdown of costs. In such cases, we can regress the company's operating income (the dependent variable) against changes in sales (the independent variable) over time to estimate the degree of operating leverage. When comparing two companies, the one with a greater slope of the least-square regression would have higher operating leverage.

Financial Risk

Financial risk refers to the risk associated with how a company chooses to finance its operations. If a company chooses to issue debt or acquire assets on long-term leases, it is obligated to make regular payments when due. Failure to perform on these obligations can lead to legal action against the company, so by taking on these fixed obligations the company increases its financial risk. On the other hand, if it uses its retained earnings or issues shares (common equity) to finance operations, the company does not incur fixed obligations. Therefore, the higher the amount of fixed financial costs taken on by a company, the greater its financial risk.

Financial risk can be measured as the sensitivity of cash flows available to owners to changes in operating income. This measure is known as the **degree of financial leverage (DFL)**.

$$DFL = \frac{\text{Percentage change in net income}}{\text{Percentage change in operating income}}$$

Tables 1-5a and 1-5b illustrate the variation in Blue Horizons' net income with different levels of fixed financial costs. We have worked with the base case operating profit scenario (operating profit = $1,600,000) and another scenario where operating profit rises by 20% to calculate changes in net income.

Table 1-5a: Sensitivity of Net Income to Fixed Financial Costs of $800,000

Fixed Financing Cost = $800,000			Percentage Change
Operating Income	1,600,000	1,920,000	20.00%
Less Interest	800,000	800,000	0.00%
Net Income	**800,000**	**1,120,000**	**40.00%**

Table 1-5b: Sensitivity of Net Income to Fixed Financial Costs of $1,200,000

Fixed Financing Cost = $1,200,000			Percentage Change
Operating Income	1,600,000	1,920,000	20.00%
Less Interest	1,200,000	1,200,000	0.00%
Net Income	**400,000**	**720,000**	**80.00%**

For simplicity we have ignored taxes from this analysis.

Notice that at higher levels of fixed financing costs ($1.2 million versus $800,000) the same percentage change in operating income (20%) leads to a higher percentage change in net income (80% versus 40%). This implies that higher fixed financial costs increase the sensitivity of net income to changes in operating income.

The degree of financial leverage (DFL) equation can be simplified into its basic elements as follows:

$$DFL = \frac{[Q(P-V)-F](1-t)}{[Q(P-V)-F-C](1-t)} = \frac{[Q(P-V)-F]}{[Q(P-V)-F-C]}$$

where:
Q = Number of units sold
P = Price per unit
V = Variable operating cost per unit
F = Fixed operating cost
C = Fixed financial cost
t = Tax rate

Blue Horizons' DFL, when operating income is $1.6 million and fixed financial costs are $800,000, is calculated as:

$$DFL = \frac{200,000 \times (20-7) - 1,000,000}{200,000 \times (20-7) - 1,000,000 - 800,000} = 2$$

Blue Horizons' DFL when operating income is $1.6 million and fixed financial costs are $1.2 million is calculated as:

$$DFL = \frac{200,000 \times (20-7) - 1,000,000}{200,000 \times (20-7) - 1,000,000 - 1,200,000} = 4$$

These calculations verify that the higher the use of fixed financing sources by a company, the greater the sensitivity of net income to changes in operating income and therefore the higher the financial risk of the company. Also note that the degree of financial leverage is also different at different levels of operating income.

The degree of financial leverage is usually determined by the company's management. While operating costs are similar among companies in the same industry, capital structures may differ to a greater extent.

Generally, companies with relatively high ratios of tangible assets to total assets or those with revenues that have below-average business cycle sensitivity are able to use more financial leverage than companies with relatively low ratios of tangible assets to total assets or those with revenues that have high business cycle sensitivity. This is because stable revenue streams and assets that can be used as collateral make lenders more comfortable in extending credit to a company. See Example 1-1.

Example 1-1: The Leveraging Role of Debt

Alpha Inc.

Expected next year's operating earnings ($)	1,000,000
Interest rate on debt	6%
Income tax rate	35%

Scenario A: Alpha has total assets of $5 million and does not use any debt financing.
Scenario B: Alpha has total assets of $5 million, financed by $2.5 million of shareholders' equity and $2.5 million of debt.

Calculate the company's net income and return on equity for the coming year assuming that operating earnings may vary as much as 50% from expectations.

Scenario A: Total Assets = $5 million Shareholders' Equity = $5 million Debt = Nil	Operating Earnings 50% Lower than Expectations	Expected Operating Earnings	Operating Earnings 50% Higher than Expectations
Earnings before interest and taxes	500,000	1,000,000	1,500,000
Interest expense	–	–	–
Earnings before taxes	500,000	1,000,000	1,500,000
Taxes	175,000	350,000	525,000
Net income	325,000	650,000	975,000
Return on equity	6.50%	13.00%	19.50%

Scenario B: Total Assets = $5 million Shareholders' Equity = $2.5 million Debt = $2.5 million	Operating Earnings 50% Lower than Expectations	Expected Operating Earnings	Operating Earnings 50% Higher than Expectations
Earnings before interest and taxes	500,000	1,000,000	1,500,000
Interest expense	150,000	150,000	150,000
Earnings before taxes	350,000	850,000	1,350,000
Taxes	122,500	297,500	472,500
Net income	227,500	552,500	877,500
Return on equity	9.10%	22.10%	35.10%

Takeaway:
The larger the proportion of debt in a company's capital structure, the greater the sensitivity of net income to changes in operating income, and therefore the greater the company's financial risk. Bear in mind that taking on more debt also magnifies earnings upward, if the company is performing well (illustrated by the higher ROEs in Scenario B).

Total Leverage

DOL looks at the sensitivity of operating income to changes in units sold, while DFL looks at the sensitivity of net income to changes in operating income. The degree of total leverage (DTL) looks at the combined effect of operating and financial leverage (i.e., it measures the sensitivity of net income to changes in units produced and sold).

Table 1-6 demonstrates the effects of a 10% change in revenues on Blue Horizons' operating income and net income. Again, we assume that the company sells all that it produces during the same period.

Table 1-6: Total Leverage of Blue Horizons

	Units Produced and Sold		
	180,000	200,000	220,000
Revenues	3,600,000	4,000,000	4,400,000
Less variable costs	1,260,000	1,400,000	1,540,000
Less fixed operating costs	1,000,000	1,000,000	1,000,000
Operating income	1,340,000	1,600,000	1,860,000
Less interest	800,000	800,000	800,000
Net income	**540,000**	**800,000**	**1,060,000**
Relative to 200,000 units produced and sold			
Percentage change in units sold	−10.00%		10.00%
Percentage change in operating profit	−16.25%		16.25%
Percentage change in net income	−32.50%		32.50%

DTL is calculated as:

$$DTL = \frac{\text{Percentage change in net income}}{\text{Percentage change in the number of units sold}}$$

$$DTL = DOL \times DFL$$

$$DTL = \frac{Q \times (P - V)}{[Q(P - V) - F - C]}$$

where:
Q = Number of units produced and sold
P = Price per unit
V = Variable operating cost per unit
F = Fixed operating cost
C = Fixed financial cost

The DTL for Blue Horizons can be calculated as:

$$DTL = 1.625 \times 2 = 3.25$$

$$DTL = \frac{200{,}000 \times (20 - 7)}{200{,}000 \times (20 - 7) - 1{,}000{,}000 - 800{,}000} = 3.25$$

This implies that a 1% change in the number of units sold will change net income by 3.25%.

Note that DTL is also different at different numbers of units produced and sold. This is because DOL is different at different levels of units produced and sold, while DFL is different at different levels of operating earnings. DTL combines the effects of DOL and DFL.

LOS 36d: Calculate the breakeven quantity of sales and determine the company's net income at various sales levels. Vol 4, pp 143–145

LOS 36e: Calculate and interpret the operating breakeven quantity of sales. Vol 4, pp 143–145

Breakeven Points and Operating Breakeven Points

A company's breakeven point occurs at the number of units produced and sold at which its net income equals zero. It is the point at which a company's revenues equal its total costs and the company goes from making losses to making profits. Figure 1-5 plots Blue Horizons' revenues and expenses against the number of units produced and sold.

Figure 1-5: Blue Horizons' Breakeven

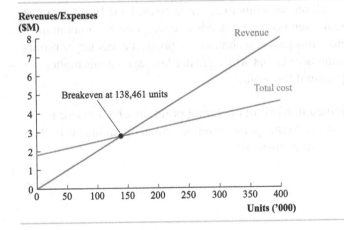

The breakeven point for a company occurs when:

$$PQ = VQ + F + C$$

where:
P = Price per unit
Q = Number of units produced and sold
V = Variable cost per unit
F = Fixed operating costs
C = Fixed financial cost

The breakeven number of units can be calculated as:

$$Q_{BE} = \frac{F + C}{P - V}$$

The breakeven number of units for Blue Horizons and Red Electronics can be calculated as:

Blue Horizons:

$$Q_{BE} = \frac{1,000,000 + 800,000}{20 - 7} = 138,461 \text{ units}$$

Red Electronics:

$$Q_{BE} = \frac{200,000 + 200,000}{20 - 14} = 66,666 \text{ units}$$

Blue Horizons must produce and sell 138,461 units in order to break even, while Red Electronics must only produce and sell 66,666 units to cover its costs. Blue Horizons must sell a higher number of units to break even because it needs to cover a higher amount of fixed costs. However, once Blue Horizons passes its breakeven point, it earns larger profits than Red Electronics. The implication here is that while greater leverage entails higher risk, it also raises the company's potential for profit.

A breakeven point can also be specified in terms of operating profit, in which case it is known as the operating breakeven point. At this point, revenues equal operating costs. The expression for operating breakeven point is given as:

$$PQ_{OBE} = VQ_{OBE} + F$$

$$Q_{OBE} = \frac{F}{P - V}$$

The operating breakeven points for Blue Horizons and Red Electronics are computed as:

Blue Horizons:

$$Q_{OBE} = \frac{1,000,000}{20-7} = 76,923 \text{ units}$$

Red Electronics:

$$Q_{OBE} = \frac{200,000}{20-14} = 33,333 \text{ units}$$

Blue Horizons also has a higher operating breakeven point compared to Red Electronics.

Note:

The farther the unit sales are from the breakeven point for high-leverage companies, the greater the magnifying effect of leverage.

The Risks of Creditors and Owners

The risk borne by creditors and owners differs because of the different rights and responsibilities associated with their investment in the company.

Creditor claims on the assets of the company are senior to those of equity holders. In return for lending money to the company, creditors demand timely interest and principal payments. Payments to creditors must be made irrespective of whether the company is profitable. Inability to make these payments may lead to the company having to declare bankruptcy. Returns for creditors are predefined; even if the company does very well, they do not see any of the upside.

On the other hand, owners only have a claim on what is left over after all the financial obligations of the company have been met. In return for the lower priority in claims, equity holders enjoy decision-making power in the company and participate in the upside if the company does well.

Legal codes in most countries provide for companies to file for bankruptcy protection. There are two main types of bankruptcy protection.

- Reorganization (Chapter 11), which provides the company temporary protection from creditors so that it can reorganize its capital structure and emerge from bankruptcy as a going concern.
- Liquidation (Chapter 7), which allows for an orderly settlement of the creditors' claims. In this category of bankruptcy, the original business ceases to exist.

Companies with high operating leverage have less flexibility in making changes to their operating structures, so bankruptcy protection does little to help reduce operating costs. On the other hand, companies with high financial leverage can use Chapter 11 protection to change their capital structure and, once the restructuring is complete, emerge as ongoing concerns.

Under both Chapter 7 and Chapter 11, providers of equity capital generally lose out. On the other hand, debt holders typically receive at least a portion of their capital, but only after the period of bankruptcy protection ends.

READING 37: WORKING CAPITAL MANAGEMENT

LESSON 1: WORKING CAPITAL MANAGEMENT

Working capital management deals with short-term aspects of corporate finance activities. Effective working capital management ensures that a company has ready access to funds that are needed for day-to-day expenses and that it invests its assets in the most productive manner at the same time. In this reading we deal with issues associated with managing working capital and look at various methods of evaluating the efficiency of a company's working capital management.

LOS 37a: Describe primary and secondary sources of liquidity and factors that influence a company's liquidity position. Vol 4, pp 157–159

Liquidity management refers to the ability of a company to generate cash when required. Sources of liquidity can be classified as:

- **Primary sources**, which are readily available resources such as cash balances and short-term funds.
- **Secondary sources**, which provide liquidity at a higher cost than primary sources. They include negotiating debt contracts, liquidating assets, or filing for bankruptcy protection.

Using primary sources of liquidity does not usually result in a change in a company's operations. On the other hand, using secondary sources of liquidity may lead to significant changes in the company's financial structure and operations, and may indicate that the company's financial position is deteriorating.

A **drag on liquidity** occurs when there is a delay in cash coming into the company. Major drags on liquidity include:

- Uncollected receivables: The longer receivables are outstanding, the greater the risk that they will not be collected at all.
- Obsolete inventory: If inventory remains unsold for a long period, it might indicate that it is no longer usable.
- Tight credit: Adverse economic conditions can make it difficult for companies to arrange short-term financing.

Drags on liquidity can be dealt with by enforcing strict credit and collection policies.

A **pull on liquidity** occurs when cash leaves the company too quickly. Major pulls on payments include:

- Making payments early instead of waiting until the due date to make them.
- Reduced credit limits as a result of a history of not being able to make payments on time.
- Limits on short-term lines of credit: These can be mandated by the government, market-related, or company-specific.
- Low existing levels of liquidity.

LOS 37b: Compare a company's liquidity measures with those of peer companies. Vol 4, pp 159–164

Creditworthiness is the perceived ability of a borrower to satisfy the payment terms on a borrowing in a timely manner. Liquidity contributes to a company's creditworthiness. See Example 1-1.

Example 1-1: Measuring Liquidity

The following table provides important liquidity ratios of Topaz Inc., along with industry averages. Evaluate the company's liquidity management.

Ratio	2008 Topaz	2008 Industry	2007 Topaz	2007 Industry
Current ratio	1.5	2.2	1	2
Quick ratio	0.8	1	0.5	0.8
Number of days of receivables	40	35	45	30
Number of days of inventory	45	38	48	30
Number of days of payables	36	38	28	36

Solution:

The changes in Topaz's ratios over 2008 suggest that its liquidity position has become more comfortable. However, the company still has room to improve, as it is still behind its peers in the industry.

The following **liquidity ratios** are used to evaluate a company's liquidity management:

The **current ratio** is the ratio of current assets to current liabilities.

$$\text{Current ratio} = \frac{\text{Current assets}}{\text{Current liabilities}}$$

- A higher current ratio means that a company is better positioned to meet its short-term obligations.
- A current ratio of less than one indicates negative working capital, which might imply that the company faces a liquidity crisis.

The **quick ratio (acid-test ratio)** is the ratio of quick assets to current liabilities. Quick assets are those that can be readily converted into cash, and exclude inventory (because it is usually the least liquid of current assets).

$$\text{Quick ratio} = \frac{\text{Cash} + \text{Short term marketable investments} + \text{Receivables}}{\text{Current liabilities}}$$

Higher quick and current ratios indicate greater liquidity. However, in order to gauge whether a given quick or current ratio is good or bad, we must look at the trend in ratios, how they compare with ratios of competitors, and available opportunities to invest in more profitable longer-term investments.

Accounts receivable turnover measures how many times, on average, accounts receivable are created by credit sales and collected over a given period. It is desirable to have an accounts receivable turnover close to the industry average.

$$\text{Accounts receivable turnover} = \frac{\text{Credit sales}}{\text{Average receivables}}$$

The number of days of receivables measures how many days it takes, on average, to collect receivables from customers. It is desirable to have a ratio close to the industry average.

$$\text{Number of days of receivables} = \frac{\text{Accounts receivable}}{\text{Average day's sales on credit}}$$

$$= \frac{\text{Accounts receivable}}{\text{Sales on credit} / 365}$$

- A collection period that is too high might imply that customers are too slow in making payments and too much of the company's capital is tied up in accounts receivable.
- A collection period that is too low might suggest that the company's credit policy is too strict, which might hurt sales.

The number of days of receivables must be evaluated in light of the credit terms offered to customers and the relation between sales and extension of credit.

Inventory turnover (TO) is a measure of how often, inventory is created and sold over a period.

$$\text{Inventory turnover} = \frac{\text{Cost of goods sold}}{\text{Average inventory}}$$

- An inventory TO ratio that is too high might indicate that the company has too little stock on hand at any given point in time, which might hurt sales.
- A low inventory TO ratio might suggest that the company has too much liquidity tied up in inventory, perhaps because the units held are obsolete.

The number of days of inventory tells us the length of the period that inventory remains with the firm before being sold. It is desirable to have this ratio close to industry norms.

$$\text{Number of days of inventory} = \frac{\text{Inventory}}{\text{Average day's cost of goods sold}}$$

$$= \frac{\text{Inventory}}{\text{Cost of goods sold} / 365}$$

Accounts payables turnover measures how many times the company theoretically pays off creditors over a period.

$$\text{Payables turnover} = \frac{\text{Purchases}}{\text{Average trade payables}}$$

- A high payables turnover ratio might indicate that the company is not making full use of available credit facilities.
- A low ratio could suggest that the company has trouble making payments on time.

The number of days of payables measures how long the company takes to pay its suppliers.

$$\text{Number of days of payables} = \frac{\text{Accounts payable}}{\text{Average day's purchases}}$$

$$= \frac{\text{Accounts payable}}{\text{Purchases} / 365}$$

The amount for purchases over the year might not be explicitly stated on the financial statements, but it can be calculated using cost of goods sold (COGS) and beginning and ending inventory balances:

$$\text{Purchases} = \text{Ending inventory} + \text{COGS} - \text{Beginning inventory}$$

LOS 37c: Evaluate working capital effectiveness of a company based on its operating and cash conversion cycles and compare the company's effectiveness with that of peer companies. Vol 4, pp 164–165

The operating cycle measures the time needed to convert raw materials into cash from sales.

$$\text{Operating cycle} = \text{Number of days of inventory} + \text{Number of days of receivables}$$

The cash conversion cycle, or the net operating cycle, is the length of the period from paying suppliers for materials to collecting cash from sales to customers. It can also be calculated as the operating cycle minus the number of days of payables.

$$\text{Net operating cycle} = \text{Number of days of inventory} + \text{Number of days of receivables}$$
$$- \text{Number of days of payables}$$

Usually, *shorter* cycles are desirable. A conversion cycle that is too long suggests that the company has too much invested in working capital.

For effective management of working capital it is important for a company to accurately forecast cash flows. Forecasts can alert financial managers to potential future cash needs ahead of time, and can provide a standard against which actual performance can be evaluated.

LOS 37d: Describe how different types of cash flows affect a company's net daily cash position. Vol 4, pp 165–167

Most companies prefer keeping a minimum cash balance to run their operations smoothly. Cash may also be needed to cater to unexpected requirements, or to capitalize on lucrative opportunities. Table 1-1 lists the typical elements of a cash flow forecast and classifies them as inflows or outflows. Table 1-2 highlights the important aspects of cash forecasting for different time horizons:

Table 1-1: Examples of Cash Inflows and Outflows[1]

Inflows	Outflows
• Receipts from operations.	• Payables and payroll disbursements.
• Funds transfer from subsidiaries, joint ventures, and third parties.	• Funds transfers to subsidiaries.
• Maturing investments.	• Investments made.
• Debt proceeds (short and long term).	• Debt repayments.
• Other income items (interest, etc.).	• Tax payments.
• Tax refunds.	• Interest and dividend payments.

Table 1-2: Aspects of Cash Forecasting[2]

	Short Term	Medium Term	Long Term
Data Frequency	Daily/weekly for 4–6 weeks	Monthly for one year	Annually for 3–5 years
Format	Receipts and disbursements	Receipts and disbursements	Projected financial statements
Techniques	Simple projections	Projection models and averages	Statistical models
Accuracy	Very high	Moderate	Lowest
Reliability	Very high	Fairly high	Not as high
Uses	Daily cash management	Planning financial transactions	Long-range financial position

Many companies face a predictable surge in demand during a particular time during the year or at a particular stage of the business cycle. For example, firms that manufacture electronic gadgets face a surge in demand for their products over the holiday shopping season. These companies have to ship a significant amount of inventory to retailers in advance, but only receive payments for sales once the season is over. As a result, they have to finance the inventory rollout. Once sales revenues come in, they use their surplus liquidity to pay back borrowed amounts and invest the excess. Predicting sales peaks caused by seasonality is very important if the company must borrow funds to cover its needs.

1 - Exhibit 5, Volume 4, CFA Program Curriculum 2019.
2 - Exhibit 6, Volume 4, CFA Program Curriculum 2019.

- If a company sets aside too much money, it will lose out on investment income (opportunity costs).
- If a company sets aside too little, it will incur higher costs to raise funds quickly.

Investing Short-Term Funds

A company maintains a daily cash position to make sure that it has the necessary funds (the target balance) to carry on its day-to-day activities. Short-term investments represent a temporary store for funds that are not needed for financing daily operations. Typical short-term investments in which businesses invest their excess cash in are highly liquid and have low risk. Table 1-3 lists some of the major instruments for short-term investments.

Table 1-3: Short-Term Investment Instruments[3]

Instruments	Typical Maturities	Features	Risks
U.S. Treasury Bills (T-bills)	13, 26, and 52 weeks	• Obligations of U.S. government (guaranteed), issued at a discount • Active secondary market • Lowest rates for traded securities	Virtually no risk
Federal agency securities	5–30 days	• Obligations of U.S. federal agencies (e.g., Fannie Mae, Federal Home Loan Board) issued as interest-bearing • Slightly higher yields than T-bills	Slight liquidity risk; insignificant credit risk
Bank certificates of deposit (CDs)	14–365 days	• Bank obligations, issued interest-bearing in $100,000 increments • "Yankee" CDs offer slightly higher yields	Credit and liquidity risk (depending on bank's credit)
Banker's acceptances (BAs)	30–180 days	• Bank obligations for trade transactions (usually foreign), issued at a discount • Investor protected by underlying company and trade flow itself • Small secondary market	Credit and liquidity risk (depending on bank's credit)
Eurodollar time deposits	1–180 days	• Time deposit with bank off-shore (outside United States, such as Bahamas) • Can be CD or straight time deposit (TD) • Interest-bearing investment • Small secondary market for CDs, but not TDs	Credit risk (depending on bank) Very high liquidity risk for TDs
Bank sweep services	1 day	• Service offered by banks that essentially provides interest on checking account balance (usually over a minimum level) • Large number of sweeps are for overnight	Credit and liquidity risk (depending on bank)

---

3 - Exhibit 7, Volume 4, CFA Program Curriculum 2019.

Table 1-3 (*continued*)

Instruments	Typical Maturities	Features	Risks
Repurchase agreements (Repos)	1 day+	• Sale of securities with the agreement of the dealer (seller) to buy them back at a future time • Typically over-collateralized at 102% • Often done for very short maturities (< 1 week)	Credit and liquidity risk (depending on dealer)
Commercial paper (CP)	1–270 days	• Unsecured obligations of corporations and financial institutions, issued at discount • Secondary market for large issuers • CP issuers obtain short-term credit ratings	Credit and liquidity risk (depending on credit rating)
Mutual funds and money market mutual funds	Varies	• Money market mutual funds commonly used by smaller businesses • Low yields but high liquidity for money market funds; mutual fund liquidity dependent on underlying securities in fund • Can be linked with bank sweep arrangement	Credit and liquidity risk (depending on fund manager)
Tax-advantaged securities	7, 28, 35, 49, and 90 days	• Preferred stock in many forms, including adjustable rate preferred stocks (ARPs), auction rate preferred stocks (AURPs), and convertible adjustable preferred stocks (CAPs) • Dutch auction often used to set rate • Offer higher yields	Credit and liquidity risk (depending on issuer's credit)

The dividend rate on adjustable-rate preferred stock is reset quarterly in line with market interest rates. These securities offer investors a tax-advantage because a high proportion of the dividend income is exempt from taxes.

When firms need to borrow over the short-term, they typically rely on bank overdrafts and commercial paper to meet their needs.

LOS 37e: Calculate and interpret comparable yields on various securities, compare portfolio returns against a standard benchmark, and evaluate a company's short-term investment policy guidelines. **Vol 4, pp 167–174**

Yields on Short-Term Investments

> Since we have already studied various measures of yields in detail in Quantitative Methods we will not spend much time on them here.

Discount instruments are instruments that are purchased at less than face value, and pay back face value at maturity. See Example 1-2.

Example 1-2: Discount Interest

A discount instrument with a face value of $1,000 pays 5% in interest and has one month remaining till maturity. At what price can the security be purchased today?

Solution:

$$\text{Purchase price} = \text{Face value} - \text{Discount in dollars}$$

$$= \$1,000 - (5\%)(1/12)(\$1,000)$$

$$= \$1,000 - \$4.167 = \$995.83$$

The difference between the face value and purchase price ($4.17) is known as **discount interest**.

Interest-bearing securities differ from discounted securities in that the investor pays the face value to purchase the security and receives the face value plus interest at maturity.

Yields on Short-Term Investments

$$\text{Money market yield} = \left(\frac{\text{Face value} - \text{price}}{\text{Price}} \right) \times \left(\frac{360}{\text{Days}} \right) = \text{Holding period yield} \times \left(\frac{360}{\text{Days}} \right)$$

$$\text{Bond equivalent yield} = \left(\frac{\text{Face value} - \text{price}}{\text{Price}} \right) \times \left(\frac{365}{\text{Days}} \right) = \text{Holding period yield} \times \left(\frac{365}{\text{Days}} \right)$$

$$\text{Discount basis yield} = \left(\frac{\text{Face value} - \text{price}}{\text{Face value}} \right) \times \left(\frac{360}{\text{Days}} \right) = \% \text{ discount} \times \left(\frac{360}{\text{Days}} \right)$$

$$\% \text{ Discount} = \frac{\text{Face value} - \text{Price}}{\text{Face value}}$$

Notice that the only difference between the money-market yield and discount-basis yield is the denominator. Money-market yield uses the purchase price, so it calculates the return an investor earns on the actual amount invested, over a 360-day year. Discount-basis yield uses the face value in the denominator and annualizes the yield for 360 days. The bond equivalent yield uses the purchase price in the denominator and uses a 365-day year. Notice that this formula for calculating BEY (for short-term instruments) is different from the one used in Quantitative Methods, where the semiannual yield was multiplied by 2 to determine BEY.

Example 1-3: Money-Market Yields, Discount-Basis Yields, and Bond Equivalent Yields

A 90-day US T-bill with a par value of $1,000 is issued at a discount of 8%. Calculate the money-market yield, discount-basis yield, and the bond equivalent yield for this security.

Solution:

Purchase price = Face value − Unannualized discount

$$= \$1,000 - (8\%)(90/360)(\$1,000) = \mathbf{\$980}$$

$$\text{Money market yield} = \left(\frac{\text{Face value} - \text{price}}{\text{Price}}\right) \times \left(\frac{360}{\text{Days}}\right) = \left(\frac{\$1,000 - \$980}{\$980}\right) \times \left(\frac{360}{90}\right) = 8.16\%$$

$$\text{Bond equivalent yield} = \left(\frac{\text{Face value} - \text{price}}{\text{Price}}\right) \times \left(\frac{365}{\text{Days}}\right) = \left(\frac{\$1,000 - \$980}{\$980}\right) \times \left(\frac{365}{90}\right) = 8.28\%$$

$$\text{Discount basis yield} = \left(\frac{\text{Face value} - \text{price}}{\text{Face value}}\right) \times \left(\frac{360}{\text{Days}}\right) = \left(\frac{\$1,000 - \$980}{\$1,000}\right) \times \left(\frac{360}{90}\right) = 8.00\%$$

Investment returns are expressed as bond equivalent yields to facilitate comparisons between various investment alternatives. The overall return on a portfolio is calculated as the weighted average of the yields of different assets in the portfolio, where an individual asset's weight is based on the proportion of the portfolio invested in that particular asset.

Investors face several different types of risks, such as credit risk, market risk, liquidity risk, foreign exchange risk, and so on. The key attributes of these risks (i.e., the conditions that lead to them) and the steps that investors may take to mitigate/eliminate associated losses are listed in Table 1-4.

Table 1-4: Types of Investment Risks and Safety Measures[4]

Type of Risk	Key Attributes	Safety Measures
Credit (or default)	• Issuer may default • Issuer could be adversely affected by economy, market • Little secondary market	• Minimize amount • Keep maturities short • Watch for "questionable" names • Emphasize government securities
Market (or interest rate)	• Price or rate changes may adversely affect return • There is no market to sell the maturity to, or there is only a small secondary market	• Keep maturities short • Keep portfolio diverse in terms of maturity, issuers
Liquidity	• Security is difficult or impossible to (re)sell • Security must be held to maturity and cannot be liquidated until then	• Stick with government securities • Look for good secondary market • Keep maturities short
Foreign exchange	• Adverse general market movement against your currency	• Hedge regularly • Keep most in your currency and domestic market (avoid foreign exchange)

Cash Management Investment Strategies

Short-term investment strategies can be categorized as passive or active.

- A passive strategy involves a limited number of transactions, and is based on very few rules for making daily investments. The focus is simply on reinvesting funds as they mature with little attention paid to yields.
- An active strategy involves constant monitoring to exploit profitable opportunities in a wider array of investments. Active strategies call for more involvement, more thorough study, evaluation, forecasts, and a flexible investment policy.
  - Matching strategies involve matching the timing of cash outflows with investment maturities. A matching strategy makes use of similar types of investments as passive strategies.
  - Mismatching strategies involve intentionally mismatching the timing of cash outflows with investment maturities. A mismatching strategy is riskier and requires very accurate and reliable cash forecasts. This strategy typically involves the use of liquid instruments and derivatives.
  - Laddering strategies involve scheduling the maturities of portfolio investments such that maturities are spread out equally over the term of the ladder.

---

4 - Exhibit 8, Volume 4, CFA Program Curriculum 2019.

Cash Management Investment Policy

Companies with short-term investment portfolios should have a formal, written policy that guides the investment decision-making process. Having such a policy protects the company and its investment manager, and effectively communicates key aspects of the portfolio to investment dealers. An investment policy has the following basic structure:

- The *purpose* of the investment policy states reasons for the existence of the portfolio and describes its general attributes, such as the investment strategy to be followed.
- It identifies the *authorities* who supervise the portfolio managers and details the actions that must be undertaken if the policy is not followed.
- It describes the types of investments that should be considered for inclusion in the portfolio. The policy also contains *restrictions* on the maximum proportion of each type of security in the portfolio and specifies the minimum credit rating of portfolio securities.

The investment policy statement should be evaluated on the basis of how well it meets the goals of short-term investments (i.e., its ability to generate competitive returns without exposing the company to undue risks). The returns on short-term investments in different instruments should be expressed as bond equivalent yields so that various investment options can be easily compared.

LOS 37f: Evaluate a company's management of accounts receivable, inventory, and accounts payable over time and compared to peer companies. Vol 4, pp 175–188

Key Elements of the Trade Credit Granting Process

A company's credit policy can have a significant impact on sales. A company may be able to enhance sales by loosening acceptance criteria, and could end up restricting sales if the terms offered to customers are too strict. An effective credit management system must follow a proper strategy that is tailored to the company's needs and reflects its goals.

Companies offer different forms of credit terms to customers depending on their financial strength, the nature of their relationship with the company, and the type of credit terms offered by competitors. Some forms of terms of credit (excluding cash) include:

- Ordinary terms
- Cash before delivery (CBD)
- Cash on delivery (COD)
- Bill-to-bill
- Monthly billing

Credit managers typically use **credit scoring models** to evaluate customers' creditworthiness. These models consider factors such as availability of ready cash, type of organization (i.e., corporation, sole proprietorship, etc.), and how quickly payments are made to suppliers. The benefit of using credit scoring models is that they allow companies to make decisions quickly, and do not require a great deal of paperwork.

Managing Customers' Receipts

A company's cash collection system depends on the types of customers it has and the methods of payment used by them. A good collection system should accelerate payments along with their information content (e.g., customer's name, identification number, etc.). This can best be achieved by establishing an electronic collection network. However, if payments cannot be converted to electronic payments, then companies may use bank lockbox services.

Companies may measure the performance for check deposits by calculating the **float factor**, which gives the average number of days it takes deposited checks to clear.

A lockbox system simplifies a company's collection and processing of accounts receivables. Under this system, customers mail their payments to a post office box from where they are collected, processed, and deposited by the company's bank. This saves the time for payments being first processed by the company's accounting system, hence, speeding up cash collection.

$$\text{Float factor} = \text{Average daily float / Average daily deposit}$$

Float = Amount of money that is in transit between payments made by the customers and funds that can be used by the company

$$\text{Average daily deposit} = \text{Total amount of check deposited / Number of days}$$

Although this measure only tells us the time it takes for checks to clear (and not how long it takes to receive those checks, deposit them, and then have them cleared), it is still very useful as it can be calculated easily for any depository account.

Evaluating Management of Accounts Receivable

An aging schedule classifies accounts receivable according to the length of time they have been outstanding. Table 1-5 provides an example of an aging schedule. It shows the accounts receivable of ABC Company at the end of the first quarter of 2008.

Table 1-5: ABC's Accounts Receivable Aging Schedule

	January 2008	February 2008	March 2008
Current (1–30 days old)	$15,000	$13,000	$10,000
1–30 days past due	$6,000	$5,000	$9,000
31–60 days past due	$5,000	$4,000	$5,000
61–90 days past due	$3,000	$3,000	$4,000
More than 90 days past due	$2,000	$2,000	$2,000
TOTAL	$31,000	$27,000	$30,000

In Table 1-6, ABC's aging schedule is presented in terms of percentages. This makes it easier to identify changes in the aging schedule over the period. Notice the change in March's aging—a lower proportion of total receivables is in the form of current receivables (33.3%), and a higher proportion of receivables is past due (66.7%). Accounts receivable have not been collected and converted to cash as rapidly in March as they were in January and February.

Table 1-6: ABC's Weighted Average Collection Period

	January 2008	February 2008	March 2008
Current (1–30 days old)	48.4%	48.1%	33.3%
1–30 days past due	19.4%	18.5%	30%
31–60 days past due	16.1%	14.8%	16.7%
61–90 days past due	9.7%	11.1%	13.3%
More than 90 days past due	6.5%	7.4%	6.7%

We can better evaluate the firm's ability to collect its receivables by calculating the **weighted average collection period**, which measures how long it takes a company to collect cash from its customers irrespective of the changes in sales and the level of sales. Exhibit 1-1 shows the calculation of ABC's weighted average collection period for February 2008 and March 2008.

Exhibit 1-1: Calculation of ABC's Weighted Average Collection Period

The average days for collecting receivables in each grouping.

The weighting from the aging schedule.

The product of collection days and weight.

February 2008

	Collection Days	Weight	Weighted days
Current (1–30 days old)	20	48.1%	9.6
31–60 days	40	18.5%	7.4
61–90 days	72	14.8%	10.7
91–120 days	95	11.1%	10.5
121+ days	123	7.4%	9.1
Weighted average collection days			**47.3**

The total of all the weighted days.

March 2008

	Collection Days	Weight	Weighted days
Current (1–30 days old)	24	33.3%	8
31–60 days	45	30%	13.5
61–90 days	78	16.7%	13
91–120 days	102	13.3%	13.6
121+ days	138	6.7%	9.2
Weighted average collection days			**57.3**

The company's weighted average collection period has increased dramatically. An analyst should scrutinize this change and determine whether it is due to an extension of credit terms by the company to promote sales or because major customers are having trouble making payments.

The only drawback of the weighted average collection method is that it requires more information than the number of days of receivables. This information may not be easily available.

Evaluating Inventory Management

The main goal of inventory management is to maintain a level of inventory that ensures smooth delivery of sales without having more than necessary invested in inventory.

- A high level of inventory is undesirable as it inflates storage costs, can result in losses from obsolescence or damage, and can squeeze liquidity from the firm.
- A shortage of inventory, on the other hand, can hurt sales as the company loses out on potential customers.

Companies may have a variety of motives for holding inventory. These include:

- The transactions motive: Inventory is just kept for the planned manufacturing activity.
- The precautionary motive: Inventory is kept to avoid any stock-out losses.
- The speculative motive: Inventory is kept to ensure its availability in the future when prices are expected to increase.

However, companies need to strike a balance in managing their inventory levels (i.e., they need to avoid costs of holding excessive inventory, and at the same time ensure that they hold sufficient stock to avoid hampering sales). Two basic approaches for managing inventory levels are economic order quantity and just-in-time.

- Economic order quantity is the order quantity for inventory that minimizes its total ordering and holding costs. Companies typically use the economic order quantity-reorder point (EOQ-ROP) method, under which the ordering point for inventory is determined on the basis of costs of ordering and carrying inventory, such that total cost associated with inventory is minimized. This method relies on expected demand, which makes it imperative that short-term forecasts are reliable.
- The just-in-time method reduces in-process inventory and associated carrying costs through evaluation of the entire system of delivery of materials and production. Under this method, the reorder point is primarily determined on the basis of historical demand.

We can evaluate a company's inventory management by analyzing the inventory turnover ratio and the number of days of inventory.

$$\text{Inventory turnover} = \frac{\text{Cost of goods sold}}{\text{Average inventory}}$$

$$\begin{aligned}\text{Number of days of inventory} &= \frac{\text{Inventory}}{\text{Average days cost of goods sold}} \\ &= \frac{\text{Inventory}}{\text{Cost of goods sold} / 365} \\ &= \frac{365}{\text{Inventory turnover}}\end{aligned}$$

As we have mentioned before, analysts should be careful when interpreting changes in these ratios. Firms in the same industry may have significantly different turnover ratios because of different strategies or product mixes. A decrease in inventory TO for a firm over time could indicate that enough stock is not being sold. On the other hand, a decrease could also indicate that a company wants to reduce the chances of inventory "stock-outs."

Evaluating Management of Accounts Payable

Managing accounts payable is an important part of working capital management, as accounts payable can be a source of working capital for the firm. By paying too early, a company loses out on interest income. If it pays late, the company risks ruining its reputation and relationships with suppliers. Further, penalties and interest charges for late payment can be very significant.

Companies should consider a variety of factors as guidelines for managing their accounts payable effectively. These include:

- Financial organization's centralization: The management of a company's payables is affected by the degree to which its core financial system is centralized or decentralized.
- Number, size, and location of vendors: The sophistication of a company's payables system is affected by its supply chain and how dependent the company is on its trading partners.
- Trade credit and cost of borrowing or alternative cost: The standardization of a company's payables procedures is dependent on the importance of credit to the company and its ability to evaluate trade credit opportunities (e.g., trade discounts).
- Control of disbursement float: The disbursement float (the amount of time between the issuance of a check and its clearance) allows companies to use their funds longer than if they had to fund their checking accounts on the day the checks were mailed.
- Inventory management: Newer management techniques and systems are required to process the increased volume of payments generated through newer inventory control techniques.
- E-commerce and electronic data interchange (EDI): Making payments electronically may be more efficient and cost-effective than making payments through checks. Checks are only more valuable when the value of the disbursement float and interest rates are high.

Evaluating Trade Discounts

A company should review its evaluation of trade discounts periodically. An early payment discount must be availed if the savings from paying suppliers early are greater than the returns that could have been earned by investing the funds instead or greater than the firm's cost of borrowing.

$$\text{Implicit rate} = \text{Cost of trade credit} = \left(1 + \frac{\text{Discount}}{1 - \text{Discount}}\right)^{\left(\frac{365}{\text{Number of days beyond discount period}}\right)} - 1$$

Terms of "2/10 net 30" mean that a 2% discount is available if the amount owed is paid within 10 days; otherwise, the full amount is due by the 30th day. See Example 1-4.

> ### Example 1-4: Evaluating Trade Discounts
>
> Calculate the cost of trade credit if terms are 2/10, net 30 and the account is paid on:
>
> - The 15th day
> - The 25th day
>
> **Solution:**
>
> $$\text{Cost of trade credit on the 15th day} = \left(1 + \frac{0.02}{1-0.02}\right)^{\left(365/5\right)} - 1 = 337.02\%$$
>
> $$\text{Cost of trade credit on the 25th day} = \left(1 + \frac{0.02}{1-0.02}\right)^{\left(365/15\right)} - 1 = 63.49\%$$
>
> Cost of credit decreases as the company approaches the net day (the 30th day).

The cost of trade credit during the discount window is zero percent, so a company should pay toward the end of the discount period if it wants to avail the discount. Once the discount period expires, the cost of credit rises significantly and then declines as the net day nears. If the company's cost of funds or short-term investment rate is less than the calculated rate, it offers a better return than the company's short-term borrowing rate.

We can evaluate a company's management of payables through its number of days of payables.

$$\text{Number of days of payables} = \frac{\text{Accounts payable}}{\text{Average day's purchases}}$$

$$\frac{\text{Accounts payable}}{\text{Purchases} / 365} = \frac{365}{\text{Payables turnover}}$$

This ratio indicates the number of days, on average, that the company takes to pay its suppliers. The number of days must be compared to the credit terms offered to the company; paying sooner than necessary has costs of credit, and paying late might affect relations with suppliers adversely.

LOS 37g: Evaluate the choices of short-term funding available to a company and recommend a financing method. Vol 4, pp 189–194

Short-term financing is available to companies from various bank and nonbank sources. Table 1-7 lists the primary features of bank sources of finance.

Table 1-7: Bank Sources of Short-Term Finance[5]

Source/Type	Users	Rate Base	Compensation	Other
Uncommitted line	Large corporations		None	Mainly in the U.S.; limited liability
Regular line	All sizes	Prime (U.S.) or base rate (other countries)	Commitment Fees	Common everywhere
Overdraft line	All sizes		Commitment Fees	Mainly outside U.S.
Revolving credit agreement	Larger corporations		Commitment fees plus extra fees	Strongest form (primarily in the U.S.)
Collateralized loan	Small, weak borrowers	Base +	Collateral	Common everywhere
Discounted receivables	Large companies	Varies	Extra fees	More overseas, but some in U.S.
Bankers' acceptances	International companies	Spread over commercial paper	None	Small volume
Factoring	Smaller	Prime ++	Service fees	Special industries

- **Uncommitted lines of credit:** A bank offers a line of credit to the company for a certain period of time, but reserves the right to refuse to lend. This makes it the weakest and least reliable form of borrowing. Its advantage is that it does not require any compensation other than interest.
- **Committed lines of credit (regular lines of credit):** These are stronger than uncommitted lines of credit as they require a formal commitment from the bank. Further, they are unsecured and are prepayable without any penalties. Borrowing rates are negotiated, and are usually stated in terms of a money-market rate (such as LIBOR) plus a spread to reflect the borrower's creditworthiness. Note that banks also typically charge a fee for a committed line of credit.
- **Revolving credit agreements:** These are the strongest form of short-term borrowing facilities. They are similar to regular lines of credit with respect to borrowing rates, compensation, and being unsecured. However, unlike regular lines of credit, they are in effect for multiple years, and may have optional medium-term loan features.

Nonbank sources of short-term finance include nonbank finance companies and commercial paper. Table 1-8 lists the features of these sources.

---

5 - Exhibit 15 - Panel A, Volume 4, CFA Program Curriculum 2019.

Table 1-8: Nonbank Sources of Short-Term Finance[6]

Source/Type	Users	Rate Base	Compensation	Other
Nonbank finance companies	Small, weak borrowers	Prime + + +	Service fees	Weak credits
Commercial paper	Largest corporations	Money-market sets rate	Back up line of credit, commissions	Lowest rates for short-term funds

Some companies take secured short-term loans, which are known as asset-based loans. These loans are collateralized by current assets of the company (usually receivables and inventory). Companies usually take asset-based loans when they do not have the required credit quality to qualify for bank loans.

Approaches to Short-Term Borrowing

Borrowers should have planned strategies for short-term borrowings. They should:

- Ensure that there is sufficient capacity to handle peak cash needs.
- Maintain sufficient sources of credit to be able to fund ongoing cash requirements.
- Ensure that the rates obtained for these borrowings are cost effective.
- Diversify to have abundant options and not be too reliant on one lender or form of lending.
- Have the ability to manage different maturities in an efficient manner.

Asset-Based Loans

If a company fails to qualify for an unsecured bank loan, it may opt for asset-based loans. These are loans that are collateralized by the company's assets. Assets that are used to secure short-term loans usually include current assets, such as receivables and inventory.

Computing the Costs of Borrowing

Firms must strive to obtain the most cost-effective source of finance. In order to find the best form of short-term financing, each of the sources have to be adjusted to a common basis for comparability.

Cost of line of credit (and other sources that require a commitment fee)

$$\text{Line of credit cost} = \frac{\text{Interest} + \text{Commitment fee}}{\text{Loan amount}}$$

Cost of banker's acceptance (and other sources whose costs are stated as "all-inclusive"):

$$\text{Banker's acceptance cost} = \frac{\text{Interest}}{\text{Net proceeds}} = \frac{\text{Interest}}{\text{Loan amount} - \text{Interest}}$$

---

6 - Exhibit 15 - Panel B, Volume 4, CFA Program Curriculum 2019.

Cost of commercial paper (and sources with dealer's fees and backup fees, which are quoted as all inclusive)

$$\frac{\text{Interest} + \text{Dealer's comission} + \text{Backup cost}}{\text{Loan amount} - \text{Interest}}$$

Example 1-5: Choosing Between Short-Term Borrowing Alternatives

Evaluate which of the following short-term financing choices should be chosen for having the lowest cost. Assume that $1,000,000 will be borrowed for one month.

1. Drawing on a line of credit at 7% with a 0.5% commitment fee on the full amount. One-twelfth of the commitment fee is allocated to each month.
2. A banker's acceptance at 8%, an all-inclusive rate.
3. Commercial paper at 6% with a dealer's commission of 1/4% and a backup line of cost of 1/2 %.

This analysis has been simplified by using a factor of 1/12 to determine the effective interest rate and a factor of 12 to annualize the effective interest rate.

Solutions:

$$\text{Line of credit cost} = \left(\frac{\text{Interest} + \text{Commitment fee}}{\text{Loan amount}}\right) \times 12$$

$$\text{Line of credit cost} = \left(\frac{(0.07 \times 1,000,000 \times 1/12) + (0.005 \times 1,000,000 \times 1/12)}{1,000,000}\right) \times 12$$

Line of credit cost = 7.5%

$$\text{Banker's acceptance cost} = \left(\frac{\text{Interest}}{\text{Loan amount} - \text{Interest}}\right) \times 12$$

$$\text{Banker's acceptance cost} = \left(\frac{(0.08 \times 1,000,000 \times 1/12)}{1,000,000 - (0.08 \times 1,000,000 \times 1/12)}\right) \times 12$$

Banker's acceptance cost = 8.05%

$$\text{Commercial paper cost} = \left(\frac{\text{Interest} + \text{Dealer's comission} + \text{Backup costs}}{\text{Loan amount} - \text{Interest}}\right) \times 12$$

$$= \left(\frac{(0.06 \times 1,000,000 \times 1/12) + (0.0025 \times 1,000,000 \times 1/12) + (0.005 \times 1,000,000 \times 1/12)}{1,000,000 - (0.06 \times 1,000,000 \times 1/12)}\right) \times 12$$

Commercial paper cost = 6.78%

Commercial paper offers the lowest cost source of short-term financing in the given scenario.

READING 38: PORTFOLIO MANAGEMENT: AN OVERVIEW

LESSON 1: PORTFOLIO MANAGEMENT: AN OVERVIEW

LOS 38a: Describe the portfolio approach to investing. Vol 4, pp 207–216

Instead of evaluating each investment in isolation, investment managers should take a portfolio perspective when evaluating an investment. Taking a portfolio perspective means evaluating each investment on the basis of its contribution to the characteristics of the portfolio as a whole.

Reasons for Taking the Portfolio Perspective

Taking the portfolio perspective offers diversification benefits. By not putting all their eggs in one basket (overinvesting in a single security or asset class), individuals can diversify away some of the risk in their investments.

> In a later reading, we will learn that portfolio standard deviation tends to be lower than the average standard deviation of its components due to the less than perfectly positive correlation between the returns on its components.

- Portfolios of securities may offer equivalent expected returns with lower volatility of returns (lower risk) compared to individual securities.
- A simple measure of the value of diversification is the diversification ratio. It is the ratio of the standard deviation of an equal-weighted portfolio to the standard deviation of a randomly selected component of the portfolio. The lower the diversification ratio, the greater the risk reduction benefits of diversification, and the greater the portfolio effect.
- The composition of the portfolio (weight of each security held in the portfolio) is an important determinant of the overall level of risk inherent in the portfolio. By varying the weights of the individual securities, investors can arrive at a portfolio that offers the same return as an equally weighted portfolio, but with a lower standard deviation (risk).

Despite the obvious benefits of subscribing to the portfolio perspective when making investments, it is important to note that portfolios do not necessarily provide downside protection. The correlation between the various components of the portfolio can change over time in a manner unfavorable to investors and reduce diversification benefits. For example, in the recent market turmoil (late 2007 to early 2009) all major market indices fell in unison.

LOS 38b: Describe types of investors and distinctive characteristics and needs of each. Vol 4, pp 216–217

LOS 38c: Describe defined contribution and defined benefit pension plans. Vol 4, pp 216–217

> An important thing to note about a defined-contribution plan is that the employee accepts the investment risk in the portfolio.

Individual Investors

Individual investors can have a variety of reasons for investing (e.g., providing for children's college education, saving for retirement, or starting a business). Most individuals accumulate wealth to provide for their needs during retirement through defined-contribution pension plans, where they contribute a part of their wages to the plan while working.

The investment needs of individuals depend on their broader financial circumstances. Younger investors tend to be more aggressive and look for capital gains, while older investors look to generate a stable income stream to meet retirement needs. See Table 1-1.

Institutional Investors

Defined-benefit pension plans: In a defined-benefit (DB) plan, the employer has an obligation to pay a certain amount to its employees every year once they retire. DB plans are long-term investors and aim to match cash flows from plan assets with the timing of future pension payments (liabilities).

Endowments and foundations: A university endowment is established to provide financial support to the university and its students. A charitable foundation invests the donations that it receives in order to fund grants that are in line with its objectives. Typically, endowments and foundations aim to maintain the inflation-adjusted capital value of their funds, while generating the necessary income to meet their objectives. They are generally established with the intent of having a perpetual useful life and must balance short-term spending needs with long-term capital preservation requirements.

Banks: A bank typically aims to earn a return on its reserves that is greater than the interest that it pays to depositors. In addition to being low risk, a bank's investments must be relatively liquid so that they can be easily sold if depositors need to withdraw funds. In the United States, there are legal restrictions on banks owning equity investments.

Insurance companies: An insurance company writes an insurance policy in return for a premium. These premiums must be invested in a manner that allows the company to meet insurance claims when they arise. Insurance companies are also relatively conservative with their investments as they need to satisfy claims when due. Life insurance companies typically have a longer time horizon than nonlife insurance companies, as they are expected to have to make payments after a longer period.

Investment companies: Investment companies and mutual funds are discussed in detail in a later reading.

Sovereign wealth funds: A sovereign wealth fund (SWF) is a government-owned investment fund. SWFs are usually established to invest revenues from finite revenue sources (e.g., oil) to benefit future generations of citizens or to manage a country's foreign exchange reserves.

Table 1-1: Summary of Investment Needs by Client Type[1]

Client	Time Horizon	Risk Tolerance	Income Needs	Liquidity Needs
Individual investors	Varies by individual	Varies by individual	Varies by individual	Varies by individual
Defined-benefit pension plans	Typically long term	Typically quite high	High for mature funds; low for growing funds	Typically quite low
Endowments and foundations	Very long term	Typically high	To meet spending commitments	Typically quite low

1 - Exhibit 14, Volume 4, CFA Program Curriculum 2019

Table 1-1 (*continued*)

Client	Time Horizon	Risk Tolerance	Income Needs	Liquidity Needs
Banks	Short term	Quite low	To pay interest on deposits and operations expenses	High to meet repayment of deposits
Insurance companies	Short term for property and casualty; long term for life insurance companies	Typically quite low	Typically low	High to meet claims
Investment companies	Varies by fund	Varies by fund	Varies by fund	High to meet redemptions

LOS 38d: Describe the steps in the portfolio management process.
Vol 4, pp 222–226

The portfolio management process involves the following steps:

- Planning
  - Understanding the client's needs.
  - Preparing the investment policy statement (IPS).
- Execution
  - Determining the asset allocation.
  - Analyzing securities.
  - Constructing the portfolio.
- Feedback
  - Monitoring and rebalancing the portfolio.
  - Measuring and reporting performance.

Planning

The planning step involves understanding the client's needs and constraints and developing an investment policy statement (IPS). The IPS is a written document that describes the objectives and constraints of the investor. It may also include a benchmark against which the portfolio manager's performance can be evaluated. An IPS should be reviewed and updated regularly, especially if there has been a drastic change in the client's circumstances.

Execution

Asset allocation: The asset allocation of a portfolio refers to the distribution of investable funds between various asset classes (e.g., equities, fixed-income securities, alternative investments, etc.). Analysts form economic and capital market expectations and allocate funds across asset classes based on how each class is expected to perform in the forecasted scenario. Although decisions regarding which individual securities are chosen do have an effect on portfolio performance, differences in asset allocation explain most of the differences between returns on portfolios.

Security analysis: Analysts use their knowledge of various companies and the industry to identify investments that offer the most attractive risk return characteristics from within each asset class.

Portfolio construction: After determining the target asset allocation and conducting a security analysis, the portfolio manager will construct the portfolio in line with the objectives outlined in the IPS. The portfolio must be well diversified, and the risk inherent in the portfolio must be in line with the client's risk tolerance level as specified in the IPS.

Once the portfolio manager has decided which securities to purchase and in what amount, she will pass instructions to a trader, who will execute the transactions.

Feedback

Portfolio monitoring and rebalancing: The portfolio must be regularly monitored. Changes in fundamental factors and client circumstances may require changes in the portfolio's composition. Rebalancing may be required when changes in security prices cause a significant change in weights of assets in the portfolio.

Performance measurement and reporting: This step involves measuring the performance of the portfolio relative to the benchmark stated in the IPS and reporting portfolio performance to the client.

LOS 38e: Describe mutual funds and compare them with other pooled investment products. Vol 4, pp 226–233

Pooled Investments

Pooled investments are investments in securities issued by entities that represent ownership in the underlying assets held by those entities. These include:

- Mutual funds and exchange traded funds, in which investors can participate with a relatively small initial investment
- Hedge funds and private equity funds, which may require a minimum investment of U.S. $1 million or more.

Mutual Funds

Mutual funds pool money from several investors and invest these funds in a portfolio of securities. Individuals and institutions invest in mutual funds to obtain diversification benefits and to avail the investment management services of qualified managers. Each investor has a pro-rata share in the income and value of the fund.

The value of a mutual fund is referred to as "net asset value" (NAV), which is calculated on a daily basis based on the closing price of the underlying securities. There are two types of mutual funds:

- *Open-end funds* accept new investment funds and issue new shares at a value equal to the fund's net asset value per share at the time of investment. These funds also allow investors to redeem their investment in the fund at the prevailing net asset value per share.

- *Closed-end funds* accept no new investment money into fund. Shares in the fund are traded in the secondary market so new investors invest in the fund by purchasing shares in the market, and investors liquidate their holdings by selling the shares in the market. Unlike open-end funds, shares of closed-end funds can trade at a discount or premium to the net asset value per share, depending on the demand and supply of shares in the market.

The structure of open-end funds makes it easy for them to grow in size, but it does pose the following problems:

- The portfolio manager needs to manage cash inflows and outflows.
- An inflow of new investment requires the manager to find new investments.
- Funds need to keep cash for redemptions.

Closed-end funds do not face these problems, but as mentioned earlier, they cannot accept new investments.

Mutual funds may also be classified into:

- *Load funds* that charge a percentage fee for investing in the fund and/or for redemptions from the fund on top of an annual fee.
- *No-load funds* that only charge an annual fee based on a percentage of the fund's NAV.

Types of Mutual Funds

- *Money-market funds*: These invest in high-quality, short-term debt instruments. Money-market mutual funds can be divided into tax-free and taxable funds.
- *Bond funds*: These invest in individual bonds and sometimes preference shares as well. Unlike money-market mutual funds, they usually invest in longer term instruments.
- *Stock funds*: These invest in equities and equity indices. Stock mutual funds can be actively or passively managed. Active portfolio management aims to outperform a benchmark portfolio or index by tilting the individual weights of stocks in the portfolio away from their weights in the benchmark. On the other hand, passive management (followed by index funds) aims to track the performance of a benchmark portfolio by attaching the same weights to individual stocks as prescribed by the benchmark.

  Active management entails higher management fees to compensate managers for the research conducted to select mispriced securities. Further, it results in a higher turnover of portfolio securities, which leads to greater capital gains tax liabilities and transaction costs relative to index funds.
- *Hybrid or balanced funds*: These invest in both bonds and equities.

Other Investment Products

Exchange Traded Funds (ETFs)

Exchange traded funds (ETFs) issue shares in a portfolio of securities and are designed to track the performance of a specified index. An ETF purchases a large number of shares in the same proportion as the index it tracks and issues shares in the ETF to investors who want to track the same index.

ETFs combine features of closed-end and open-end mutual funds. They are similar to closed-end funds in that they are traded in the secondary market. However, like open-end funds, their prices stay close to the NAV per share.

ETFs differ from index mutual funds in the following ways:

- Investors in index mutual funds purchase shares directly from the fund, while investors in an ETF purchase shares from other investors (just like buying or selling shares of stock). Investors are allowed to short ETF shares and even purchase them on margin.
- ETFs have lower costs, but unlike index mutual funds, investors do incur brokerage costs when trading ETFs.
- ETFs are constantly traded throughout the business day. Each trade occurs at the prevailing market price at that time. All purchases and redemptions for a mutual fund for a given day occur at the end of a trading day, at the same price.
- ETFs pay out dividends, while index mutual funds usually reinvest dividends.
- The minimum required investment is usually smaller for an ETF.
- ETFs are generally considered to have a tax advantage over index mutual funds.

Separately Managed Accounts (SMAs)

A separately managed account (also called a managed account, wrap account, or individually managed account) is a fund management service for wealthy investors. The portfolio manager manages the account exclusively for the benefit of the client and aims to meet the needs of the client in relation to investment objectives, risk tolerance, and tax situation. The client may also receive personalized investment advice in return for an annual fee.

SMAs differ from mutual funds in the following ways:

- Unlike investors in mutual funds, investors in SMAs directly own the shares and therefore have control over which assets are bought and sold and over the timing of transactions.
- Unlike mutual funds, in which no consideration is given to the tax position of the investor, transactions in SMAs take into account the specific tax needs of the investor.
- The required minimum investment for an SMA is usually much higher than for a mutual fund.

Hedge Funds

Hedge funds and venture capital funds are discussed in greater detail in Alternative Investments.

Hedge funds were originally meant to offer plays against the market and hedge against a downside, usually through short selling and using derivatives. Today, the term hedge funds has evolved to encompass a host of funds that simply look to generate absolute returns for investors (as compared to other funds that define a specific benchmark whose return they try to match or exceed).

- Hedge funds differ from mutual funds in that most hedge funds are exempt from many of the reporting requirements for a typical public investment company.
- They require a minimum investment that is typically U.S. $250,000 for new funds and U.S. $1 million or more for well-established funds.
- They usually place restrictions on investors' ability to make withdrawals from the fund.
- Total management fee also has a performance-based component.

Hedge fund strategies may involve significant risk due to the use of leverage and derivatives. Some of these strategies are discussed below:

- Convertible arbitrage funds purchase securities, such as convertible bonds, and simultaneously take short positions in related equity securities.
- Dedicated short bias funds take more short positions than long positions.
- Emerging market funds invest in companies in emerging markets by purchasing corporate or sovereign securities.
- Equity market neutral funds eliminate exposure to overall market movements by taking short positions in overvalued securities and long positions (of nearly equal value) in undervalued securities.
- Event driven funds attempt to take advantage of specific company events, such as mergers and acquisitions.
- Fixed-income arbitrage funds take opposing positions in debt securities to profit from arbitrage opportunities and to limit interest rate risk.
- Global macro funds attempt to profit from changes in the overall macroeconomic environment using derivatives on currencies and interest rates.
- Long/short funds go long on securities that are expected to increase in value and short securities that are expected to decrease in value. These differ from equity market neutral funds in that they attempt to profit from movements in the broader market, as well as from identifying overvalued or undervalued securities.

Buyout and Venture Capital Funds

Leveraged buyout (LBO) funds raise money specifically for the purpose of buying public companies, taking them private, and restructuring them to make them more efficient and profitable concerns. The purchase of company shares is usually financed with a significant amount of debt. The idea is to service the debt by increasing the company's cash flow and then to exit the investment through an IPO or sale to another company.

A venture capital (VC) fund does not buy out a company, but provides financing to startups.

Buyout and venture capital funds have the following characteristics:

- They take equity positions in companies and play a very active role in managing those companies.
- The eventual exit strategy is an important consideration when funds evaluate potential investments.

LBO and VC funds are similar to hedge funds in that they have relatively high minimum investment requirements, investors are unable to withdraw money from these funds for a specified period, and management fees have a performance-based component.

READING 39: PORTFOLIO RISK AND RETURN: PART I

LESSON 1: INVESTMENT CHARACTERISTICS OF ASSETS

LOS 39a: Calculate and interpret major return measures and describe their appropriate uses. Vol 4, pp 244–267

LOS 39b: Describe characteristics of the major asset classes that investors consider in forming portfolios. Vol 4, pp 244–267

LOS 39c: Calculate and interpret the mean, variance, and covariance (or correlation) of asset returns based on historical data. Vol 4, pp 244–267

Financial assets are generally defined by their risk and return characteristics. This makes it easier to value them and simplifies the process of determining which assets should be included in a portfolio.

Return

Financial assets may provide one or both of the following types of returns:

- Periodic income (e.g., dividends and interest income)
- Capital gains or losses resulting from changes in market price.

Holding Period Return

Holding period return is simply the return earned on an investment over a single specified period of time. It is calculated as:

$$R = \frac{P_t - P_{t-1} + D_t}{P_{t-1}} = \frac{P_t - P_{t-1}}{P_{t-1}} + \frac{D_t}{P_{t-1}} = \text{Capital gain} + \text{Dividend yield}$$

$$= \frac{P_T + D_T}{P_0} - 1$$

where:
P_t = Price at the end of the period
P_{t-1} = Price at the beginning of the period
D_t = Dividend for the period

Note: We have assumed that the dividend is paid at the end of the period. If the dividend is paid any time before t, we would also have to account for the return earned by investing the dividend for the remainder of the period. This would lead to a higher holding period return.

Holding period returns may also be calculated for more than one period by compounding single period returns:

$$R = \left[(1 + R_1) \times (1 + R_2) \times \ldots \times (1 + R_n) \right] - 1$$

where:
$R_1, R_2, \ldots, R_n$ are sub-period returns

Arithmetic or Mean Return

The arithmetic or mean return is a simple average of all holding period returns. It is calculated as:

$$R = \frac{R_{i1} + R_{i2} + \ldots + R_{iT}}{T} = \frac{1}{T}\sum_{t=1}^{T} R_{iT}$$

Arithmetic return is easy to calculate and has known statistical properties such as standard deviation, which is used to evaluate the dispersion of observed returns. However, the arithmetic mean return is biased upward as it assumes that the amount invested at the beginning of each period is the same. This bias is particularly severe if holding period returns are a mix of both positive and negative returns.

Geometric Mean Return

> Basically, the geometric mean reflects a "buy-and-hold" strategy, whereas the arithmetic mean reflects a constant dollar investment at the beginning of each time period.

The geometric mean return accounts for compounding of returns, and does not assume that the amount invested in each period is the same. The geometric mean is lower than the arithmetic mean (due to the effects of compounding) unless there is no variation in returns, in which case they are equal.

The geometric mean return is calculated as:

$$R = \left\{ \left[(1+R_1) \times (1+R_2) \times \ldots \times (1+R_n) \right]^{1/n} \right\} - 1$$

Money-Weighted Return or Internal Rate of Return

Unlike the return measures discussed above, the money-weighted return accounts for the amount of money invested in each period and provides information on the return earned on the actual amount invested. The money-weighted return equals the internal rate of return of an investment.

A drawback of the money-weighted return is that it does not allow for return comparisons between different individuals or different investment opportunities. For example, two investors in the same mutual fund could have different money-weighted returns if they invested varying amounts in different periods.

Example 1-1: Computation of Returns

An analyst gathered the following information regarding a mutual fund's returns over 5 years:

Year	Assets Under Management at the Beginning of the Year	Net Return
1	$40 million	25%
2	$35 million	10%
3	$55 million	−10%
4	$70 million	5%
5	$30 million	20%

---

1. Calculate the holding period return for the 5-year period.
2. Calculate the arithmetic mean annual return.
3. Calculate the geometric mean annual return. How does it compare with the arithmetic mean annual return?
4. Calculate the money-weighted annual return.

Solution:

1. Holding period return = $[(1.25)\,(1.1)\,(0.9)\,(1.05)\,(1.2)] - 1 = 55.93\%$
2. Arithmetic mean annual return = $(0.25 + 0.1 - 0.1 + 0.05 + 0.2)\,/\,5 = 10\%$
3. Geometric mean annual return = $\{[(1.25)\,(1.1)\,(0.9)\,(1.05)\,(1.2)]^{1/5}\} - 1 = 9.29\%$
4. In order to calculate the money-weighted annual return, we need to determine cash inflows and outflows. From the investor's perspective, amounts invested in the fund are negative cash flows and amounts withdrawn from the fund are positive cash flows. The dollar value of the holdings at the end of the investment horizon is also treated as a cash inflow to the investor.

Year	1	2	3	4	5
Balance from previous year	0	50	38.5	49.5	73.5
Net investment*	40	–15	16.5	20.5	–43.5
Net balance at the beginning of year	40	35	55	70	30
Investment return for the year	25%	10%	–10%	5%	20%
Investment gain/loss	10	3.5	–5.5	3.5	6
Balance at the end of year	50	38.5	49.5	73.5	36

*Net investment = Net balance at the beginning of year – Ending balance from previous year.

The following cash flows are used to compute the money-weighted rate of return.

$CF_0 = -\$40$; $CF_1 = \$15$; $CF_2 = -\$16.5$; $CF_3 = -\$20.5$; $CF_4 = \$43.5$; $CF_5 = \$36$

Use the following TI calculator key strokes to calculate the money-weighted annual return:

[CF] [2ND] CE|C]
40 [+/–] [ENTER] [↓]
15 [ENTER] [↓] [↓]
16.5 [+/–] [ENTER] [↓][↓]
20.5 [+/–] [ENTER] [↓][↓]
43.5 [ENTER] [↓] [↓]
36 [ENTER] [IRR] [CPT]
IRR = 7.97%

Annualized Return

An investment may have a term less than one year long. In such cases, the return on the investment is annualized to enable comparisons across investment instruments with different maturities. Annualized returns are calculated as:

$$r_{annual} = (1 + r_{period})^n - 1$$

where:
r = Return on investment
n = Number of periods in a year

The assumption here is that the returns earned over these short investment horizons can be replicated over the year. However, this is not always possible.

Example 1-2: Annualized Returns

An analyst obtained the following rates of return for three investments:

Investment 1 offers a 5.5% return in 120 days
Investment 2 offers a 6.2% return in 16 weeks
Investment 3 offers a 7.3% return in 4 months

Calculate the annualized rates of return for these investments.

Solution:

Investment 1:
$R = (1 + 0.055)^{365/120} - 1 = 17.69\%$

Investment 2:
$R = (1 + 0.062)^{52/16} - 1 = 21.59\%$

Investment 3:
$R = (1 + 0.073)^{12/4} - 1 = 23.54\%$

Portfolio Return

The return on a portfolio is simply the weighted average of the returns on individual assets. For example, the return of a two-asset portfolio can be calculated as:

$$R_p = w_1 R_1 + w_2 R_2$$

where:
R_p = Portfolio return
w_1 = Weight of Asset 1
w_2 = Weight of Asset 2
R_1 = Return of Asset 1
R_2 = Return of Asset 2

Other Return Measures and Their Applications

Gross and Net Returns

Gross returns are calculated before deductions for management expenses, custodial fees, taxes, and other expenses that are not directly linked to the generation of returns. Note that trading expenses (e.g., commissions) are accounted for in the computation of gross returns. Gross returns are an appropriate measure to evaluate portfolio performance.

Net returns deduct all managerial and administrative expenses that reduce an investor's return. Investors are primarily concerned with net returns.

Pre-Tax and After-Tax Nominal Returns

Pretax nominal returns do not adjust for taxes or inflation. Unless otherwise stated, always assume that stated returns are pretax nominal returns.

After-tax nominal returns account for taxes. Most investors are concerned with returns on an after-tax basis.

Real Returns

Nominal returns consist of the real risk-free rate of return, a premium for risk, and a premium for inflation. Investors calculate the real return because:

- It is useful in comparing returns across time periods as inflation rates may vary over time.
- It is useful in comparing returns among countries when returns are expressed in local currencies in which inflation rates vary between countries.
- The after-tax real return is what an investor receives as compensation for postponing consumption and assuming risk after paying taxes on investment returns.

Real after-tax returns are not usually computed by investment managers because it is difficult to estimate a general tax rate that is applicable to all investors.

Leveraged Return

The leveraged return is computed when an investor uses leverage (by either borrowing money or using derivative contracts) to invest in a security.

Leverage enhances returns, but also magnifies losses. See Example 1-3.

Example 1-3: Computation of Special Returns

Continuing from Example 1-1, suppose that the mutual fund spends a fixed amount of $600,000 every year on expenses that are unrelated to the manager's performance. Given that an investor faces a tax rate of 25% and that the inflation rate is 3%, answer the following questions:

1. What is the annual gross return for the fund in Year 1?
2. What is the after-tax net return for the investor in Year 2? Assume that all gains are realized at the end of the year and that taxes are paid immediately at that time.
3. What is the expected after-tax real return for the investor in Year 5?
4. What is the net return earned by investors in the fund over the 5-year period?

Solutions:

1. The fixed expenses of $600,000 would cause the gross return to be higher than net return by 1.5% (600,000 / 40,000,000). Therefore, gross return would equal 26.5%(1.5% + 25%).
2. After-tax return (Year 2) = 10% × (1 − 0.25) = 7.5%
3. After-tax return (Year 5) = 20% × (1 − 0.25) = 15%

$$\text{After-tax real return (Year 5)} = \frac{(1+0.15)}{(1+0.03)} - 1 = 1.1165 - 1 = 0.1165 = 11.65\%$$

4. The HPY for the fund over the 5-year period is computed after considering all direct and indirect expenses. The net return is 55.93%.

Variance and Covariance of Returns

The risk of an asset or a portfolio of assets can be measured by its standard deviation, which is the positive square root of variance.

Variance of a Single Asset

Variance equals the average squared deviation of observed values from their mean. A higher variance indicates higher volatility or dispersion of returns. The population variance is calculated as follows:

$$\sigma^2 = \frac{\sum\limits_{t=1}^{T}(R_t - \mu)^2}{T}$$

where:
R_t = Return for the period t
T = Total number of periods
μ = Mean of T returns

If only a representative sample of the population is available, we may calculate the sample variance as:

$$s^2 = \frac{\sum\limits_{t=1}^{T}(R_t - \bar{R})^2}{T-1}$$

where:
$\bar{R}$ = mean return of the sample observations
s^2 = sample variance

Standard Deviation of an Asset

The population and sample standard deviations are calculated as:

$$\sigma = \sqrt{\frac{\sum\limits_{t=1}^{T}(R_t - \mu)^2}{T}} \qquad s = \sqrt{\frac{\sum\limits_{t=1}^{T}(R_t - \bar{R})^2}{T-1}}$$

Variance of a Portfolio of Assets

Earlier in this reading, we learned that the expected return on a portfolio of securities equals the weighted average of the individual securities, returns. However, calculation of portfolio variance and standard deviation is not as straightforward. In addition to being a function of individual asset variances and their weights in the portfolio, portfolio variance also depends on the covariance (and correlation) between the assets in the portfolio. The variance of a two-asset portfolio can be calculated as:

$$\sigma_p^2 = w_1^2 \sigma_1^2 + w_2^2 \sigma_2^2 + 2w_1 w_2 \sigma_1 \sigma_2 \rho_{1,2} \ \text{ or } \ w_1^2 \sigma_1^2 + w_2^2 \sigma_2^2 + 2w_1 w_2 Cov_{1,2}$$

The standard deviation of a portfolio of two risky assets is calculated as:

$$\sigma_p = \sqrt{w_1^2 \sigma_1^2 + w_2^2 \sigma_2^2 + 2w_1 w_2 \sigma_1 \sigma_2 \rho_{1,2}} \ \text{ or } \ \sqrt{w_1^2 \sigma_1^2 + w_2^2 \sigma_2^2 + 2w_1 w_2 Cov_{1,2}}$$

The first part of the formula for the two-asset portfolio standard deviation $(w_1^2 \sigma_1^2 + w_2^2 \sigma_2^2)$ tells us that portfolio standard deviation is *a positive* function of the standard deviation and weights of the individual assets held in the portfolio. The second part $(2w_1 w_2 Cov_{1,2})$ shows us that portfolio standard deviation is also dependent on how the two assets move in relation to each other (covariance or correlation). See Example 1-4.

Example 1-4: Mean Return, Variance of Returns, Covariance of Returns, and Correlation

An analyst gathered the following information regarding the returns on two stocks:

Year	Stock 1 Return	Stock 2 Return
2006	0.200	0.100
2007	0.100	0.150
2008	–0.150	–0.050
2009	–0.200	0.100
2010	0.050	0.050
2011	0.100	0.200

Calculate the mean return, sample variance, sample covariance, and correlation of returns for these two stocks.

Solution:

Year	Stock 1 Return	Stock 2 Return	$R_t - \overline{R}_1$	$R_t - \overline{R}_2$	$(R_t - \overline{R}_1)(R_t - R2)$
2006	0.200	0.100	0.183	0.008	0.002
2007	0.100	0.150	0.083	0.058	0.005
2008	–0.150	–0.050	–0.167	–0.142	0.024
2009	–0.200	0.100	–0.217	0.008	–0.002
2010	0.050	0.050	0.033	–0.042	–0.001
2011	0.100	0.200	0.083	0.108	0.009
Sum	**0.100**	**0.550**			**0.036**

Stock 1:

The mean return is calculated by dividing the sum of the individual annual returns by the number of years in the sample.

$$\text{Mean Return} = \overline{R}_1 = \frac{\sum R_1}{n} = \frac{0.1}{6} = 1.67\%$$

Sample variance is calculated by dividing the sum of the squared deviations from the mean (sum of the contents of Column 4) by the number of years in the sample minus 1.

$$\text{Sample variance} = s^2 = \sum_{n=1}^{N}\left(R_t - \overline{R}_1\right)^2 / (N-1)$$

$$s_1^2 = \frac{\left[(0.183)^2 + (0.083)^2 + (-0.167)^2 + (-0.217)^2 + (0.033)^2 + (0.083)^2\right]}{(6-1)}$$

$$s_1^2 = 0.0247$$

Sample standard deviation is calculated as the square root of sample variance.

$$\text{Sample standard deviation} = s_1 = (0.0247)^{1/2} = 0.1572$$

Stock 2:

$$\text{Mean Return} = \bar{R}_2 = \frac{0.55}{6} = 9.17\%$$

$$\text{Sample variance} = s_2^2 = \frac{[(0.008)^2 + (0.058)^2 + (-0.142)^2 + (0.008)^2 + (-0.042)^2 + (0.108)^2]}{(6-1)}$$

$$s_2^2 = 0.0074$$

$$\text{Sample standard deviation} = s_2 = (0.0074)^{1/2} = 0.0860$$

Sample covariance is calculated by dividing the sum of the products of the deviations from the mean for the stocks (sum of the contents of Column 6) by the number of years in the sample minus 1.

$$\text{Sample covariance} = \text{Cov}_{1,2} = \frac{[\Sigma(R_t - R_1)(R_t - R_2)]}{(n-1)}$$

$$= \frac{0.036}{(6-1)}$$

$$= 0.0072$$

Finally, sample correlation is calculated by dividing the covariance of returns by the product of the standard deviations of returns of the two stocks.

$$\text{Sample correlation} = \frac{\text{Cov}_{1,2}}{s_1 s_2} \quad \frac{0.0072}{(0.1572 \times 0.0860)} = 05326$$

Historical Return and Risk

Historical Mean Return and Expected Return

Historical return refers to the return that was actually earned in the past, while expected return refers to the return that an investor expects to earn in the future. Historical returns are calculated from historical data, while expected returns are determined by the real risk-free interest rate, expected inflation, and expected risk.

Even though investors sometimes use historical returns to forecast expected returns, one must bear in mind that there is no guarantee that returns earned in the past will be earned in the future.

Risk-Return Trade-off

Every investment decision involves a trade-off between risk and return. Empirical evidence has shown that over the long run, market prices reward higher risk with higher returns.

Other Investment Characteristics

In order to evaluate investments using mean (expected return) and variance (risk), we need to make the following assumptions:

- Returns follow a normal distribution (which is fully described by its mean and variance).
- Markets are informationally and operationally efficient.

When these assumptions are violated we need to consider additional investment characteristics.

Distributional Characteristics

We have discussed the characteristics of a normal distribution in Quantitative Methods. The mean-variance framework is only appropriate for evaluating investments whose returns are normally distributed. In reality, however, returns are not always normally distributed. Deviations from normality may occur because of either skewness or kurtosis.

- *Skewness* refers to the asymmetry of a returns distribution.
  - When most of the distribution is concentrated on the left, it is referred to as right skewed or positively skewed.
  - When most of the distribution is concentrated to the right, it is referred to as left skewed or negatively skewed.
- *Kurtosis* refers to fat tails or higher-than-normal probabilities for extreme returns. This leads to an increase in an asset's risk that is not captured by the mean-variance framework.

Market Characteristics

Markets are not always operationally efficient. One limitation on operational efficiency in markets is liquidity. Liquidity has an impact on the bid-ask spread (illiquid stocks have a wider spread) and on the price impact of a trade (illiquid stocks suffer a greater price impact).

Informational efficiency is discussed in later readings on market efficiency.

LESSON 2: RISK AVERSION, PORTFOLIO SELECTION, AND PORTFOLIO RISK

LOS 39d: Explain risk aversion and its implications for portfolio selection.
Vol 4, pp 267–276

The Concept of Risk Aversion

Suppose an investor is offered two alternatives:

Option 1: He is guaranteed $25 in one year.
Option 2: There is a 50% chance that he will get $50 in one year, and a 50% chance that he will get nothing.

The expected value in both these cases is $25, but there are three possibilities regarding the investor's preferences.

1. The investor may play it safe and go with Option 1. This behavior is indicative of **risk aversion**. Risk-averse investors aim to maximize returns for a given level of risk and minimize risk for a given level or return. Historically, there has been a positive relationship between risk and return, which suggests that market prices are primarily determined by investors who are predominantly risk averse.
2. The investor may choose to gamble and go with Option 2. Such **risk-seeking** investors get extra utility or satisfaction from the uncertainty associated with their investments. Even though most individuals do exhibit risk-seeking behavior in isolated situations (e.g., gambling at casinos when the expected value of the payoff can even be negative), risk aversion is the standard assumption in the investment arena.
3. The investor may be indifferent between the two options. Such risk-neutral investors seek higher returns irrespective of the level of risk inherent in an investment.

Risk tolerance refers to the level of risk that an investor is willing to accept to achieve her investment goals.

- The lower the risk tolerance, the lower the level of risk acceptable to the investor.
- The lower the risk tolerance, the higher the risk aversion.

Utility Theory and Indifference Curves

In the investment management arena, utility is a measure of the relative satisfaction that an investor derives from a particular portfolio. For example, a risk-averse investor obtains a higher utility from a definite outcome relative to an uncertain outcome with the same expected value. In order to quantify the preferences for investment choices using risk and return, utility functions are used. An example of a utility function is:

$$U = E(R) - \frac{1}{2}A\sigma^2$$

where:
  U = Utility of an investment
$E(R)$ = Expected return
  σ^2 = Variance of returns
  A = Additional return required by the investor to accept an additional unit of risk

"A" is a measure of risk aversion. It is higher for investors who are more risk averse, as they require larger compensation for accepting more risk.

The utility function assumes the following:

- Investors are generally risk averse, but prefer more return to less return.
- Investors are able to rank different portfolios based on their preferences and these preferences are internally consistent. This means that if Investment A is preferred to Investment B, and Investment B is preferred to Investment C, Investment A must be preferred to Investment C.

We can draw the following conclusions from the utility function:

- Utility is unbounded on both sides—it can be highly negative or highly positive.
- Higher return results in higher utility.
- Higher risk results in lower utility.
- The higher the value of "A," the higher the negative effect of risk on utility.

Note that utility is not an absolute level of satisfaction. A portfolio with a utility, "U," of 2.5 is not necessarily two times as satisfying as a portfolio with a "U" of 1.25. However, the former would definitely be preferred to the latter.

Important Notes Regarding the Risk Aversion Coefficient, "A"

- "A" is positive for a risk-averse investor. Additional risk reduces total utility.
- It is negative for a risk-seeking investor. Additional risk enhances total utility.
- It equals zero for a risk-neutral investor. Additional risk has no impact on total utility.

Indifference Curves

The risk-return tradeoff that an investor is willing to bear can be illustrated by an indifference curve. An investor realizes the same total utility or satisfaction from every point on a given indifference curve. Since each investor can have an infinite number of risk-return combinations that generate the same utility, indifference curves are continuous at all points. Two points relating to indifference curves for risk-averse investors are worth noting:

1. They are *upward sloping*. This means that an investor will be indifferent between two investments with different expected returns only if the investment with the lower expected return entails a lower level of risk as well.
2. They are *curved*, and their slope becomes steeper as more risk is taken. The increase in return required for every unit of additional risk increases at an increasing rate because of the diminishing marginal utility of wealth.

Figure 2-1 illustrates two indifference curves. While an investor would be equally happy at any point on IDC_1, she would prefer any point on IDC_2 to any point on IDC_1. This is because IDC_2 offers a higher level of return for every given level of risk compared to IDC_1. The utility of risk-averse investors increases as we move northwest.

Figure 2-1: Indifference Curves and Risk Aversion

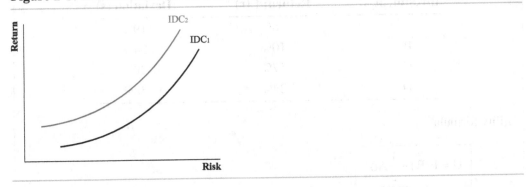

The slope of an indifference curve represents the extra return required by the investor to accept an additional unit of risk. See Figure 2-2.

- A risk-averse investor would have a relatively steep indifference curve (significant extra return required to take on more risk).
- A less risk-averse investor would have a flatter indifference curve (lower extra return required to take on more risk).
- A risk-seeking investor would have an indifference curve with a negative slope. Her utility increases with higher return and higher risk.
- A risk-neutral investor would have a perfectly horizontal indifference curve. Her utility does not vary with risk.

> The risk aversion coefficient (in the utility function) and the slope of the indifference curve are positively related.

Figure 2-2: Indifference Curves of Various Types of Investors

For the remainder of the section on portfolio management, we shall assume that all investors are risk-averse. See Example 2-1.

Example 2-1: Computation of Utility

Answer the questions below based on the following information:

Investment	Expected Return; E(r)	Standard Deviation (s)
A	8%	19%
B	10%	24%
C	17%	28%
D	24%	32%

Utility formula:

$$U = E(R) - \frac{1}{2}A\sigma^2$$

1. Which investment will a risk-averse investor with a risk aversion coefficient of 5 choose?
2. Which investment will a risk-averse investor with a risk aversion coefficient of 3 choose?
3. Which investment will a risk-neutral investor choose?
4. Which investment will a risk-loving investor choose?

Solution:

The following table shows the utility for risk-averse investors with A = 5 and A = 3.

Investment	Expected Return; E(r)	Standard Deviation (σ)	Utility at A = 5	Utility at A = 3
A	8%	19%	−0.010	0.0259
B	10%	24%	−0.044	0.0136
C	17%	28%	−0.026	0.0524
D	24%	32%	−0.016	0.0864

1. A risk-averse investor with a risk aversion coefficient of 5 would choose Investment A.
2. A risk-averse investor with a risk aversion coefficient of 3 would choose Investment D.
3. A risk-neutral investor's risk aversion coefficient is 0. She wants the highest return possible. Therefore, she would choose Investment D.
4. A risk-loving investor likes both higher risk and higher return. Therefore, she would choose Investment D as well.

Application of Utility Theory to Portfolio Selection

The Risk-Free Asset

The expected return on a risk-free asset is entirely certain and therefore the standard deviation of its expected returns is zero ($\sigma_{RFR} = 0$). The return earned on the risk-free asset is the risk-free rate (RFR).

The relevant portion of the CFA Program curriculum invests a weight of w_i in the risk-free asset. We assume that w_i equals the weight of the risky asset in the portfolio. The conclusion of the analysis is the same.

Expected Return for a Portfolio Containing a Risky Asset and the Risk-Free Asset

Let's assume that we invest a proportion of our investable funds (w_i) in a risky asset (i) that has an expected return, $E(R_i)$, and variance, σ_i^2, and the remainder ($1 - w_i$) in the risk-free asset that has an expected return of RFR and a variance of zero.

The expected return for the portfolio that includes the risk-free asset and a risky asset is simply the weighted average of their expected returns.

$$E(R_p) = w_i E(R_i) + (1 - w_i)RFR \text{ or } E(R_p) = RFR + w_i[E(R_i) - RFR]$$

Equation 1

where:

w_i = Proportion of funds invested in the risky asset.
$E(R_i)$ = The expected rate of return on the risky asset.

Standard Deviation of a Portfolio Containing a Risky Asset and the Risk-Free Asset

Recall that the variance for a two-asset portfolio is given as:

$$\sigma_{portfolio}^2 = w_1^2 \sigma_1^2 + w_2^2 \sigma_2^2 + 2w_1 w_2 \sigma_1 \sigma_2 \rho_{1,2}$$

Substituting the risk-free asset for Asset 1, and the risky asset (i) for Asset 2, this formula becomes:

$$S_{portfolio}^2 = (1 - w_i)^2 S_{RFR}^2 + w_i^2 \sigma_i^2 + 2(1 - w_i)w_i S_{RFR} \sigma_i R_{RFR,i}$$

The variance of the risk-free asset is zero because it has a guaranteed return. Further, the return on the risk-free asset does not vary with the return on any risky asset. Therefore, the correlation between the risk-free asset and the risky asset is also zero ($R_{RFR,i} = 0$). Hence, the expression for the variance of a portfolio becomes:

$$\sigma_{port}^2 = w_i^2 \sigma_i^2$$

The standard deviation of a portfolio that combines a risk-free asset with a risky asset is a linear proportion of the standard deviation of the risky asset.

$$\sigma_{port} = w_i \sigma_i$$

The expression for the standard deviation of the portfolio can be reorganized to get an expression for w_i:

$$w_i = \frac{\sigma_{port}}{\sigma_i} \longrightarrow \boxed{Equation\ 2}$$

Replacing w_i with $\frac{\sigma_{port}}{\sigma_i}$ in Equation 1, we can state the expected return on the portfolio as a function of portfolio risk:

$$E(R_p) = RFR + w_i[E(R_i) - RFR] \quad (Equation\ 1)$$

$$E(R_p) = RFR + \frac{\sigma_{port}}{\sigma_i}[E(R_i) - RFR]$$

$$E(R_p) = RFR + \sigma_{port}\frac{[E(R_i) - RFR]}{\sigma_i}$$

This equation that relates the return on a portfolio composed of the risk-free asset and a risky asset to the standard deviation of the portfolio is known as the capital allocation line (CAL). The CAL has an intercept of RFR and a constant slope that equals:

$$\boxed{\frac{[E(R_i) - RFR]}{\sigma_i}}$$

The expression for the slope of the CAL is the extra return required for each additional unit of risk and is also known as the market price of risk. See Figure 2-3.

Figure 2-3: Capital Allocation Line with Two Assets

- At Point RFR, the portfolio consists only of the risk-free asset. Therefore, its expected return equals RFR and variance equals zero.
- At Point A, the portfolio consists only of the risky asset. Therefore its expected return equals $E(R_i)$ and variance equals σ_i^2
- Risk-return combinations beyond Point A can be obtained by borrowing at the risk-free rate $(1 - w_i < 0)$ and investing in the risky asset $(w_i > 1)$.

The next question is which of these numerous portfolios that lie along the CAL will actually be chosen by the investor? The answer lies in combining indifference curves with the CAL. Indifference curves represent the investor's utility function, while the CAL represents the risk-return combinations of the set of portfolios that the investor can invest in. Portfolios that lie below the CAL may be invested in, but then the investor would not be maximizing the potential return given the level of risk she is willing to take. Portfolios that lie above the CAL are desirable, but cannot be attained with the given assets.

From Figure 2-4 notice that:

- IDC_3, which lies above the CAL, is most desirable but cannot be attained with the available assets.
- IDC_1 intersects the CAL at two different points, Point B and Point C. Both these points offer the same level of satisfaction to the investor, as they lie on the same indifference curve.
- IDC_2 is tangential to the CAL at Point M.

Figure 2-4: Portfolio Selection

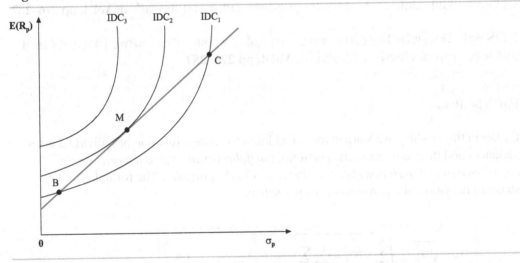

Given a choice between investing in a portfolio on IDC_1 (Points B or C) or in a portfolio on IDC_2 (Point M) an investor would choose the portfolio on IDC_2 as it offers a higher level of satisfaction (it lies to the northwest of IDC_1). Therefore, Point M (the point of tangency between the investor's indifference curve and the CAL) represents the optimal portfolio for this investor.

Portfolio Selection for Two Investors with Different Levels of Risk Aversion

The indifference curve of a relatively more risk-averse investor (Harry) would lie to the left of the indifference curve of a less risk-averse investor (Bob) because he has a lower tolerance for risk. Notice that Harry's optimal portfolio has a lower expected return and a lower level of risk than Bob's optimal portfolio. Further, for the same level of return, Harry's indifference curve has a higher slope, which suggests that he needs a greater incremental return than Bob for taking additional risk. See Figure 2-5.

Figure 2-5: Optimal Portfolios

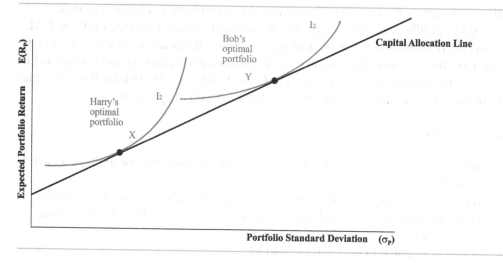

LOS 39e: Calculate and interpret portfolio standard deviation. **Vol 4, pp 276–287**

LOS 39f: Describe the effect on a portfolio's risk of investing in assets that are less than perfectly correlated. **Vol 4, pp 276–287**

Portfolio Risk

Earlier in this reading, we learned that in addition to being a function of individual asset variances and their weights in the portfolio, *portfolio variance also depends on the covariance (and correlation) between the assets in the portfolio*. The formula for the standard deviation of a portfolio of risky assets is:

$$\sigma_p = \sqrt{\sigma_p^2} = \sqrt{\sum_{i=1}^{n} w_i^2 \sigma_i^2 + \sum_{i=1}^{n}\sum_{j=1}^{n} w_i w_j Cov_{i,j}} \qquad i \neq j$$

The formula for the standard deviation of a portfolio consisting of two risky assets is:

$$\sigma_p = \sqrt{w_1^2 \sigma_1^2 + w_2^2 \sigma_2^2 + 2w_1 w_2 \sigma_1 \sigma_2 \rho_{1,2}} \text{ or } \sqrt{w_1^2 \sigma_1^2 + w_2^2 \sigma_2^2 + 2w_1 w_2 Cov_{1,2}}$$

The formula for the standard deviation of a portfolio consisting of three risky assets is:

$$\sigma_p = \sqrt{w_1^2 \sigma_1^2 + w_2^2 \sigma_2^2 + w_3^2 \sigma_3^2 + 2w_1 w_2 Cov_{1,2} + 2w_2 w_3 Cov_{2,3} + 2w_3 w_1 Cov_{3,1}}$$

The first part of the formula for the two-asset portfolio standard deviation () tells us that portfolio standard deviation is *a positive* function of the standard deviation and weights of the individual assets held in the portfolio. The second part ($2w_1 w_2 Cov_{1,2}$) shows us that portfolio standard deviation is also dependent on how the two assets move in relation to each other (covariance or correlation).

From the two-asset portfolio standard deviation formula it is also important to understand that:

- The maximum value for portfolio standard deviation will be obtained when the correlation coefficient equals +1.
- Portfolio standard deviation will be minimized when the correlation coefficient equals −1.
- If the correlation coefficient equals zero, the second part of the formula will equal zero and portfolio standard deviation will lie somewhere in between.

Implications

- When asset returns are *negatively* correlated, the final term in the standard deviation formula is negative and serves to *reduce* portfolio standard deviation.
- If the correlation between assets equals zero, portfolio standard deviation is *greater* than when correlation is negative.
- When asset returns are positively correlated, the second part of the formula for portfolio standard deviation is also positive and portfolio standard deviation is higher than when the correlation coefficient equals zero. With a correlation coefficient of +1 (perfect positive correlation) there are no diversification benefits.

Let's go through a brief example to highlight some important points. Assets A and B have the following expected returns, portfolio weights, variances, and standard deviations:

Asset	E(R)	Weight	σ^2	σ
A	0.10	0.5	0.0081	0.09
B	0.05	0.5	0.0049	0.07

Portfolio standard deviations in various correlation scenarios are given below.

Scenario	Correlation Between Assets	Portfolio Standard Deviation
a	−1	0.01
b	−0.5	0.0409
c	0	0.057
d	0.5	0.0695
e	1	0.08

First of all, remember that the portfolio's expected return does *not* vary with the correlation coefficient of the two assets. The expected return for this portfolio equals 0.075 or 7.5%.

a. With perfectly negative correlation, the standard deviation of the portfolio is at its lowest (1%). The negative covariance term significantly offsets the individual asset variance terms.

b. With a correlation of −0.5 the standard deviation of the portfolio is not at its lowest, but is still relatively low (4.09%) due to the negative covariance term.

c. With zero correlation, portfolio standard deviation (5.7%) is higher than it is with negative correlation, but lower than it is with positive correlation.

d. With a correlation of 0.5 the standard deviation of the portfolio is still higher (6.95%).

e. With perfect positive correlation, the standard deviation of the portfolio (8%) is at its highest possible level. There are no diversification benefits from investing in the portfolio when correlation is +1. In this scenario, portfolio standard deviation is simply the weighted average of the standard deviations of the individual assets. This is because the expression for portfolio standard deviation is in the form of:

$$\sigma_{port} = \sqrt{(w_A\sigma_A)^2 + (w_B\sigma_B)^2 + 2(w_A\sigma_A)(w_B\sigma_B)(1)}$$

which can be simplified to:

$$\sigma_{port} = \sqrt{[(w_A\sigma_A) + (w_B\sigma_B)]^2} \Rightarrow \sigma_{port} = (w_A\sigma_A) + (w_B\sigma_B)$$

Conclusion: The risk (standard deviation) of a portfolio of risky assets depends on the asset weights and standard deviations, *and most importantly on the correlation of asset returns*. The *higher* the correlation between the individual assets, the *higher* the portfolio's standard deviation.

Constant Correlation with Changing Weights

Using the same two assets, now let's change the weights of the individual assets in the portfolio, and use a constant correlation coefficient of zero to gauge the impact on portfolio standard deviation.

Portfolio	w_A	w_B	$E(R_{port})$	σ_{port}
f	0	1	0.05	0.07
g	0.25	0.75	0.0625	0.0571
h	0.5	0.5	0.075	0.57
i	0.75	0.25	0.0875	0.0697
j	1	0	0.1	0.09

From Figure 2-6, notice the following:

- The set of risk-return combinations for the 5 portfolios traces an ellipse that starts at Portfolio f (Asset B's risk-return profile), and goes through the 50–50 point onto Portfolio j (Asset A's risk-return profile).
- With assets that have a correlation of less than +1, it is possible to form portfolios that have a *lower* risk than either of the individual assets. This holds true for Portfolios g, h, and i in our example.
- A conservative investor can experience both a higher return and a lower risk by diversifying into a higher-risk, higher-return asset if the correlation between the assets is fairly low. Suppose a conservative investor is fully invested in Asset B (Portfolio f), where she expects a return of 5% with a portfolio standard deviation of 7%. By shifting 25% of her assets into the higher-risk asset (Asset A) and investing in Portfolio g, she can increase her expected return to 6.25% and lower the standard deviation of her portfolio to 5.71%.

Figure 2-6: Risk Return Tradeoff

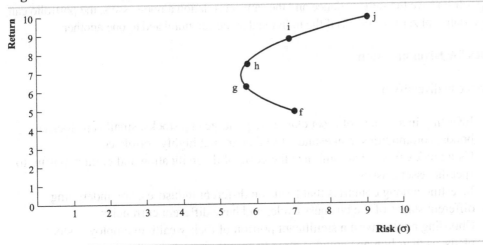

Figure 2-7 shows the change in curvature of the risk-return relationship between assets depending on their weights, as a function of the correlation between the two assets.

Figure 2-7: Effect of Correlation on Portfolio Risk and Return

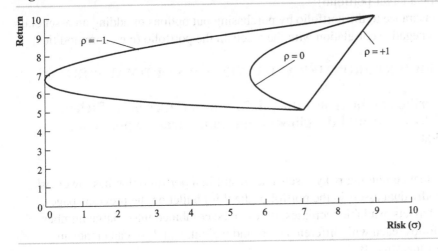

Notice that for any mix of asset weights, the maximum value that the portfolio standard deviation can take is equal to the higher of the individual assets' standard deviations.

Notice the following from Figure 2-7:

- When correlation equals +1, the risk-return combinations that result from altering the weights lie along a straight line between the two assets' risk-return profiles.
- As correlation falls, the curvature of this line increases.
- When correlation equals −1, the curve is represented by two straight lines that meet at the vertical axis. This point represents a zero-risk portfolio where portfolio return must equal the risk-free rate to prevent arbitrage.

Portfolios of Many Risky Assets

As more and more assets are added to a portfolio, the contribution of each individual asset's risk to portfolio risk diminishes. The covariance among the assets in the portfolio accounts for the bulk of portfolio risk.

Further, given that there are a large number of assets in the portfolio, if we assume that all assets in the portfolio have the same variance and the same correlation among assets, the portfolio can have a variance of zero (zero risk) if the individual assets are unrelated to one another.

Avenues for Diversification

Investors can diversify by:

- Investing in a variety of asset classes (e.g., large cap stocks, small cap stocks, bonds, commodities, real estate, etc.) that are not highly correlated.
- Using index funds that minimize the costs of diversification and grant exposure to specific asset classes.
- Investing among countries that focus on different industries, are undergoing different stages of the business cycle, and have different currencies.
- Choosing not to invest a significant portion of their wealth in employee stock plans, as their human capital is already entirely invested in their employing companies.
- Only adding a security to the portfolio if its Sharpe ratio is greater than the Sharpe ratio of the portfolio times the correlation coefficient.
- Only adding a security to the portfolio if the benefit (additional expected return, reduced portfolio risk) is greater than the associated costs (trading costs and costs of tracking a larger portfolio).
- Adding insurance to the portfolio by purchasing put options or adding an asset class that has a negative correlation with the assets in the portfolio (e.g., commodities).

LESSON 3: EFFICIENT FRONTIER AND INVESTOR'S OPTIMAL PORTFOLIO

LOS 39g: Describe and interpret the minimum-variance and efficient frontiers of risky assets and the global minimum-variance portfolio. Vol 4, pp 288–300

We have learned that combining risky assets may result in a portfolio that has lower risk than any of the individual assets in the portfolio (the third bullet on the previous page). As the number of assets available increases, they can be combined into a large number of different portfolios (each with different assets and weights), and we can create an opportunity set of investments.

Combinations of these assets can be formed into portfolios that entail the lowest level of risk for each level of expected return. An envelope curve that plots the risk-return characteristics of the lowest risk "domestic assets only" portfolios is labeled MVF_{DA} (minimum-variance frontier—domestic assets) on Figure 3-1. As international assets are added to the portfolio, portfolio risk for each level of return can be reduced further given that international assets are not perfectly positively correlated with domestic assets. Therefore, the minimum-variance frontier that includes international assets (MVF_{IA}) lies to the left of MVF_{DA}. Similarly, once all possible investments and asset classes are considered, the minimum-variance frontier (MVF) that plots the risk-return characteristics of portfolios that minimize portfolio risk at each given level of return lies further to the left. We will work with this minimum-variance frontier as we move forward, and assume that all assets and asset classes have been considered in deriving this minimum-variance frontier. Note that no risk-averse investor would invest in any portfolio that lies to the right of the MVF, as it would entail a higher level of risk than a portfolio that lies on the MVF for a given level of return.

Figure 3-1: Investment Opportunity Set

In Figure 3-2, notice that Portfolios A, B, and C all have the same expected return, E(R1). Portfolio A entails the lowest level of risk, but lies to the left of the minimum variance frontier, so it cannot be attained given the investment opportunity set. The minimum risk that the investor can take to earn $E(R_1)$ is by investing in Portfolio B. A risk-averse investor would invest in Portfolio B over Portfolio C, as it entails lower risk for the same expected return. Portfolio D defines the global minimum-variance portfolio. It is the portfolio of risky securities that entails the lowest level of risk among all the risky asset portfolios on the minimum-variance frontier.

> Note the emphasis on "risky" assets. Later, the introduction of the risk-free asset will allow us to relax this constraint.

Figure 3-2: Minimum-Variance Frontier

The minimum-variance frontier represents portfolios with the lowest level of risk for each level of expected return. Investors aim to maximize expected return for each level of risk. Given a choice between Portfolios B and E (that entail the same level of risk and lie on the minimum-variance frontier), an investor would prefer Portfolio B as it offers a higher return. Therefore, all portfolios on the MVF that lie above and to the right of the global minimum-variance portfolio dominate all portfolios on the MVF that lie below and to the right of the global minimum-variance portfolio.

This dominant portion of the MVF (the one above and to the right of the global minimum-variance portfolio) is known as the Markowitz efficient frontier. It contains all the possible portfolios that rational, risk-averse investors will consider investing in.

An important thing to note about the efficient frontier is that the slope of the curve decreases as we move to the right. The additional return attained as investors take on more risk (by successively moving to the right along the Markowitz efficient frontier to portfolios with more and more risk) declines.

A Risk-Free Asset and Many Risky Assets

Now let's bring the risk-free asset into our analysis. The risk-free asset has zero risk (so it plots on the y-axis), an expected return of RFR, and zero correlation with risky assets. Further, the risk-return characteristics of portfolios that combine the risk-free asset with a risky asset or a portfolio of risky assets lie along a straight line.

An investor can attain any point along CAL_A by investing a certain portion of her funds in the risk-free asset and the remainder in a portfolio of risky assets (Portfolio A). The set of portfolios that lies on CAL_A (combinations of the risk-free asset and Portfolio A with varying weights) dominates all the risky-asset portfolios on the efficient frontier below Point A because portfolios along CAL_A have a higher return than the portfolios on the efficient frontier with the same risk (standard deviation).

> The difference between the CALs that we are using here and the CAL described earlier in the reading is that back then we were combining the risk-free asset with a risky asset. Now that we are working with the Markowitz efficient frontier, we are combining the risk-free asset with different portfolios of risky assets.

Likewise, any position can be attained along CAL_B by investing in some combination of the risk-free asset and Portfolio B of risky assets. Again, these potential combinations of the risk-free asset and Portfolio B dominate all portfolio possibilities on the efficient frontier below Point B. Further, any portfolio that lies on CAL_B dominates any portfolio on CAL_A because portfolios that lie on CAL_B offer a higher expected return for any given level of risk compared to those on CAL_A.

Therefore, as the investor combines the risk-free asset with portfolios further up the efficient frontier, she keeps attaining better portfolio combinations. Each successive portfolio on the efficient frontier has a steeper line (higher slope) joining it to the risk-free asset. The slope of this line represents the additional return per unit of extra risk. The steeper the slope of the line, the better risk-return tradeoff the portfolio offers. The line with the steepest slope is the one that is drawn from the risk-free asset to Portfolio M (which occurs at the point of tangency between the efficient frontier and a straight line drawn from the risk-free rate). This particular line offers the best risk-return tradeoff to the investor. Any combination of the risk-free asset and Portfolio M dominates all portfolios below CAL_M.

It is essential to understand what we have accomplished here. By adding the risk-free asset, we have narrowed down the risky asset portfolio that an investor would invest in to a single optimal portfolio, Portfolio M, which is at the point of tangency between CAL_M and the efficient frontier.

- At Point RFR, an investor has all her funds invested in the risk-free asset.
- At Point M she has all of her funds invested in Portfolio M (which is entirely composed of risky securities).
- At any point between RFR and M, she holds both Portfolio M and the risk-free asset (i.e., she is lending some of her funds at the risk-free rate).

However, an investor may want to attain a higher expected return than available at Point M, where all her funds are invested in the risky-asset portfolio. Adding leverage to the portfolio by borrowing money at the RFR and investing it in the risky asset portfolio will allow her to attain risk-return profiles beyond (to the right of, or above) Point M on the CAL_M (e.g., Point L). See Figure 3-3.

Figure 3-3: Optimal Risky Portfolio

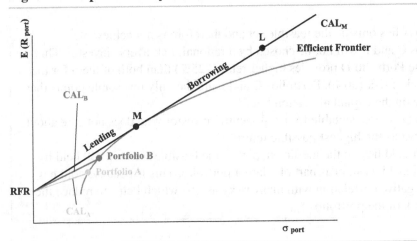

The Two-Fund Separation Theorem

The two-fund separation theorem states that regardless of risk and return preferences, all investors hold some combination of the risk-free asset and an optimal portfolio of risky assets. Therefore, the investment problem can be broken down into two steps:

1. The investing decision, where an investor identifies her optimal risky portfolio.
2. The financing decision, in which she determines where exactly on the optimal CAL she wants her portfolio to lie. Her risk preferences (as delineated by her indifference curves) determine whether her desired portfolio requires borrowing or lending at the risk-free rate.

Example 3-1: Choosing the Right Portfolio

Based on the information in Figure 3-4 and the table that follows, answer the following questions:

Figure 3-4: Choosing the Right Portfolio

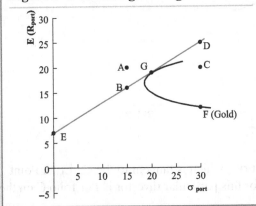

Point	Return (%)	Risk (%)
A	20	15
B	16	15
C	20	30
D	25	30
E	7	0
F (Gold)	12	30
G	19	20

1. Which of the above points is not achievable?
2. Which of the portfolios will not be chosen by a rational, risk-averse investor?
3. Which of these portfolios is most suitable for a risk-neutral investor?
4. Why is gold held by many rational investors as part of a larger portfolio, when it is shown in the graph to lie on the inefficient part of the feasible set?

Solution:

1. Portfolio A lies outside the feasible set and therefore is not achievable.
2. Portfolios C and F will not be chosen by a rational, risk-averse investor. This is because Portfolio D provides higher return (25%) than both of them for the same level of risk (30%). Portfolios C and F are the only investable points that do not lie on the capital allocation line.
3. Portfolio D is most suitable for a risk-neutral investor who does not care about risk and wants the highest possible return.
4. Although gold lies on the inefficient part of the feasible set, it is still held by many rational investors as part of a larger portfolio. This is because gold has low or negative correlation with many risky assets, which helps to reduce the overall risk of the portfolio.

LOS 39h: Explain the selection of an optimal portfolio, given an investor's utility (or risk aversion) and the capital allocation line. Vol 4, pp 294–300

Optimal Investor Portfolio

The line CAL_M in Figures 3-3 and 3-5 represents the best portfolios available to an investor. The portfolios along this line contain the risk-free asset and the optimal portfolio, Portfolio M, with varying weights. An individual's optimal portfolio depends on her risk-return preferences, which are incorporated into her indifference curves.

Figure 3-5: Optimal Investor Portfolio

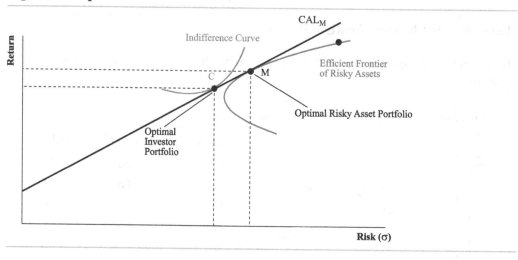

Figure 3-5 shows an investor's indifference curve, which is tangent to the CAL_M at Point C. Therefore, the optimal investor portfolio for this particular investor is Portfolio C on the CAL_M.

For a more risk-averse investor, the optimal investor portfolio would lie closer to the y-axis (a higher proportion invested in the risk-free asset), while a less risk-averse investor's optimal portfolio would lie closer to Portfolio M, and further away from the y-axis. An investor with an even higher tolerance for risk might borrow money at the risk-free rate to invest in Portfolio M. Her optimal portfolio would lie to the right of Portfolio M on CAL_M.

The thing to notice is that we have been able to account for all types of investors' risk preferences by using just two items—the risk-free asset and Portfolio M that consists of risky assets. Portfolio M is the optimal risky asset portfolio and will be selected by a rational, risk-averse investor regardless of her preferences. The only decision that the investor makes is how to divide her funds between the risk-free asset and the Portfolio M.

READING 40: PORTFOLIO RISK AND RETURN: PART II

LESSON 1: CAPITAL MARKET THEORY

Before getting into the LOS for this reading, we summarize some of the important takeaways from the previous sections on portfolio management:

- Risky assets can be combined into portfolios that may have a lower risk than each of the individual assets in the portfolio if assets are not perfectly positively correlated.
- An investor's investment opportunity set includes all the individual risky assets and risky asset portfolios that she can invest in.
- The minimum-variance frontier reduces the investment opportunity set to a curve that contains only those portfolios that entail the lowest level of risk for each level of expected return.
- The global minimum-variance portfolio is the portfolio of risky assets that entails the lowest level of risk among all portfolios on the minimum-variance frontier.
- Investors aim to maximize return for every level of risk. Therefore, all portfolios above and to the right of the global minimum-variance portfolio dominate those that lie below and to the right of the global minimum-variance portfolio.
- The section of the minimum-variance frontier that lies above and to the right of the global minimum-variance portfolio is referred to as the Markowitz efficient frontier.

LOS 40a:
Describe the
implications
of combining
a risk-free
asset with a
portfolio of
risky assets.
Vol 4, pp 314–321

A risk-free asset has an expected return of the risk-free rate (RFR), a standard deviation (risk) of zero, and a correlation with any risky asset of zero. Once the risk-free asset is introduced into the mix:

- Any portfolio that combines a risky asset portfolio that lies on the Markowitz efficient frontier and the risk-free asset has a risk-return tradeoff that is linear (CAL is represented by a straight line).
- The point at which a line drawn from the risk-free rate is tangent to the Markowitz efficient frontier defines the optimal risky asset portfolio. This line is known as the optimal CAL.
- Each investor will choose a portfolio (optimal investor portfolio) that contains some combination of the risk-free asset and the optimal risky portfolio. The weights of the risk-free asset and the optimal risky portfolio in the optimal investor portfolio depend on the investor's risk tolerance (indifference curve).
- The optimal investor portfolio is defined by the point where the investor's indifference curve is tangent to the optimal CAL.

LOS 40b: Explain the capital allocation line (CAL) and the capital market line (CML). Vol 4, pp 318–326

Going forward, we shall assume that all investors have homogenous expectations. Given that all investors in the market have identical expectations regarding the risk-return distribution for each asset, only one optimal risky portfolio exists. If investors have different expectations regarding various assets, there would be different optimal risky portfolios.

If markets are **informationally efficient** (i.e., market price is an unbiased estimate of the sum of the discounted values of a security's expected cash flows), investors would not be able to earn a rate of return that exceeds the required rate of return from the investment. In this case, investors should adopt passive investment strategies as they entail lower costs and are easy to administer.

If, however, an investor has more confidence in her abilities to forecast cash flows and estimate growth rates and discount rates, she might consider an active investment strategy. She would use her forecasts to determine whether an asset is fairly priced by the market and trade on any perceived mispricing.

When we refer to the "market," we are referring to all assets (e.g., stocks, bonds, real estate, commodities, etc.) that are tradable and investable. For our purposes going forward, we will define the term "market" quite narrowly as the S&P 500 Index. The terms "market return" and "market risk premium" therefore refer to the return on the S&P 500 and the U.S. equity risk premium (difference between the S&P 500 return and the U.S. long-term interest rate) respectively.

The Capital Market Line

A capital allocation line (CAL), includes all combinations of the risk-free asset and **any risky asset portfolio**. The capital market line (CML) is a special case of the capital allocation line where the risky asset portfolio that is combined with the risk-free asset is the **market portfolio**.

Graphically, the market portfolio occurs at the point where a line from the risk-free asset is tangent to the Markowitz efficient frontier. The market portfolio is the optimal risky asset portfolio, given homogenous expectations. All portfolios that lie below the CML offer a lower return than portfolios that plot on the CML for each level of risk.

An interesting point is that the slopes of the CML and CAL are constant even though they represent combinations of two assets. The important thing to note is that they are not combinations of two risky assets, but of a risk-free asset and a risky portfolio.

The risk and return characteristics of portfolios that lie on the CML can be computed using the risk and return formulas for two-asset portfolios.

Expected return on portfolios that lie on CML

$$E(R_p) = w_f R_f + (1 - w_f)E(R_m)$$

Variance of portfolios that lie on CML

$$\sigma^2 = w_f^2 \sigma_f^2 + (1 - w_f)^2 \sigma_m^2 + 2w_f(1 - w_f)Cov(R_f, R_m)$$

Equation of CML

> The derivation of this expression relating the expected return of portfolios that lie on the CML to their variance (risk) is very similar to the derivation of the CAL equation in an earlier reading. The only difference is that the risky asset, i, in the CAL is replaced by the market portfolio, m, in the CML.

$$E(R_p) = R_f + \frac{E(R_m) - R_f}{\sigma_m} \times \sigma_p$$

where:

y-intercept = R_f = risk-free rate

slope = $\dfrac{E(R_m) - R_f}{\sigma_m}$ = market price of risk

Figure 1-1 illustrates the CML.

Figure 1-1: Capital Market Line

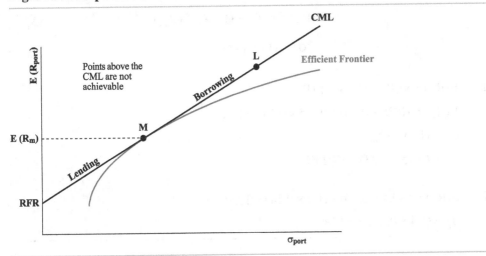

- At Point RFR, an investor has all her funds invested in the risk-free asset.
- At Point M she has all of her funds invested in the market portfolio (which only contains risky securities).
- At any point between RFR and M, she holds both the market portfolio and the risk-free asset (i.e., she is lending some of her funds at the risk-free rate).

However, an investor may want to attain a higher expected return than available at Point M, where all her funds are invested in the market portfolio. Adding leverage to the portfolio by borrowing money at the RFR and investing it in the market portfolio will allow her to attain a risk-return profile beyond (to the right of, or above) Point M on the CML (e.g., Point L).

The particular point that an investor chooses on the CML depends on her utility function, which in turn is determined by her risk and return preferences. See Example 1-1.

Example 1-1: Risk and Return of a Leveraged Portfolio

Sasha Miles is evaluating how to allocate funds between the risk-free asset and the market portfolio. She gathers the following information:

- Risk-free rate of return = 6%
- Expected return on the market portfolio = 14%
- Standard deviation of returns of the market portfolio = 23%

Calculate the expected risk and return of a portfolio that is:

a. 75% invested in the market portfolio.
b. 140% invested in the market portfolio.

Solution:

Portfolio return and standard deviation can be calculated using the following equations:

$$E(R_p) = w_1 R_f + (1 - w_1)E(R_m)$$

$$\sigma_p = (1 - w_1)\sigma_m$$

a. $E(R_p) = w_1 R_f + (1 - w_1)E(R_m)$

$E(R_p) = (0.25 \times 0.06) + (0.75 \times 0.14) = 12\%$

$\sigma_p = (1 - w_1)\sigma_m$

$\sigma_p = (0.75 \times 0.23) = 17.25\%$

b. $E(R_p) = (-0.4 \times 0.06) + (1.4 \times 0.14) = 17.2\%$

$\sigma_p = (1.4 \times 0.23) = 32.2\%$

Leveraged Positions with Different Lending and Borrowing Rates

In the previous section, we assumed that an investor could borrow or lend unlimited amounts of funds at the risk-free rate. Practically speaking, an investor's ability to repay is not as certain as that of the U.S. government, so the rate at which she would be able to borrow would be higher than the rate at which she would be able to lend. Given the disparity in borrowing and lending rates, the CML would no longer be a straight line (see Figure 1-2).

The slope of the CML to the left of Point M (when she invests a portion of her portfolio in the risk-free asset at R_f) would be:

$$\frac{E(R_m) - R_f}{\sigma_m}$$

While the slope CML to the right of Point M (where she is borrowing at R_b) would be:

$$\frac{E(R_m) - R_b}{\sigma_m}$$

All passively managed portfolios would lie on the kinked CML, even though an investor's investment in the risk-free asset may be:

- Positive (the investor's optimal portfolio would lie between RFR and Point M)
- Zero (the investor's optimal portfolio would lie at Point M)
- Negative (the investor's optimal portfolio would lie to the right of Point M)

The risk and return for a leveraged portfolio is higher than that of an unleveraged portfolio. Further, given that the investor's borrowing rate is higher than the risk-free rate, for each additional unit of risk taken beyond Point M (when the portfolio is leveraged), the investor gets a lower increase in expected return compared with portfolios to the left of Point M (where the portfolio is not leveraged).

Figure 1-2: CML with Different Lending and Borrowing Rates

LESSON 2: PRICING OF RISK AND COMPUTATION OF EXPECTED RETURN

LOS 40c: Explain systematic and nonsystematic risk, including why an investor should not expect to receive additional return for bearing nonsystematic risk. Vol 4, pp 326–328

Systematic and Nonsystematic Risk

When investors diversify across assets that are not perfectly positively correlated, the portfolio's risk is lower than the weighted average of the individual assets' risks. In the market portfolio, all the risk unique to individual assets comprising the portfolio has been diversified away. The risk that disappears due to diversification in the portfolio construction process is known as **nonsystematic risk** (also known as unique, diversifiable, or firm-specific risk). The risk inherent in all risky assets (caused by macroeconomic variables) that cannot be eliminated by diversification is known as **systematic risk** (also known as nondiversifiable or market risk).

> Total Risk = Systematic risk + Unsystematic risk

Complete diversification of a portfolio requires the elimination of all nonsystematic or diversifiable risk. Once nonsystematic risk has been eliminated and only systematic risk remains, a completely diversified portfolio would correlate perfectly with the market.

By adding assets to a portfolio that are not perfectly correlated with the assets already in the portfolio, we can reduce the overall standard deviation of the portfolio. However, we cannot eliminate the variability and uncertainty of macroeconomic factors that affect returns on all risky assets. We do not have to include all risky assets in the market portfolio to diversify away nonsystematic risk. Studies have shown that a portfolio consisting of 12 to 30 different stocks can diversify away 90% of nonsystematic risk. Whatever the exact number of different stocks required to eliminate nonsystematic risk, it is significantly lower than *all* the risky assets comprising the market portfolio. Further, we can attain a lower level of systematic risk by diversifying globally versus only diversifying within one country, because some of the domestic systematic risk factors (such as monetary policy) are not perfectly correlated with systematic risk variables in other countries.

In capital market theory, taking on a higher degree of nonsystematic risk will not be compensated with a higher return because nonsystematic risk can be eliminated, without additional cost, through diversification. Only if an investor takes on a higher level of risk that cannot be easily diversified away (systematic risk) should she expect to be rewarded in the form of a higher return. Systematic risk is measured as the contribution of a security to the risk of a well-diversified portfolio.

This conclusion has very important implications for asset pricing and expected returns. If risk is measured in terms of the standard deviation of returns of a stock, the riskiest stock will not necessarily have the highest expected return. For example, consider a tech firm whose entire business is reliant on the success of one particular technology. If the innovation is a success, the returns on the company's stock would be phenomenal, but if its product does not penetrate the market, the company would go out of business. The two scenarios facing this company are extreme. It is a stock with a high standard deviation of expected returns and high total risk.

Compare an investment in this tech company to an investment in a large manufacturing company that has a relatively well-known brand. This company may not seem to be a very risky investment in terms of total risk (standard deviation of expected returns), but it is relatively more sensitive to changes in the macroeconomic environment than the tech company.

Most of the risk inherent in the tech company's stock is firm specific in nature. Market factors like the rate of economic growth make up a relatively small proportion of the total risk of this company. The major chunk of its total risk (measured by standard deviation) can be diversified away by adding other stocks to the portfolio. For the manufacturing company, most of its standard deviation in expected returns (total risk) arises from macroeconomic risk factors that cannot be diversified away.

Even though the tech stock has a higher level of total risk, capital market theory dictates that the market will expect a higher return on the investment that has a higher level of systematic risk, regardless of total risk. Nonsystematic risk is not rewarded by an efficient market because it can be diversified away at no cost. *Therefore, the expected return on an individual security only depends on its systematic risk.*

As we have seen earlier, portfolios on the CML offer a better risk-return tradeoff than portfolios that plot below it, so it effectively becomes the new efficient frontier for investors. The CML leads all investors to invest in the same risky asset portfolio, Portfolio M. Investors only differ regarding their exact position on the CML, which depends on their risk preferences.

LOS 40d: Explain return-generating models (including the market model) and their uses. Vol 4, pp 328–331

Return-Generating Models

A return-generating model is a model that is used to forecast the return on a security, given certain parameters. A multifactor model uses more than one variable to estimate returns.

- Macroeconomic factor models use economic factors (e.g., economic growth rates, interest rates, and inflation rates) that correlate with security returns to estimate returns.
- Fundamental factor models use relationships between security returns and underlying fundamentals (e.g., earnings, earnings growth, and cash flow growth) to estimate returns.

- Statistical factor models use historical and cross-sectional returns data to identify factors that explain returns and use an asset's sensitivity to those factors to project future returns.

A general return-generating model may be expressed as:

$$E(R_i) - R_f = \sum_{j=1}^{k} \beta_{ij} E(F_j) = \beta_{i1}[E(R_m) - R_f] + \sum_{j=2}^{k} \beta_{ij} E(F_j)$$

where:

$E(F_1), E(F_2), \ldots E(F_k)$ = Various factors in the model. There are k number of factors in the model

B_{ij} = Factor weights, or loads associated with each factor.

$E(R_i) - R_f$ = Excess return

$E(R_m)$ = Market return

The Market Model

The market model is an example of a single-index return-generation model. It is used to estimate beta risk and to compute abnormal returns. The market model is given as:

$$R_i = \alpha_i + \beta_i R_m + e_i$$

First, the intercept α_i and slope coefficient β_i are estimated using historical asset and market returns. These estimates are then used to predict returns in the future. See Example 2-1.

Example 2-1: Using the Market Model to Calculate Abnormal Returns

A regression of ABC Stock's historical monthly returns against the return on the S&P 500 gives an α_i of 0.002 and a β_i of 1.05. Given that ABC Stock rises by 3% during a month in which the market rose 1.25%, calculate the abnormal return on ABC Stock.

Solution:

ABC Stock's expected return for the month = $0.002 + 1.05 \times 0.0125 = 0.015125$ or 1.51%

ABC's company-specific return (abnormal return) = $0.03 - (0.015125) = 0.014875$ or 1.49%

LOS 40e: Calculate and interpret beta. **Vol 4, pp 331–335**

Calculation and Interpretation of Beta

Beta is a measure of the sensitivity of an asset's return to the market's return. It is computed as the covariance of the return on the asset and the return on the market divided by the variance of the market. See Example 2-2.

$$\beta_i = \frac{Cov(R_i, R_m)}{\sigma_m^2} = \frac{\rho_{i,m}\sigma_i\sigma_m}{\sigma_m^2} = \frac{\rho_{i,m}\sigma_i}{\sigma_m}$$

Example 2-2: Calculating Asset Beta

Given that the standard deviation of the returns on the market is 18%, calculate beta for the following assets:

- Asset A, which has a standard deviation twice that of the market and zero correlation with the market.
- Asset B, which has a standard deviation of 24% and its correlation of returns with the market equals −0.2.
- Asset C, which has a standard deviation of 20% and its covariance of returns with the market is 0.035.

Solution:

We use the following formula for calculating beta:

$$\beta_i = \frac{\rho_{i,m}\sigma_i}{\sigma_m}$$

Since the correlation of Asset A with the market equals zero, its beta also equals zero.

Asset B's beta = (−0.2 × 0.24) / 0.18 = −0.267

Asset C's beta = 0.035 / 0.18^2 = 1.08

Important Points Regarding Beta
- Beta captures an asset's systematic or nondiversifiable risk.
- A positive beta suggests that the return on the asset follows the overall trend in the market.
- A negative beta indicates that the return on the asset generally follows a trend that is opposite to that of the current market trend.
- A beta of zero means that the return on the asset is uncorrelated with market movements.
- The market has a beta of 1. Therefore, the average beta of stocks in the market also equals 1.

Estimating Beta Using Regression Analysis

The market model described previously can also be used to compute beta. Historical market and asset returns are used to determine α_i and β_i (see Figure 2-1.). The length of the period from which the inputs to the regression model are drawn from is extremely important. If data over a short time period are used, beta estimates may be affected by special events during that period. If data over a longer time period are used, they can be a poor gauge of future performance if major changes have occurred in the asset.

Figure 2-1: Beta Estimation with a Plot of Security and Market Returns

LESSON 3: THE CAPITAL ASSET PRICING MODEL

LOS 40f: Explain the capital asset pricing model (CAPM), including its assumptions, and the security market line (SML). Vol 4, pp 335–340

LOS 40g: Calculate and interpret the expected return of an asset using the CAPM. Vol 4, pg 340

The Capital Asset Pricing Model

The capital asset pricing model (CAPM) is a single-index model that is widely used to estimate returns, given security betas. The CAPM is expressed as:

$$E(R_i) = R_f + \beta_i[E(R_m) - R_f]$$

Assumptions of the CAPM
- Investors are utility-maximizing, risk-averse, rational individuals.
- Markets are frictionless and there are no transaction costs and taxes.
- All investors have the same single-period investment horizon.
- Investors have homogenous expectations and therefore arrive at the same valuation for any given asset.
- All investments are infinitely divisible.
- Investors are price-takers. No investor is large enough to influence security prices.

The Security Market Line

The SML illustrates the CAPM equation. Its y-intercept equals the risk-free rate and its slope equals the market risk premium, $(R_m - R_f)$.

> Efficient portfolios are those that offer the highest return for each level of risk.

Recall that the CAL and the CML are only applied to efficient portfolios, not to individual assets or inefficient portfolios. They used total risk on the x-axis, and since only systematic risk is priced, they could only be used for efficient portfolios (those with no nonsystematic risk and whose total risk therefore was the same as their systematic risk).

The SML and the CAPM, on the other hand, apply to any security or portfolio, regardless of whether it is efficient. This is because they are based only on a security's systematic risk, not total risk.

The CAPM equation tells us that the expected (required) rate of return for a risky asset is determined by the risk-free rate plus a risk premium. The risk premium for an asset is determined by the systematic risk of the asset, (β_i), and the prevailing market risk premium, $(R_m - R_f)$. See Example 3-1.

Example 3-1: Using the SML to Compute Expected Returns

Assume that the risk-free rate in an economy is 5% and the return on the market portfolio is expected to be 10%. Compute the expected rates of return for the following 5 securities:

Stock	Beta
A	0.75
B	1.00
C	1.15
D	1.5
E	−0.25

Solution:

$$E(R_i) = R_f + \beta_i[E(R_m) - R_f]$$

$$E(R_A) = R_f + \beta_A[E(R_m) - R_f] = 0.05 + 0.75(0.10 - 0.05) = 8.75\%$$

$$E(R_B) = R_f + \beta_B[E(R_m) - R_f] = 0.05 + 1.00(0.10 - 0.05) = 10\%$$

$$E(R_C) = R_f + \beta_C[E(R_m) - R_f] = 0.05 + 1.15(0.10 - 0.05) = 10.75\%$$

$$E(R_D) = R_f + \beta_D[E(R_m) - R_f] = 0.05 + 1.5(0.10 - 0.05) = 12.5\%$$

$$E(R_E) = R_f + \beta_E[E(R_m) - R_f] = 0.05 + (-0.25)(0.10 - 0.05) = 3.75\%$$

- Security C and D's betas are greater than market beta (1). These securities have a higher level of systematic risk than the market, meaning that they are more risky than the market portfolio. The expected return on these assets is therefore greater than the return on the market.
- Security A and E's betas are lower than market beta. These securities have a lower level of systematic risk than the market, meaning that they are less volatile than the market portfolio. Therefore, the expected return on these assets is lower than the return on the market.

- A security with a negative beta (Stock E) is quite rare in practice. Notice that its required or expected return is even lower than the risk-free rate. This is because its negative beta *reduces* systematic portfolio risk.
- Stock B's beta equals market beta, so its expected return equals the rate of return expected from the market (10%).

Portfolio Beta

The CAPM can also be applied to portfolios of assets.

- The beta of a portfolio equals the weighted average of the betas of the securities in the portfolio.
- The portfolio's expected return can be computed using the CAPM (see Example 3-2):

$$E(R_p) = R_f + \beta_p[E(R_m) - R_f]$$

Example 3-2: Portfolio Beta and Return

Allison invests 25% of her money in the risk-free asset, 35% in the market portfolio, and 40% in Alpha Corp, a U.S. stock that has a beta of 1.5. Given that the risk-free rate and the expected return on the market are 5% and 14% respectively, calculate the portfolio's beta and expected return.

Solution:

The beta of the risk-free asset and that of the market equal 0 and 1 respectively. The beta of the portfolio is calculated as:

$$\beta_{Portfolio} = w_1\beta_1 + w_2\beta_2 + w_3\beta_3$$

$$\beta_{Portfolio} = (0.25 \times 0) + (0.35 \times 1) + (0.4 \times 1.5) = 0.95$$

Expected return of the portfolio = $R_f + \beta(R_m - R_f)$

Expected return of the portfolio = 5% + 0.95 (14% − 5%) = 13.55%

LOS 40h: Describe and demonstrate applications of the CAPM and the SML. Vol 4, pp 337–351

Applications of the CAPM

Estimate of expected return: The expected rate of return computed from the CAPM is used by investors to value stocks, bonds, real estate, and other assets. In capital budgeting, where the NPV is used to make investing decisions, the CAPM is used to compute the required rate of return, which is then used to discount expected future cash flows. See Example 3-3.

> **Example 3-3: Application of the CAPM to Capital Budgeting**
>
> The directors of Mercury Inc. are considering investing in a new project. The project requires an initial investment of $550 million in one year. The probability of success is 60%. If it is successful, the project will provide an income of $350 million at the end of Year 2, but will also require a further investment of $200 million. Further, it will generate net income of $250 million in each of Years 3 and 4. At the end of Year 4, the company will sell the project for $300 million. If the project is unsuccessful, the company will not earn anything. Given that the market return is 14%, risk-free rate is 4%, and beta of the project is 1.5, answer the following questions:
>
> 1. Calculate the annual cash flows using the probability of success.
> 2. Calculate the expected return.
> 3. Calculate the net present value.
>
> **Solution:**
>
> 1. Year 1 = −$550m
>   Year 2 = 0.6 × ($350m − $200m) = $90m
>   Year 3 = 0.6 × $250m = $150m
>   Year 4 = 0.6 × ($250m + $300m) = $330m
>
> 2. Using the CAPM, the expected or required rate of return is calculated as:
>
>   Required return = 4% + [1.5 × (14% − 4%)] = 19%
>
> 3. Use the following TI calculator keystrokes to calculate NPV.
>
>   [CF] [2ND] [CE|C]
>   [↓] 550 [+/−] [ENTER] [↓][↓]
>   90 [ENTER] [↓][↓]
>   150 [ENTER] [↓][↓]
>   330 [ENTER] [NPV]
>   19 [ENTER] [↓] [CPT]
>
>   NPV = −$145.06 million

Portfolio Performance Evaluation

The *Sharpe ratio* is used to compute excess returns per unit of total risk. It is calculated as:

$$\text{Sharpe ratio} = \frac{R_p - R_f}{\sigma_p}$$

Notice that the Sharpe ratio basically equals the slope of the CAL. A portfolio with a higher Sharpe ratio is preferred to one with a lower Sharpe ratio, given that the numerator of the portfolios being compared is positive. If the numerator is negative, the ratio will be closer to zero (less negative) for riskier portfolios, resulting in distorted rankings. Two drawbacks of the Sharpe ratio are that it uses total risk as a measure of risk even though only systematic risk is priced, and that the ratio itself is not informative.

The *Treynor ratio* basically replaces total risk in the Sharpe ratio with systematic risk (beta). It is calculated as:

$$\text{Treynor ratio} = \frac{R_p - R_f}{\beta_p}$$

For the Treynor ratio to offer meaningful results, both the numerator and the denominator must be positive. Neither the Sharpe nor the Treynor ratio offer any information about the significance of the differences between the ratios for portfolios.

M-squared (M^2) is also based on total risk, not beta risk. It is calculated as:

$$M^2 = (R_p - R_f)\frac{\sigma_m}{\sigma_p} - (R_m - R_f)$$

M^2 offers rankings that are identical to those provided by the Sharpe ratio. However, these rankings are easier to interpret as they are in percentage terms. A portfolio that matches the market's performance will have an M^2 of zero, while one that outperforms the market will have a positive M^2. The M^2 also enables us to tell which portfolios beat the market on a risk-adjusted basis.

Jensen's alpha is based on systematic risk (like the Treynor ratio). It first estimates a portfolio's beta risk using the market model, and then uses the CAPM to determine the required return from the investment (given its beta risk). The difference between the portfolio's actual return and the required return (as predicted by the CAPM) is called Jensen's alpha. Jensen's alpha is calculated as:

Jensen's alpha is the maximum that an investor should be willing to pay the portfolio manager.

$$\alpha_p = R_p - [R_f + \beta_p(R_m - R_f)]$$

Jensen's alpha for the market equals zero. The higher the Jensen's alpha for a portfolio, the better its risk-adjusted performance (see Example 3-4).

Example 3-4: Portfolio Performance Evaluation

The following table provides information about the portfolio performance of three investment managers:

Manager	Return	σ	β
A	13%	20%	0.6
B	11%	15%	1.1
C	12%	10%	0.8
Market (M)	10%	16%	
Risk-free rate (R_f)	4%		

1. Calculate the following for each of the investment managers:
   a. Expected return
   b. Sharpe ratio
   c. Treynor ratio
   d. M^2
   e. Jensen's alpha
2. Comment on your answers and rank the managers' performance.

Solution:

1. We illustrate the calculations for Manager A. The table that follows summarizes the results for all managers.

   Manager A

   Expected return $= R_f + \beta(R_m - R_f) = 4\% + [0.6 \times (10\% - 4\%)] = 7.6\%$

   $$\text{Sharpe ratio} = \frac{R_A - R_f}{\sigma_A} = \frac{13\% - 4\%}{20\%} = 0.45$$

   $$\text{Treynor ratio} = \frac{R_A - R_f}{\beta_A} = \frac{13\% - 4\%}{0.6} = 0.15$$

   $$M^2 = (R_A - R_f)\frac{\sigma_m}{\sigma_A} - (R_A - R_f) = (13\% - 4\%)\frac{16\%}{20\%} - (10\% - 4\%) = 1.2\%$$

   Jensen's alpha $= R_A - [R_f + \beta(R_m - R_f)] = 13\% - [4\% + 0.6(10\% - 4\%)] = 5.4\%$

Manager	Expected Return	Sharpe Ratio	Treynor Ratio	M^2	Jensen's Alpha
A	7.6%	0.45	0.150	1.20%	5.4%
B	10.6%	0.47	0.064	1.47%	0.4%
C	8.8%	0.8	0.1	6.80%	3.2%
Market	10%	0.375	0.060	0	0
R_f	4%	–	–	–	0

Ranking of portfolios by performance

Rank	Sharpe Ratio	Treynor Ratio	M^2	Jensen's Alpha
1	C	A	C	A
2	B	C	B	C
3	A	B	A	B
4	M	M	M	M
5	–	–	–	R_f

2. When considering total risk (relevant when the portfolio is not fully diversified), we look at the Sharpe ratio and M^2. C performs the best as she has both the highest Sharpe ratio (0.8) and the highest M^2 (6.8).

When we consider systematic risk (relevant when the portfolio is well diversified), we look at the Treynor ratio and Jensen's alpha. Manager A performs the best as she has both the highest Treynor ratio (0.15) and the highest Jensen's alpha (5.4%).

Notice that all three managers outperform the benchmark as the risk-return profiles of their performance lie above the SML, as shown in Figure 3-1:

Figure 3-1: Portfolio Performance Versus SML

We can see from the graph that A performs the best on a risk-adjusted basis, as it lies northwest relative to the other portfolios.

A question arises as to when analysts should use measures like the Sharpe ratio and M^2 (that are based on total risk) and when they should use the Treynor ratio or Jensen's alpha (that are based on beta risk). Total risk is relevant when an investor holds an inefficient portfolio (one that is not fully diversified)

Security Characteristic Line

The security characteristic line (SCL) plots the excess returns of a security against the excess returns on the market. The equation of the SCL is given as:

$$R_i - R_f = \alpha_i + \beta_i(R_m - R_f)$$

Note that Jensen's alpha is the y-intercept, and beta is the slope of the SCL.

Security Selection: Identifying Mispriced Securities

Table 3-1 uses the same five stocks that we used in Example 2-1. We now calculate the expected return on these five securities based on their expected dividends, expected prices in one year, and current market prices.

Table 3-1: Calculation of Expected Return

Stock	Beta	Required Return from SML	Current Price (P0)	Expected Dividend (D1)	Expected Price (P1)	Expected Return [(P1 + D1)/P0] − 1
A	0.75	8.75%	25	1	26.31	[(26.31+1)/25] −1 = **9.24%**
B	1.00	10%	32	0.75	34.45	[(34.45+0.75)/32] −1 = **10%**
C	1.15	10.75%	15	0.80	15.7	[(15.70+0.80)/15] −1 = **10%**
D	1.5	12.5%	7	Nil	7.95	[(7.95+0)/7] −1 = **13.57%**
E	−0.25	3.75%	48	1.5	48.3	[(48.30+1.50)/48] −1 = **3.75%**

To determine whether a security is undervalued or overvalued, we compare the return that the security offers (based on its expected future price and dividend payments over the holding period) to the return it should offer to compensate investors for its systematic risk (beta). For example, based on our forecasts, Stock A offers a return of 9.24%. Based on the CAPM, the return required from Stock A to compensate for its beta risk is 8.75%. Stock A's current price is too low, which is why its expected return is higher than the required return (according to the CAPM). Therefore, Stock A is *undervalued* and investors should buy it.

Our forecasted return for Stock C (10%) is lower than the return required by investors for investing in a stock with a beta of 1.15 (10.75%). Stock C's current price is too high. Therefore, investors should *sell* the stock based on the given forecasts.

- If the expected return using price and dividend forecasts is *higher* than the investor's required return given the systematic risk in the security, the security is *undervalued* and the investor should *buy* it.
- If the expected return using price and dividend forecasts is *lower* than the investor's required return given the systematic risk in the security, the security is *overvalued* and the investor should *sell* it.

Let's plot the forecasted returns on these securities on the same graph as the SML (which illustrates the required return from securities with various levels of systematic risk). See Figure 3-2.

Figure 3-2: Mispriced Securities

- Notice from Figure 3-2 that Stock A and D plot *above* the SML. This is because the expected return on these stocks is *greater* than their required return. Securities that plot *above* the SML are *undervalued* and should be *purchased*.
- Stock B and E plot on the SML. This means that the expected return on these securities equals the return required from these securities. These stocks are *fairly valued*.
- Stock C plots below the SML. The expected return for this stock falls short of the return required to compensate investors for the systematic risk inherent in the security. This stock is *overvalued* and should be *sold*.

Constructing a Portfolio

The CAPM tells us that investors should hold a portfolio that combines the risk-free asset with the market portfolio. Let's assume that we begin with the S&P 500 as our risky asset portfolio. The S&P 500 index contains only large-cap U.S. stocks, but does not encompass the entire global market. Therefore, we might want to consider a security not included in the S&P 500 for inclusion in the portfolio. The decision regarding whether the particular security should be included in our portfolio depends on the α_i of the security (based on the CAPM and the S&P 500 as the market portfolio). Positive α_i securities (even if they are correctly priced) should be added to the portfolio.

Further, within the set of securities included in the S&P 500, some may be undervalued (expected to generate positive alpha) and others may be overvalued (expected to generate negative alpha) based on investor expectations. The weight of undervalued securities should be increased and that of overvalued securities should be reduced. See Example 3-5.

The weight of each nonmarket security in the portfolio should be proportional to:

> The information ratio
>
> $\left(\dfrac{\alpha_i}{\sigma_{ei}}\right)$ measures
>
> the abnormal return per unit of risk added by the security to a well-diversified portfolio. The larger the information ratio is, the more valuable the security.

$$\frac{\alpha_i}{\sigma_{ei}^2}$$

where:

α_i = Jensen's alpha

σ_{ei}^2 = Nonsystematic variance of the security

Example 3-5: Optimal Investor Portfolio with Heterogeneous Beliefs

An investor gathers the following information regarding three stocks, which are not in the market portfolio:

Stocks	Expected Return	Standard Deviation	Beta
A	16%	29%	1.7
B	20%	24%	1.4
C	18%	21%	1.2

Given that the return on the market portfolio is 13% with a standard deviation of 15%, and the risk-free rate of return is 5%, answer the following questions:

1. Calculate Jensen's alpha for Stocks A, B, and C.
2. Calculate nonsystematic variance for A, B, and C.
3. If an investor holds the market portfolio, should she add any of these three stocks to her portfolio? If so, which stock should have the highest weight in the portfolio?

Solution:

1. $\alpha_A = R_A - [R_f + \beta(R_m - R_f)] = 13\% - [4\% + 0.6(10\% - 4\%)] = 5.4\%$

   $\alpha_A = 16\% - [5\% + 1.7(13\% - 5\%)] = -0.026$

   $\alpha_B = 20\% - [5\% + 1.4(13\% - 5\%)] = 0.038$

   $\alpha_C = 18\% - [5\% + 1.2(13\% - 5\%)] = 0.034$

2. Nonsystematic variance = Total variance − Systematic variance

   $$\sigma_{ei}^2 = \sigma_i^2 - \beta_i^2 \sigma_m^2$$

   A's nonsystematic variance $= (0.29)^2 - (1.7^2 \times 0.15^2) = 0.0191$

   B's nonsystematic variance $(0.24)^2 - (1.4^2 \times 0.15^2) = 0.0135$

   C's nonsystematic variance $(0.21)^2 - (1.2^2 \times 0.15^2) = 0.0117$

3. Stock A should not be included in the portfolio as it has a negative alpha. It should only be included if the investor can short the stock.

   On the other hand, Stocks B and C have positive alphas and should be included in the portfolio. Their weights are determined as follows:

   Weight of Stock B = 0.038 / 0.0135 = 2.815

   Weight of Stock C = 0.034 / 0.0117 = 2.906

   In relative terms, the weight of Stock C will be greater than that of Stock B by 3.23% (2.906 / 2.815 − 1).

Beyond the CAPM

Limitations of the CAPM

Theoretical limitations
- The CAPM is a single-factor model; only systematic risk is priced in the CAPM
- It is only a single-period model.

Practical limitations
- A true market portfolio is unobservable, as it would also include assets that are not investable (e.g., human capital).
- In the absence of a true market portfolio, the proxy for the market portfolio used varies across analysts, which leads to different return estimates for the same asset (not permissible in the CAPM world).

Extensions of the CAPM
Theoretical models, like the arbitrage pricing theory (APT), expand the number of risk factors.
Practical models use extensive research to uncover risk factors that explain returns.

READING 41: BASICS OF PORTFOLIO PLANNING AND CONSTRUCTION

LESSON 1: PORTFOLIO PLANNING

LOS 41a: Describe the reasons for a written investment policy statement (IPS). Vol 4, pp 368–369

In order to construct a portfolio that satisfies the client's investment objectives, investment managers first need to devise a plan. This plan is documented in an investment policy statement (IPS).

The Investment Policy Statement

An investment policy statement is an invaluable planning tool that adds discipline to the investment process. Before developing an IPS, an investment manager must conduct a fact-finding discussion with the client to learn about the client's risk tolerance and other specific circumstances.

The IPS can be thought of as a road map that serves the following purposes:

- It helps the investor decide on realistic investment goals after learning about financial markets and associated risks.
- It creates a standard according to which the portfolio manager's performance can be judged.
- It guides the actions of portfolio managers, who should refer to it from time to time to assess the suitability of particular investments for their clients.

A typical investment policy statement specifies investment objectives and constraints, and the types of risks that the investor is willing to take in order to meet those goals.

Investment goals are expressed in terms of both risk and return. This is because every investment decision involves a trade-off between risk and return. An investor's willingness and ability to take more risk in pursuit of higher returns depends on her individual situation and preferences. However, a manager must ensure that a client's return objectives and risk tolerance are consistent with each other. A client should not expect to earn a relatively high return without taking a relatively high level of risk.

Investment constraints are factors that the investment manager needs to consider when making investments for the client's portfolio. These typically include the following:

- Liquidity requirements.
- Time horizon.
- Tax concerns.
- Regulatory requirements.
- Unique needs and circumstances.

The investment policy statement should be reviewed on a regular basis and updated when there are major economic changes or changes in the client's needs and circumstances.

LOS 41b: Describe the major components of an IPS. Vol 4, pg 369

An investment policy statement does not have a single standard format. It generally includes the following sections:

- An introduction that describes the client.
- A statement of purpose.
- A statement of duties and responsibilities, which describes the duties and responsibilities of the client, the custodian of the client's assets, and the investment manager.
- Procedures that outline the steps required to keep the IPS updated and steps required to respond to various contingencies.
- The client's investment objectives.
- The client's investment constraints.
- Investment guidelines regarding how the policy should be executed (e.g., whether use of leverage and derivatives is permitted) and specific types of assets that must be excluded.
- Evaluation and review guidelines on obtaining feedback on investment results.
- Appendices that describe the strategic asset allocation and the rebalancing policy.

> The sections that are most closely linked to a client's distinctive needs, and probably the most important from a planning perspective, are those dealing with investment objectives and constraints.

LOS 41c: Describe risk and return objectives and how they may be developed for a client. Vol 4, pp 370–376

Risk Objectives

It is very important for the portfolio manager to ensure that the risk of the portfolio is suitable for the client. Quantitative risk objectives may be absolute, relative, or a combination of both.

- An example of an absolute risk objective would be that the client does not want to lose more than 5% of her capital over a particular period. A more practical way of stating the same objective would be as a probability statement (e.g., the portfolio should not lose more than 5% of its value over a 12-month period with 95% probability). Measures of absolute risk include the variance, standard deviation, and value at risk.
- Relative risk objectives relate risk to a certain benchmark that represents an appropriate level of risk. For example, investments in large-cap U.K. equities could be benchmarked to the FTSE 100. Tracking risk or tracking error is the appropriate measure of risk relative to a benchmark.

> Note that this objective is not related to investment market performance, good or bad, and is absolute in the sense of being self-standing.

Risk objectives for institutional clients may be stated in terms of minimizing the probability of failing to meet their liabilities when they are due.

Risk tolerance is a function of both a client's ability to take risk and her willingness to take risk. The ability to take risk is a function of several factors including time horizon, expected income, and net worth. Generally speaking, a client with a longer time horizon, high expected income, and greater net worth has a greater ability to bear risk. A client's willingness to bear risk, on the other hand, is based on more subjective factors including her psychological makeup and level of understanding of financial markets.

LOS 41d:
Distinguish
between the
willingness
and the ability
(capacity)
to take risk
in analyzing
an investor's
financial risk
tolerance.
Vol 4, pp 381–384

- When the client's ability to take risk is below average and her willingness to take risk is also below average, the investor's overall risk tolerance is below average.
- When the client's ability to take risk is above average and her willingness to take risk is also above average, the investor's overall risk tolerance is above average.
- When the client's ability to take risk is below average and her willingness to take risk is above average, the investor's overall risk tolerance is below average.
- When the client's ability to take risk is above average and her willingness to take risk is below average, the investment manager should explain the conflict and implications to the client.

When there is a mismatch between a client's ability and willingness to take risk, the prudent approach is to conclude that the client's tolerance for risk is the lower of the two factors. Further, any decisions made must be documented.

Return Objectives

Return objectives may also be stated in absolute or relative terms.

- Absolute return objectives state the percentage return desired by the client. The return may be expressed on a real or nominal basis.
- Relative return objectives express the required return relative to a stated benchmark. A good benchmark should be investable (i.e., an investor should be able to replicate it).

The return objective may be stated before or after fees and on a pre-or post-tax basis. Further, it could also be expressed in terms of a required return (i.e., the amount an investor needs to earn over the investment horizon to meet a specified future goal).

The portfolio manager must ensure that the client's return objective is realistic in light of her tolerance for risk.

LOS 41e: Describe the investment constraints of liquidity, time horizon, tax concerns, legal and regulatory factors, and unique circumstances and their implications for the choice of portfolio assets. Vol 4, pp 376–381

Liquidity

This refers to the ability to readily convert investments into cash at a price close to fair market value. Investors may require ready cash to meet unexpected needs and could be forced to sell their assets at unfavorable terms if the investment plan does not consider their liquidity needs. Therefore, an IPS should state any likely requirements to withdraw funds from the portfolio.

Time Horizon

This refers to the time period between putting funds into an investment and requiring them for use. A close relationship exists between an investor's time horizon, liquidity needs, and ability to take risk. The shorter the time horizon, the harder it would be for an investor to overcome losses. Therefore, low-risk investments are more appropriate for investors with short time horizons.

Tax Concerns

Taxes play a very important role in investment planning because, unlike tax-exempt investors, taxable investors are really only concerned with after-tax returns on their portfolios. The tax code in most countries is very complex. For example, dividend income, interest income, and rental income may be taxed at the investor's marginal tax rate, while capital gains might be taxed at a different rate. Further, capital gains are only taxable after the asset has been sold (the capital gain realized), but unrealized capital gains are not taxable (the tax liability can be deferred indefinitely).

Legal and Regulatory Factors

Investors also need to be aware of legal and regulatory factors. For example, some countries impose a limit on the proportion of equity securities in a pension fund's portfolio. Further, an individual working for a company may be constrained from selling her shares for a period of time if she has access to material nonpublic information about the company (e.g., members of a company's board of directors are prohibited from trading the company's stock before financial results are released).

Unique Circumstances

There may be a number of individual and unusual considerations that affect investors. For example, many investors may want to exclude certain investments from their portfolios based on personal or socially conscious reasons. Because each investor is unique, the implications of this constraint differ for each investor. For example, an investor may not want to invest additional funds in the company she works for if she already has stock options in the company.

LESSON 2: PORTFOLIO CONSTRUCTION

LOS 41f: Explain the specification of asset classes in relation to asset allocation. Vol 4, pp 384–393

LOS 41g: Describe the principles of portfolio construction and the role of asset allocation in relation to the IPS. Vol 4, pp 384–398

> An asset class is a category of assets that have similar characteristics, attributes, and risk-return relationships.

Portfolio Construction

Once the IPS has been compiled, the investment manager begins constructing the portfolio. How the portfolio funds are allocated across different asset classes is referred to as the portfolio's strategic asset allocation (SAA). A portfolio's SAA is important because it is a portfolio's allocation across various asset classes (not its allocation across securities within those asset classes) that is the primary determinant of portfolio returns.

Capital Market Expectations

Capital market expectations refer to a portfolio manager's expectations regarding the risk and return prospects of various asset classes. Capital market expectations are quantified in terms of expected returns, standard deviation of returns, and correlations among asset classes. Return expectations can be developed from historical data, economic analysis, or valuation models, while standard deviation and correlation estimates are primarily obtained from historical data.

The Strategic Asset Allocation

The strategic asset allocation defines how the investor's funds are divided across different asset classes. Traditionally, cash, equities, bonds, and real estate were defined as the major asset classes. Recently, hedge funds, private equity, and commodities have been added to the list. Further, each asset class can be subdivided into several subclasses. For example, bonds can be divided into government and corporate debt. Further, government bonds can be subdivided into domestic and foreign government bonds, while corporate bonds can be divided into investment-grade and high-yield bonds.

When defining asset classes, the following must be considered:

- Each asset class should contain assets that carry a similar expected return and risk, and correlations among the assets within a class should be relatively high.
- Each asset class should provide diversification benefits. The correlation of an asset class with other asset classes should be relatively low.
- Asset classes should be mutually exclusive and should cover all investment alternatives.

Sometimes asset classes will be subdivided into smaller classes, which are relatively highly correlated with each other. For example, the European and U.S. equity markets have a relatively high correlation, but they may still be treated as separate asset classes for the purposes of portfolio construction, because different managers/products may be used to manage investments in U.S. equities and European equities.

The risk-return characteristics of the strategic asset allocation depend on the expected returns and risk of the individual asset classes, and on the correlations between the asset classes. Typically, risk-averse investors will place a higher weight on government bonds and cash in their SAAs, while those with a higher risk tolerance will have a higher weight invested in equities.

A theoretical framework for developing the SAA for a client is by developing the client's utility function and using capital market expectations to determine the risk-return profiles of all investable portfolios available to the client. The utility function can be used to draw up indifference curves, while capital market expectations can be used to determine the efficient frontier. The point of tangency between the two represents the optimal asset allocation for the investor. A change in capital market expectations would cause a movement in the efficient frontier, while a change in the investor's objectives or constraints would result in a shift in her indifference curves. A change in either of both the efficient frontier and the investor's indifference curves would require the strategic asset allocation to be adjusted.

Note that the framework described above may not be followed exactly in practice due to the following reasons:

- An IPS does not explicitly express the client's investment objectives and constraints in terms of a utility function. It usually only provides threshold levels of risk and return along with a description of constraints.
- The constraints listed in the IPS make it more appropriate to use multiperiod models. This framework is a single-period model.

Steps Toward an Actual Portfolio

1. Risk budgeting: This is the process of subdividing the desired level of portfolio risk (which has been determined in the IPS) across the different sources of investment returns (i.e., the strategic asset allocation, tactical asset allocation, and security selection).

2. Tactical asset allocation: This refers to an allocation where the manager deliberately deviates from the strategic asset allocation for the short term. For example, if a manager believes that equities are in for a difficult few months, she might invest more (than stated in the SAA) of the portfolio in bonds on a temporary basis to enhance portfolio return.

3. Security selection: A manager may be able to outperform the asset class benchmark by investing in particular securities within the asset class that she expects to do well (better than the benchmark).

4. Portfolio rebalancing: Changes in security prices will lead to changes in the weights of different asset classes in the portfolio and cause them to deviate or "drift" from policy weights. Therefore, the portfolio should be rebalanced periodically and brought in line with policy weights. The set of rules that lay out guidelines for rebalancing the portfolio is known as the rebalancing policy and is an important element of risk management.

> Deviating from the prescribed weights and aiming to select securities that will outperform the benchmark leads to additional risk over and above the risk in the policy portfolio.

Additional Portfolio Organizing Principles

The top-down investment framework described in this reading has two drawbacks:

- If several managers are hired to manage different subclasses within the same asset class, it may result in underutilization of the risk budget.
- Each manager would trade within the portfolio under her management so the portfolio overall may not be efficient from a capital gains tax point of view.

In order to avoid this, managers invest most of their funds in passive investments and trade a minority of assets actively. This approach is known as the "core-satellite" approach.

READING 42: RISK MANAGEMENT: AN INTRODUCTION

LESSON 1: THE RISK MANAGEMENT PROCESS AND RISK GOVERNANCE

LOS 42a: Define risk management. Vol 4, pp 409–411

The Risk Management Process

Risk encompasses all of the uncertain environmental variables that lead unpredictability of outcomes. Taking risk is an integral part of conducting business and managing investment portfolios. While risk is generally seen in an unfavorable light, the challenge for companies and investment managers lies in carefully choosing, understanding, and managing the risks entailed by their decisions. In the investment management arena, many managers focus on return, which is actually not as easily managed or controlled as risk.

Risk exposure refers to the extent to which the underlying environmental or market risks result in actual risk borne by a business or an investor.

Risk management is the process by which an organization or individual defines the level of risk that should be taken, measures the level of risk actually being taken, and then continually ensures that the latter is consistent with the former, with the aim of maximizing the company's or portfolio's value. Stated differently, risk management refers to all the decisions and actions that must be taken in order to achieve return/performance objectives while taking on an acceptable level of risk.

For example, suppose that a U.S. investor has a long position on the GBP worth £1,000,000. It is expected that an upcoming economic data release will result in the GBP either appreciating or depreciating by exactly 1% versus the USD.

- The risk here is the uncertain result of the announcement, as the USD-denominated value of this investor's GBP position can rise or fall by 1%.
- The risk exposure, in this case, is 1% of £1,000,000 or £10,000.
- Risk management would include quantifying and understanding this risk exposure, deciding whether the investor should bear the risk, how much of the risk exposure she should bear, and then possibly mitigating or modifying this risk.

Very important:

- Risk management is not about minimizing risk. It is about actively understanding and embracing those risks that offer the best chance of achieving an organization's goals with an acceptable chance of failure.
- Risk management is not even about predicting risks. It is about being prepared for (positive or negative) unpredictable events such that their impact would have already been quantified and considered in advance.

Good risk management does not prevent losses, but constantly provides management with the knowledge and insight to navigate as efficiently as possible (in terms of taking risks) toward the goals set by the governing body. Good risk management may also enable managers to more quickly or effectively act in the face of a crisis. But note that even the best risk management may not stop a portfolio from losing money in a bear market or prevent a business from reduced profits in a recession.

LOS 42b: Describe features of a risk management framework.
Vol 4, pp 411–417

A **risk management framework** refers to the infrastructure, process, and analytics required to support the risk management function in an organization. Every organization must have a customized risk management framework based on its individual objectives and requirements. An effective risk management framework should address the following areas:

- Risk governance.
- Risk identification and measurement.
- Risk infrastructure.
- Defined policies and processes.
- Risk monitoring, mitigation, and management.
- Communications.
- Strategic analysis or integration.

Risk governance comes from the board of directors. It is the top-down process and guidance that directs risk management activities to align with the organization's goals and risk appetite. To attain the best results, risk governance should take an enterprise-wide view of risk (enterprise risk management) as opposed to having each business division or segment manage the risks it faces individually. Risk governance is discussed in more detail later in the reading.

Risk identification and measurement form the core of risk management. Risk identification and measurement are an ongoing process that entails analyzing the business or portfolio to identify risk exposures, tracking changes in those risk exposures, calculating risk metrics to gauge the significance of those risks under various scenarios, as well as keeping an eye on the business environment for potential risk drivers. A risk driver refers to any fundamental underlying factor that gives rise to a risk that is relevant to the entity. The different types of risk are discussed later in the reading.

Bear in mind that even though technological innovations have made risk analysis and management more quantitative and timely, technology should be used only in conjunction with experienced business judgment when identifying and measuring risk.

Risk infrastructure refers to the people, systems, and technology required to track risk exposures and conduct quantitative risk analysis. It includes the process (known as risk capture) through which risk exposures are populated in the risk management system, as well as the databases, models, and skilled personnel needed to develop and maintain the risk framework.

Policies and processes translate risk governance into the organization's day-to-day operations and decision-making processes in order to ensure that risky activities are kept in line with the entity's risk tolerance levels. They include commonsense business practices such as updating and protecting data, controlling cash flows, conducting due diligence on investments, and making checklists to support important decisions.

Risk monitoring, mitigation, and management make up one of the most difficult facets of a risk framework.

This facet requires pulling together risk governance, identification and measurement, infrastructure, and policies and processes, continually reviewing and reevaluating them in the face of changing risk exposures and risk drivers. Further, it requires recognizing when the entity's risk exposure is not aligned with its predetermined risk tolerance, and then taking action to bring them back into alignment. Risk mitigation and management are discussed in detail toward the end of this reading.

Communication of critical risk issues must happen continuously across all levels of the organization.

- Governance parameters, such as risk tolerances and associated constraints, must be clearly communicated to managers.
- Risk metrics must be reported in a clear and timely manner.

Figure 1-1: The Risk Management Framework in an Enterprise

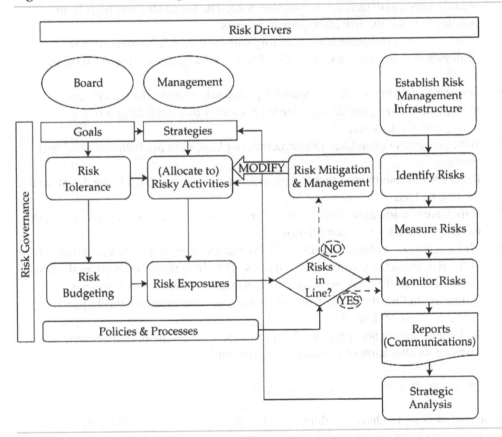

Figure 1-1 illustrates the process of risk management for an enterprise, pulling together all the described elements of the risk framework. Although there are a very high number of risks faced by every organization, most organizations are primarily affected by a small number of key risk drivers, or primary underlying factors that create risk. Along the left side is risk governance, which represents board-level decisions and encompasses and affects the boxes immediately to its right. The governance body, often called a board, defines the goals of the organization and, in turn, decides on its risk tolerance. It may additionally provide guidance on how or where that risk is taken (risk budgeting). The board is also involved in setting high-level policies that will affect most risk management processes. These risk governance activities are a crucial keystone of the risk framework and will be discussed in detail in the next section. When the rest of the risk framework hinges off of these top-down governance elements and is focused on the goals of the entire enterprise (as shown here), the end result is effective enterprise risk management.

- Risk issues must be reviewed and discussed as a standard part of decision making.
- Changes in risk exposures must be discussed so that action can be taken as appropriate.
- There should also be a feedback loop with the governance body so that top-level risk guidance is continually validated/updated and communicated back to the rest of the organization.

Strategic analysis and integration of a risk management framework into the business can help management better understand the how and why of performance and help sort out which activities are adding value and which are not. When it comes to portfolio management, thorough analysis can support better investment decisions and improve risk-adjusted returns.

- It is the governance body or board's responsibility to define the goals of the organization and determine its risk tolerance. The board also sets high-level policies to guide the risk management process.
- Management is responsible for planning and executing value-maximizing strategies that are consistent with the objectives and guidance provided by the board.
- In order to develop a risk management program to support the entity's goals, management must provide the required resources by establishing a risk management infrastructure.
- With processes defined and infrastructure in place, risks are then identified and measured.
- Risks are constantly monitored to ensure that they are not outside the limits set in the risk budget.
- If they are outside these limits, mitigation and management actions must be taken to bring them back into compliance.
- These actions/modifications will result in changes to management's actual allocation of the risk budget to various risky activities. The circle must then be started again to ensure that modified risk exposures are consistent with the entity's policies.
- If they are in line, the process moves forward to continuous monitoring and communicating risk levels.
- Risk management also plays a role in strategic analysis, helping management improve its allocation of capital and the risk budget.

Benefits of Establishing Good Risk Management

An organization is said to have developed an effective **risk culture** when effective risk management is truly integrated at all levels of management and into every step of the decision-making process. An effective risk culture brings the following benefits:

- There is a lower probability of management being surprised by an event, and even if it is a surprise, management has a better idea regarding the extent of the damage.
- There is more discipline leading to better consideration of trade-offs and better risk-return relationships.
- Management is able to respond to unfavorable events more promptly and is able to mitigate losses more effectively.
- There are fewer operational errors from deficiencies in policies and procedures, transparency, and risk awareness.
- There is a stronger level of trust between the governing body and management, which generally results in more effective delegation.

- The company enjoys a better image or reputation because analysts and investors perceive a company as prudent and value-focused.

Together, all these benefits should lead to higher value for the enterprise.

LOS 42c: Define risk governance and describe elements of effective risk governance. Vol 4, pp 417–419

Risk Governance

As mentioned earlier, risk governance is the top-down process and guidance from the board that directs management activities to align with the goals of the overall entity.

An Enterprise View of Risk

The governing body or board performs the following roles within the risk management framework:

- It determines the organization's goals and priorities, which form the basis of enterprise risk management.
- It determines the organization's risk appetite and tolerance; that is, it defines which risks are acceptable, which risks must be mitigated and to what extent, and which risks are unacceptable.
- It is responsible for overseeing risk management to continually ensure that it is functioning properly and is consistent with the goal of maximizing value.

Desirable Properties of Good Risk Governance

- Good risk governance should provide a sense of the worst loss that the organization can manage in various scenarios.
- It should provide clear guidance, but at the same time leave enough flexibility for management to execute strategy.
- The focus should be on enterprise risk management (that focuses on the objectives, health, and value of the organization as a whole). The entire economic balance sheet of the business should be considered, not just individual divisions or departments of the business. For example:
  - A pension fund manager should not just try to maximize the value of assets under management, but should also consider the nature of its liabilities (duration, etc.). Further, the manager should also consider the sponsor's business profile. If the overall business is not performing well, the sponsor will find it more difficult to make contributions to the plan.
  - In the context of portfolio management for individuals, the asset allocation decision should be based on a more holistic analysis rather than a simple exercise in optimizing the risk-return trade-off. For example, if an individual's career is related to real estate, her optimal portfolio should ideally have a lower allocation to real estate than the portfolio of an otherwise identical individual whose human capital is not related to real estate in any way.

- The board should provide a regular forum (e.g., a risk management committee) where the risk framework and key risk issues are discussed at management level. This ensures that risk at the operational level is kept within the boundaries defined by the board.
- It should provide for the appointment of a chief risk officer (CRO) who is responsible for building and implementing the risk framework for the enterprise and managing all related activities. Further, the CRO's insight should be used in making key strategic decisions.

LOS 42d: Explain how risk tolerance affects risk management.
Vol 4, pp 419–421

Risk Tolerance

Risk tolerance identifies the extent to which the entity is willing to experience losses or opportunity costs and to fail in meeting its objectives. At the governance level, the idea is not really to select activities that will maximize value or produce the highest returns given an acceptable level of risk (this duty falls on management), but to define the entity's risk appetite.

Defining an organization's risk tolerance calls for answering the following questions:

- What shortfalls within the organization would cause it to fail to achieve critical goals? This question looks to address internal risk factors.
  - For example, a company may identify liquidity and revenue shortfalls as key internal risk drivers. In order to mitigate these risks, it could set tolerance bands on its revenue and cash flow variation.
- What uncertain forces is the organization exposed to? This question focuses on outside risk factors.
  - For example, a company may recognize foreign exchange rate fluctuations and interest rate changes as its primary outside risk drivers. In response, it may then engage in hedging strategies to mitigate or eliminate these risks, depending on how uncomfortable it is with continued exposure to these risks.

Once it has answers to these two questions, the board can define the dimensions of risk it is not willing to accept, and then communicate them throughout the organization (ideally *before* a crisis, not after).

In providing governance guidance, the board should recognize that the organization has certain core competencies, and therefore it should take risks that offer the best chance of success and value creation. Companies should abstain from retaining significant exposure to risks in areas where they do not have expertise by limiting or hedging those noncore risks.

Factors That Affect a Company's Risk Tolerance

- The more dynamic a company is in its ability to respond to adverse events, the higher its risk tolerance.
- The greater the loss a company can bear without impairing its status as a going concern, the higher its risk tolerance.
- The stronger the company's competitive position, the higher its risk tolerance.
- The overall competitive landscape in the industry and the regulatory landscape also influence a company's risk tolerance.

Factors That Should Not Determine Risk Tolerance

There are other factors that should not determine risk tolerance, but unfortunately do in some cases. Personal motivations, beliefs, and agendas of board members (the agency problem), as well as company size, short-term pressures, and management compensation often affect risk tolerance in ways that do not always align with owners' interests.

LOS 42e: Describe risk budgeting and its role in risk governance.
Vol 4, pp 421–424

Risk Budgeting

Risk tolerance focuses on determining the organization's risk appetite and which risks are acceptable or unacceptable. **Risk budgeting** focuses on how risk is taken by quantifying and allocating tolerable risk to various activities and/or investments based on their characteristics. The risk budget provides the means for taking board-level risk tolerance guidance to management decision making and operations.

Risk budgets can be complex and multidimensional or simple and one-dimensional.

- Single-dimensional risk measures include standard deviation, beta, value at risk (VaR), and scenario loss.
- Multidimensional risk approaches include one where portfolio risk is evaluated based on the risk profiles of underlying asset classes (equity, fixed income, etc.), and another risk-factor approach where exposure to various risk factors is used to capture associated risk premiums (value stocks versus growth stocks).

The benefit of risk budgeting lies in the fact that it forces the organization into thinking about risk trade-offs and fosters a culture where risk is an important consideration in all key decisions. Every step or decision the organization takes is based on the philosophy of maximizing value added while remaining within the confines of its risk tolerance.

LESSON 2: IDENTIFICATION OF RISKS AND MEASURING AND MODIFYING RISKS

LOS 42f: Identify financial and nonfinancial sources of risk and describe how they may interact. Vol 4, pp 424–433

Identification of Risks

Now that we have understood risk management and risk governance, we move into the implementation side of things, which starts with identification of risks. Risks can be categorized as **financial** or **nonfinancial risks**.

Financial Risks

Financial risks are those that originate in financial markets, such as changes in prices or interest rates. The primary types of financial risks are market risk, credit risk, and liquidity risk.

- **Market risk** arises from changes in interest rates, stock prices, exchange rates, and commodity prices.
  - Generally speaking, the underlying risk drivers of market risk are fundamental economic conditions or events in the overall economy, the industry, or the company itself.
- **Credit risk** (**default risk** or **counterparty risk**) is the risk of loss if one party fails to pay an amount owed on an obligation (e.g., bond or derivative).
  - Generally speaking, the underlying risk drivers of credit risk tend to be fundamental weakness in the economy or industry, or in demand for a company's products.
- **Liquidity risk** (or **transaction cost risk**) is the risk of a substantial downward valuation adjustment when trying to sell an asset. It refers to the possibility that the seller will have to reduce the price of the asset to a level below its true market value in order to liquidate or sell it.
  - In many transactions, there is a bid–ask spread that is known at the time of purchase. This spread is simply a transaction cost. Liquidity risk would arise if this spread widened when the asset was being sold.
  - Generally speaking, the primary drivers of liquidity risk are (1) changes in market conditions or the market for the individual asset and (2) the size of the position (i.e., large positions are typically more difficult and costly to offload).

NonFinancial Risks

Nonfinancial risks arise from outside the financial markets. They emanate from a variety of sources, such as the relationship between the organization and its peers, regulators, governments, the environment, suppliers, employees, and customers.

- **Settlement risk** (also known as **Herstatt risk**) is related to default risk, but has more to do with settlement of payments just before a default. For example, consider a forward contract where Party A has committed to purchase 1,000 shares of ABC Company from Party B for a total of $500,000. At expiration, Party A would be expected to wire the funds, while Party B would transfer the shares. However, if Party A were to wire the funds and Party B were to declare bankruptcy and not transfer the shares, Party A would not be able to recover the money, except perhaps through a slow and tedious bankruptcy process. Essentially, this settlement risk arises from the timing of the payment process, typically due to significant time zone differences.

- **Legal risk** is of two types. First, there is the risk of being sued for something the entity does or fails to do. Second, there is the risk of the terms of a contract not being upheld by the legal system. For example, the company might have a position on a derivative contract with an underlying asset that has witnessed a favorable change in price since initiation of the contract, thereby holding positive value for the company. There is a risk, however, that the counterparty (which has been adversely affected by the price change) refuses to pay up based on some legal issue with the contract. There is always a risk with litigation that even seemingly frivolous arguments can hold up on court.

- **Compliance risk** encompasses **regulatory risk**, **accounting risk**, and **tax risk**. It refers to the risk of the organization incurring significant unexpected costs, back taxes owed, financial restatements, and penalties.

- **Model risk** is the risk of a valuation error resulting from using an incorrectly specified model or improperly using a valid model.

  - **Tail risk** is related to model risk, and can even be viewed as a form of model risk. It refers to the risk of events captured by the tail of a distribution occurring more frequently than expected by the model. The following examples illustrate tail risk:

    - Severe market crashes have occurred more frequently than predicted by the normal distribution (which is commonly used in modeling). While this risk is a part of market risk, it also affects valuations and models if it is not handled correctly.

    - Several quantitative models (e.g., option pricing models) and asset allocation models used in portfolio management use standard deviation, thereby ignoring the existence of fat tails in returns and the asymmetric nature of payoffs. This results in an overly simplistic approach toward analyzing market risk.

- **Operational risk** is used to describe all internal risks that arise from the people and processes that work together in an organization to produce its output. Examples include the risk of hackers breaking into the company's computer systems, its computers becoming infected with a virus, programming errors, and bugs. Note that even though the factors that give rise to such risks can arise externally, the risks themselves are largely internal to an organization because it is the organization's responsibility to ensure that its people and processes are functioning efficiently regardless of the threats posed by external forces.

> Terrorism is another form of operational risk that poses a threat to organizations and individuals.

Employees are also major sources of potential internal risks. Examples of risks that arise from employees include senior management manipulating reported financial statements to inflate the company's performance or position, and rogue traders (e.g., Nick Leeson of Barings Bank) undertaking risky speculative transactions without regard for trading limits and controls. Note that the motivation behind these activities may or may not be personal gain (they could be honest mistakes). Either way, employees remain an internal source of risk for companies.

Companies are also threatened by business interruptions; for example, due to inclement weather or security threats. Even though these threats are posed by external forces outside their control, organizations bear the responsibility for establishing internal procedures to deal with related disruptions. For example, airlines are typically able to make the necessary adjustments to their schedules in response to weather-related disruptions.

- **Solvency risk** is the risk that the entity runs out of cash, and is therefore unable to survive or succeed, even if it is otherwise solvent. Note that, in practice, solvency risk as defined here is referred to as liquidity risk. For the purpose of the CFA exam, however, bear in mind that liquidity risk is the risk of a valuation shock when trying to sell a security, whereas solvency risk is the risk relating to the cash position of an entity.

While excessive leverage was a key factor in the failure of Lehman Brothers, it was solvency risk that forced the company into bankruptcy. As panic spread across the financial system, Lehman's liquidity disappeared overnight because most funding sources were no longer willing to bear Lehman's counterparty risk. Since the 2008 crisis, businesses have become increasingly wary of poor solvency management, and have taken measures such as using less leverage, securing more stable sources of financing, investing in models to provide more transparency on solvency risk, incorporating solvency risk at an enterprise level in risk governance, and holding more cash equivalents and assets with less liquidity risk.

Moving on to individuals, they also face a number of operational risks. Examples include:

- The risk of burglary or identity theft.
- Health risk. Note that some individuals take steps to address only their financial exposure to health risk (via health insurance) but do not take any proactive steps to directly address the risk (by eating healthy, exercising regularly, etc.).
- Mortality risk, the risk of dying relatively young.
- Property and casualty risks, which are typically insured against.
- Risk of being cheated by a financial adviser.

Interactions between Risks

Some risks can be classified into more than one category. Further, there are several interactions between risks, as illustrated in the examples that follow:

Suppose Party A buys an out-of-the-money put option from Party B. The underlying asset is the return on an equity index. Assume that the put premium takes into account a 3% probability of default on behalf of Party B, and assumes (erroneously) that the possibility of default is independent of the performance of the equity index. In reality, Party B's default risk might rise if the equity market falls. Party A's expected payoff would then be lower than what it initially thought because it actually faces a credit risk that is compounded by market risk. This type of risk interaction is known as wrong-way risk.

Many banks and hedge funds experienced interacting risks during the financial crisis of 2008. Some highly leveraged institutions were battered by movements in the market (i.e., market risk), which interacted with liquidity and solvency risk to infest the entire financial system. The crisis provided an example of systemic risk, as stresses and failures in one sector transmitted stresses and failures to other sectors, ultimately impacting the entire economy.

Risks interact when it comes to individuals as well. For example, individuals have a tendency to invest more than an "allocatively efficient" amount in their employer's stock (either through employee stock ownership programs or by purchases from the market). This results in highly concentrated portfolios and exposes individuals to a potentially disastrous interaction between market risk and human capital risk. Enron provided an example of this interaction, as many honest employees lost their jobs and a significant chunk of their retirement savings when the company went bankrupt.

The point is that it is important for organizations to recognize that risks interact, and that the interaction is more toxic in stressed market conditions. When different sources of risk come together, the combined risk is almost always nonlinear in that the total risk faced is much greater than the simple sum of the individual risks, and this makes the situation even worse. Unfortunately, most risk models and systems do not directly account for risk interactions. Governance bodies, company management, and financial analysts must be cognizant of the potential risk and damage of risks in combination, and be aware of the dangers of treating risks as separate and unrelated.

LOS 42g: Describe methods for measuring and modifying risk exposures and factors to consider in choosing among the methods. Vol 4, pp 434–447

Measuring and Modifying Risks

Risk Metrics
- **Probability** is a measure of the relative frequency with which one would expect an outcome, series of outcomes, or range of outcomes to occur. On its own, probability does not communicate everything we need to know regarding the risk, such as the magnitude of loss.
- **Standard deviation** measures the range over which a certain percentage of the outcomes would be expected to occur.
  - Standard deviation is not an appropriate measure of risk for nonnormal distributions.
  - Standard deviation may not exist for return distributions with fat tails.
  - When it comes to modern portfolio theory, standard deviation captures systematic and nonsystematic risk. Since nonsystematic risk can easily be diversified away, standard deviation overstates the risk associated with an asset's returns.
- **Beta** is a measure of a security's systematic risk, which is actually the risk that investors can expect to be compensated for in the form of a higher expected return.
  - Formally, beta is a measure of the sensitivity of a security's returns to the returns on the market portfolio.
  - It captures the market risk that a particular asset contributes to a well-diversified portfolio.

When it comes to derivatives, there are several specialized measures of risk. These include the following "Greeks":

- **Delta** measures the sensitivity of the value of a derivative to a small change in the underlying asset.
- **Gamma** captures the impact of relatively large changes in the underlying asset on the value of the derivative.
- **Vega** captures the impact of changes in the volatility of the underlying asset on the value of an option contract.
- **Rho** measures the sensitivity of the value of a derivative contract to changes in interest rates.

> These Greeks are discussed in detail at Level II. You will see some of them in the Level I derivatives readings as well.

Other asset classes have their own special metrics to describe risk. For example, the interest rate sensitivity of a fixed-income instrument is measured by **duration**. The point is that each asset class has some risk measures that are specific to it, but with the increased sophistication of financial institutions and global bank capital regulation, there was a need for an approach to measure financial risk across all asset classes. As a result, **value at risk** (or **VaR**) was introduced.

Value at Risk (VaR)

Value at risk or **VaR** is a measure of the size of the tail of the distribution of profits on a portfolio or for an entity. A VaR measure is composed of (1) a currency amount, (2) a time period, and (3) a probability. If a bank states that its VaR is $4 million at 3% for one day, it means that the bank expects to lose a minimum of $4 million in one day 3% of the time.

- VaR is a minimum extreme loss metric.
- There is no ultimate maximum loss that is stated in the measure. However, the statistics used to compute VaR can be used to estimate average extreme losses.
    - Conditional VaR or CVaR is calculated as the weighted average of all loss outcomes in a statistical distribution that exceed the VaR loss.
    - Expected loss given default (which is used to measure credit risk) measures the average expected loss if the underlying company defaults.
- VaR can be measured in several different ways, resulting in highly diverse estimates.
- VaR is subject to model risk as well.
    - VaR is based on a particular assumption about the probability distribution of returns or profits. If that assumption is incorrect, the VaR estimate will be incorrect.
    - VaR also requires certain inputs. If those inputs are incorrect, the VaR estimate will be incorrect.

VaR can understate actual risk. Under the normal distribution, extreme negative returns are accounted for, but they are offset by extreme positive returns. However, actual historical returns have exhibited a tendency for more extreme negative returns than assumed by the normal distribution (tail risk). In response, statisticians have developed extreme value theory to help them gauge the likelihood of outcomes that exceed those that would normally be expected.

Due to its shortcomings, critics have argued that naive users of VaR can be lulled into a false sense of security. A presumably tolerable VaR can give the illusion that risk is under control, even when it is actually not. Nonetheless, VaR is accepted as a risk measure by most banking regulators and is approved for disclosure purposes in accounting standards.

As with any risk measure, one should supplement VaR with other measures. Two measures in particular that are often used to complement VaR are scenario analysis and stress testing. Although scenario analysis and stress testing can provide useful information (and banks are required to perform them) they are also subject to model risk.

The measures that we have discussed so far all relate primarily to market risk. Credit risk is covered in detail in the fixed income section. Aside from the information provided by credit rating agencies and their own analysis on creditors, risk managers also look at market pricing of credit default swaps (CDSs) to gauge the *ex ante* risk cost of default. Similarly, put options, exotic options, insurance contracts, and other financial instruments can convey important information regarding the cost of default.

Just like credit risk events, operational risk and compliance risk events are relatively rare and potential losses are difficult to quantify. For example:

- If a company's credit card database is hacked, estimating the potential losses would be very difficult. Further, the threat of litigation would exist for years to come.
- Changes in accounting rules, tax rules, and regulations are generally driven by politics, and there are no real numeric measures to quantify these risks.

Nonetheless, risk managers should try to obtain at least a subjective sense of the probability, frequency, and cost of these events, and modify the organization's exposure to these risks accordingly.

Methods of Risk Modification

Once the required analysis has been performed, and the organization has determined which risks it is exposed to and which ones are acceptable/unacceptable and to what degree, the risk management proceeds to align actual risk with acceptable risk.

Note that risk modification is not always an exercise in risk reduction. For example, if a portfolio with a 50–50 equity–cash split sees an outperformance of cash, the weight of cash will outweigh that of equity. The risk manager would then have to rebalance the portfolio by investing more in equity, thereby increasing portfolio risk.

Most risk management, however, does focus on risk reduction or hedging. Hedging can be geared toward reducing the risk to an acceptable level, or eliminating it entirely. We now move to a discussion of methods of risk modification.

Risk Prevention and Avoidance

Avoiding risk completely is difficult. Further, avoiding every risk would be unwise, as the benefits from taking certain risks can outweigh associated costs. For example, an investor may invest her entire retirement savings in cash, but that would come at the cost of giving up protection from inflation and losing out on potentially higher returns.

From the point of view of the risk bearer, every risk taken has a benefit to it. Gambling, for example, carries the risk of substantial financial loss and addiction, but for the consumer who incurs the risk, it is acceptable because of the adequate utility she derives from gambling.

In organizations, the board typically decides which business or investment activities are not worth pursuing based on the organization's goals and the perceived risk-return trade-off. Areas where the board believes management has a better chance of adding value are the ones whose risks are taken, but they are still managed via (1) self-insurance, (2) risk transfer, or (3) risk shifting.

Risk Acceptance: Self-Insurance and Diversification

- Self-insurance refers to retaining exposure to a risk that is considered undesirable but is too costly to eliminate by external means. An example of self-insurance can be found in the banking industry, where self-insurance is obtained by setting aside sufficient capital and loan loss reserves to cover losses.
- Diversification is another form of accepting risk, but it does so in the most efficient manner possible. When it comes to portfolio risk management, diversification is the key to eliminating nonsystematic risk, but other forms of risk management may be needed to mitigate other risks.

Risk Transfer

Risk transfer is the process of passing on a risk to another party, usually in the form of an insurance policy. Insurance is a legal contract in which the insurer agrees to compensate the insured for the loss incurred from a specific event in return for a premium payment from the insured.

Insurance companies work on the basis of diversification or pooling of risks. They aim to sell as many policies as possible with risks that have low correlations. Insurance premiums are carefully calculated, and the aim is to have premiums collected exceed expected aggregate losses and operating costs so that the company can earn a profit.

Other than staying away from writing too many policies with similar and potentially correlated risks, insurers manage their risk exposure through the following:

- They may transfer some of the risk to another insurer, a practice known as reinsurance.
- They may write provisions into contracts to exclude coverage of special cases (e.g., a war may nullify insurance coverage in affected areas).
- Most insurance policies also contain provisions to guard against moral hazards, such as suicide or destroying one's own property.

- Some insurance companies have issued bonds (known as catastrophe bonds) that permit them to legally avoid paying principal and/or interest if insurance claims exceed a certain amount. These instruments transfer some of the insurance risk to the investors who buy the bonds.
- It is common for policies to contain a deductible, a monetary amount of the loss that will be covered by the insured before any claims are paid. Deductibles serve the following purposes:
  - Because insurers incur fixed costs for each claim, they benefit if deductibles reduce the number of small claims.
  - Deductibles also encourage good risk management by the insured parties.
  - They offer the insured the opportunity to combine risk transfer with self-insurance and thereby achieve a potentially better trade-off of risk and reward.

For unique risks that are not easy to pool, the insurer would have to bear that risk without the benefit of diversification. Specialized coverage for such risks is offered by institutions such as Lloyds of London. They do so by organizing groups of investors (known as syndicates) who are willing to bear the unique risk for a premium. Institutions that offer specialized coverage are able to attain diversification by insuring several different types of unique (presumably uncorrelated) risks, such as an actor not being able to complete a big-budget movie, and a global sports event being canceled.

Other variations of insurance include the following:

- Surety bonds, where an insurer promises to pay the insured a certain amount of money if a third party fails to fulfill its obligation. They are popular in commercial contracts where one party bears the risk of potentially suffering a huge cost if another party does not perform.
- Fidelity bonds, which cover against losses that result from employee dishonesty.
- Indemnity clauses and hold harmless arrangements, where one of the parties to a contract agrees to hold the other harmless and/or indemnify the other in the event of loss.

Note that in the case of surety and fidelity bonds, the word "bond" does not refer to a debt obligation issued by a borrower to lenders, but instead refers to assuring one party that it bears no risk for the actions of a specified other party.

Risk Shifting

Risk shifting refers to actions that change the distribution of risk outcomes. While risk transfer is typically associated with insurance, risk shifting is associated with derivative contracts and risk modification vehicles. Risk shifting mechanisms are used when the organization wants to modify the probability distribution of returns, or adjust the payoff diagram of its risk exposures.

For example, consider an investor who is bullish on the stock market, but wants to protect herself from losing too much money if the market falls. Such an investor would buy a put option on her portfolio. Without getting into the specifics of options and other derivatives-based hedging strategies (that you will be studying in great depth in the derivatives readings), this strategy will result in her making a slightly smaller profit if the market goes up (due to the cost of purchasing the put option), but will set a floor on the amount she could lose if the market falls.

> Types of derivatives, forward commitments versus contingent claims, and derivatives markets are all discussed in detail in the derivatives readings. We will not get into this material here.

How to Choose a Method for Modifying Risk

When deciding on which risk modification method(s) to use, the organization must weigh the costs versus benefits in light of its risk tolerance. For example, many companies operate outside their home countries, which exposes them to foreign exchange risk. Different companies use different approaches to manage this risk.

- Some companies prefer forwards or swaps, others prefer options, while still others use multiple instruments.
- Some companies choose to simply balance their foreign assets and liabilities.
- Some set up operations in foreign countries (as opposed to manufacturing domestically and shipping abroad) so that their costs and revenues are denominated in the same currency. This is another example of how risks interact. Companies must evaluate the trade-off between currency risk and the political and operational risks of operating in a foreign country.

Generally speaking:

- Management should try to avoid risks that lie outside the core competencies of the organization. But, if the potential value added is too great to ignore, then management must at least take adequate precautions.
- Organizations that have large amounts of free cash flow should self-insure as much as possible because self-insurance reduces costs and enables the company to retain flexibility. At the same time, organizations should aim to diversify as much as possible.
- Self-insurance and risk avoidance should be addressed at the board level to ensure consistency and adherence to the organization's risk tolerance.
- Insurance works best when risks can be pooled, but this is not the case for many types of risks, particularly those that can affect a large number of parties at the same time since premiums can be prohibitively high.
- For financial risks that exceed risk appetite, risk shifting is a very common choice. However, risk shifting tools such as derivatives may not be available for all types of risks.

An important point is that the various risk management methods are not equal in terms of the risk reduction and the risk profile that remains. For example:

- Contingent claims, such as insurance or options, offer flexibility in that they leave open the opportunity to profit from favorable movements, while reducing a loss in the case of adverse movements. However, they require a cash payment up front.
- On the other hand, forward commitments lock in an outcome so they provide little flexibility, but they do not require an initial cash payment.

READING 43: FINTECH IN INVESTMENT MANAGEMENT

LESSON 1: THE PRIMARY COMPONENTS OF FINTECH

LOS 43a: Describe "fintech". Vol 4, pp 456–457

"Fintech" refers to the use of technology-based innovations that are changing the way financial services and products are being designed and delivered to clientele. Fintech began with simple data processing and automation of tasks, but has evolved significantly to involve decision-making systems and programs that learn over time. This evolution has been facilitated by technological advances that are capable of extracting market-related information that is ever-growing and changing in terms of types, sources, and quality. Fintech is revolutionizing the way financial advisers, financial planners, and lenders provide services to clientele.

Primary areas of fintech relevant to the financial industry include:

- Analysis of large data sets
  - Fintech can be used to analyze large amounts of data such as security prices, financial statements, and economic indicators to help investment managers sift through information. Fintech is also used to examine social media and sensor network data to provide managers additional insights in the hopes of generating more alpha and reducing risk.
- Analytical tools
  - Artificial intelligence (AI) has advanced to a stage that it can perform tasks that would otherwise require human analysis, such as qualitative and statistical analysis and identifying complex investor/security relationships. For example, AI can sort through company filings, annual reports, and earnings calls to help find trends and create insights into investor sentiment and behavior.
- Automated trading
  - Computer algorithms can be used to generate automated trading systems that are designed to provide more efficient trading, lower transaction costs, manager anonymity, and greater liquidity to portfolios.
- Automated advice (robo-advisers)
  - Robo-advisers can be used for retail wealth management services to provide investors lower-cost advice than a human financial adviser model could.
- Financial recordkeeping
  - Distributed ledger technology (DLT) is a new way to track the ownership of financial assets on a peer-to-peer (P2P) basis. This means that investors can make transactions directly between one another without the use of a third party, thereby reducing costs.

LOS 43b: Describe Big Data, artificial intelligence, and machine learning. Vol 4, pp 457–460

Big Data

The term *Big Data* has been around since the late 1990s and refers to the massive amounts of data produced by financial markets (i.e., securities and derivatives), businesses (i.e., financial statements), governments (i.e., economic data), individuals (i.e., purchases, social media, and Internet searches), and sensor networks (i.e., satellites, radio frequency identification readers, and wireless sensors).

Big Data is characterized by large volumes of data (i.e., millions to quadrillions of data bytes), rapid delivery of data (i.e., real- or near-real-time data), and a wide variety of data (i.e., SQL tables, CSV files, and HTML code, to name a few).

There are three general types of Big Data: structured data that can be stored in database tables, unstructured data that cannot be stored in tables, and semi-structured data than can have both characteristics.

Historically, investment analysts have relied on traditional data sources to perform statistical analysis to measure performance, create predictive models, analyze sector and market trends, and make decisions. These traditional data sources have included security-related data, corporations' financial and regulatory filings, and economic data provided by governments.

However, more recently, quantitative investment analysts have been seeking new ways to determine factors that affect security prices, improve security selection and trading processes, and uncover industry and security trends. To accomplish these goals, analysts are incorporating "alternative" data into their analytical and decision-making processes. This data can include information about retail sales, social media, and satellite imagery, which can potentially provide insights into consumer behavior, business performance, trends, and other factors affecting investments.

There are three main sources of alternative data:

1. Individuals
   - This type of data tends to be unstructured and is growing rapidly as people increasingly make personal data available through various electronic trails such as emails, web searches, website activity, social media activity, e-commerce, and online reviews of products, services, and companies.
2. Business processes
   - This type of data tends to be structured and includes sales/credit card data and "corporate exhaust," which includes supply chain data, banking records, and point-of-sale scanner data.
   - These data can be used as leading and real-time business indicators as opposed to corporate filings, which are lagging indicators of quarterly or annual performance.
3. Sensors
   - This type of data tends to be unstructured and is growing exponentially due to the prevalence of networking technology in personal and commercial devices. These data are collected from smartphones, cameras, radio frequency identification readers, and satellites connected via wireless networks.
   - Sensor data can also include information drawn from the Internet of Things, which refers to networked devices in vehicles, smart office buildings, and homes that can interact and share information.

Aside from the potential legal and ethical issues associated with collecting information that may be captured without the explicit knowledge and consent of the parties involved, Big Data poses many analytical challenges, such as the volume, quality, and appropriateness of data. Analysts must consider whether the data is sufficient, misleading, incomplete, or suffers from selection bias and outliers. The process of analyzing and interpreting alternative data can be very difficult because it is not usually quantitative in nature and is voluminous and complex. As a result, the use of AI and machine learning is growing to support the use of these types of data.

Artificial Intelligence

In a nutshell, AI is designed to perform cognitive or decision-making tasks in a comparable or superior manner to human intelligence. AI has been around since the early 1980s, but has evolved significantly since then due to greater computer and network processing speeds. Early stages of AI development involved the use of "if-then" rules to develop an "expert system" that could simulate the knowledge base and analytical capabilities of humans in problem solving. Beginning in the 1980s, financial firms used AI, in the form of neural networks based on how human brains learn and process information, to detect fraudulent credit card claims and charges. Since the late 1990s, AI has helped financial firms in data mining and financial analysis and continues to evolve through the technology of machine learning, as discussed next.

Machine Learning

Machine learning (ML) basically consists of computer programs that use algorithms to learn how to complete tasks over time so that greater experience translates into better performance. ML programs have been around for many years, but have been limited in their usefulness due to a lack of sufficient data to train the programs. However, with the growth of Big Data for training purposes, ML techniques are improving their predictive accuracy and becoming more useful.

The way ML works is simple in theory. Computer algorithms are fed sets of variables and data/inputs and are expected to produce certain target/output data. ML algorithms learn and refine their processes by identifying relationships between inputted and targeted data based on historical patterns. More specifically, these programs split data into two sets— training and validation/evaluation—to test out relationships. Eventually, the ML algorithms learn enough from this process to predict outcomes based on data inputs. Nonetheless, ML algorithms still require human oversight to select the inputted data and appropriate data analysis techniques. For example, people must ensure that inputs for algorithms are free of any biases or spurious data and that sufficiently large amounts of data are provided to train and validate the ML model.

Analysts using ML programs must also be wary of overfitting data, which is when the program learns inputs and targeted outputs too precisely, or has been overtrained on a particular data set. This can create errors that produce false relationships and unsubstantiated patterns, resulting in an ML program that is unable to make accurate predictions using different data sets. On the other hand, analysts must also prevent underfitting data, which occurs when a program is too simplistic. In these instances, an ML program interprets true parameters as being noise and cannot identify relationships and patterns when training with a dataset.

Another issue associated with ML programs is that they can essentially become "black box" approaches, given that their operations are not explicitly programmed (i.e., AI works on its own), which can create results that are inexplicable or hard to understand.

Types of Machine Learning

Supervised learning involves labeling or identifying inputs and outputs to the algorithm so that it can be trained to identify relationships for labeled data and work with other data sets. An example of this technique is finding variables that forecast whether securities and markets will produce up, down, or flat performance from one business day to the next.

Unsupervised learning does not involve giving programs labeled data, but instead requires algorithms to describe the data and its structure on its own. An example of this technique is creating company peer groups based on their characteristics instead of relying on how an index classifies them.

Deep learning (or deep learning nets) is a technique that uses neural networks to perform multistage, nonlinear processing to identify patterns and relationships in data through a supervised or unsupervised approach. Deep learning has evolved from improvements in the underlying algorithms used in neural networks to better learn from data and understand simple concepts. This leads to discovering more complex relationships that would otherwise be too difficult or time-consuming to find. These algorithms are improving image, pattern, and speech recognition and are progressively consuming less computing power than previous neural networks did.

ML, greater availability of data, improvements in computing power, reductions in data storage costs, and advancements in algorithms have reached a point where they can be relied upon to provide investment research analysts with the ability to use Big Data in meaningful ways. For example, advancements in ML image-recognition algorithms can provide data on the number of people parking at retail locations, shipping activity, and even crop yields. Moreover, ML techniques can provide valuable information to investment managers for analyzing individual firms, creating security valuation models, predicting market trends, and even modeling national and global economic conditions.

LESSON 2: APPLICATIONS OF FINTECH IN THE INVESTMENT INDUSTRY

LOS 43c: Describe fintech applications to investment management.
Vol 4, pp 465–469

Text analytics is the use of programs to retrieve and analyze information from unrelated sources to conduct predictive analysis and find indicators of future performance. For example, text analytics can be used to form opinions about consumer sentiment. Text analytics usually analyzes large, unstructured text-based data sets, which can include corporate financials, corporate earnings, conference call transcripts, social media, emails, and other related postings found on the Internet. This sort of analysis can also include lexical analysis, which involves looking at documents for keywords, phrases, and the frequency of certain words used.

Natural language processing (NLP) is the analysis and interpretation of language using artificial intelligence, including translation, speech recognition, and text mining. NLP alongside ML algorithms can be used in many ways, such as scouring through corporate annual reports, corporate earnings calls, news articles, social media, and text- and audio-based data. Because NLP can analyze massive amounts of data, it can provide analytics on a scale beyond the capacity of human investment research teams.

For example, NLP can be used in the analysis of stock analyst reports to catch subtleties and nuances in commentary to produce sentiment indicators on the future direction of buy/hold/sell recommendations. Similarly, NLP can also be used to analyze communications from major central banks, such as the Federal Reserve or European Central Bank to provide insights on such things as the future direction of interest rates, GDP growth, or inflationary expectations. Given that human research teams generally tend to focus on topline data such as earnings per share (EPS) and current interest rates, inflation, and GDP growth, NLP can be a very effective complement to traditional research through its ability to pick up on the subtleties of language.

Robo-Advisory Services

Robo-advisory services emerged in 2008 with the goal of providing cost-effective and easily accessible investment solutions through the Internet without the interaction of human financial advisers. Similar to human advisers, robo-advisers are regulated in the United States by the Securities and Exchange Commission, with other countries following suit.

As is the case with human advisers, clients must answer a series of questions to receive the most appropriate advice. The goals of these questions are to establish knowledge regarding a client's assets, liabilities, risk preferences, and targeted return goals; a list of these types of questions can be found in Figure 2-1. Once this information has been gathered, algorithms use historic investment data and inputted client data to produce investment recommendations. Thereafter, robo-advisers can automatically optimize asset allocations, execute trades, engage in tax-loss harvesting, and even rebalance portfolios.

Figure 2-1: Typical Questions Required by Robo-Advisers

General Information	Risk Tolerance
Income	Age
Investment Amount	Association with Investing
Job Description	Association with Risk
Other	Choose Portfolio Risk Level
Source of Income	Comfort Investing in Stock
Spendings	Credit Based Investments
Time to Retirement	Dealing with Financial Decisions
Type of Account	Degree of Financial Risk Taken
Working Status	Education
Risk Capacity	Ever Interested in Risky Asset for Thrill
Dependence on Withdrawal of Investment Amount	Experience of Drop/Reaction on Drop/Max Drop before Selling
Income Prediction	Family and Household Status
Investment Amount/Savings Rate Ratio	Financial Knowledge
Investment Amount/Total Capital Ratio	Gender
Investment Horizon	Investment Experience
Liabilities	Investment Goal
Savings Rate	Investor Type/Self-Assessment Risk Tolerance
Total Capital	Preference Return vs. Risk

Source: Michael Tertilt and Peter Scholz, "To Advise, or Not to Advise—How Robo-Advisers Evaluate the Risk Preferences of Private Investors," Working paper (13 June 2017): Table 1: Categories and Subcategories for Questionnaires.

Robo-advisers have low fees and account minimums and, in line with the goal of reducing costs, tend to recommend passive investment management for stocks, bonds, commodities, futures, and real estate through low-cost index and exchange-traded funds. These reduced costs, relative to traditional actively managed funds and human advisers, allow firms to provide advice to otherwise underserved market segments. There are two primary types of robo-advisory services:

1. **Fully automated digital wealth managers** that do not rely on any assistance from human advisers to keep costs down.
2. **Adviser-assisted digital wealth managers** that provide automated services, but include access to a virtual financial adviser that can provide basic financial advice and periodic reviews by phone.

Criticisms of robo-advisers include:

1. They would not be helpful to clients during times of financial crisis, when people truly need human expertise.
2. They do not provide the transparency of advice and rationale for recommendations that a human adviser can provide.
3. Clients may have trust issues and fear that robo-advisers may make inappropriate recommendations.
4. They may not be able to keep pace with client portfolios as they grow in size and complexity, especially with respect to alternative investments such as hedge funds, private equity, and real estate.

Risk Analysis

Fintech can help analyze and manage risks in a variety of ways, including, but not limited to, the following examples:

Stress-testing financial institutions. Fintech can analyze massive amounts of quantitative and qualitative data, including balance sheet positions, credit exposures, liquidity, risk parameters, and capital planning procedures, to name a few.

Identifying adverse near-term market trends. Through Big Data, fintech can provide real-time insights into market conditions and potentially identify adverse trends in advance so managers can employ appropriate risk management and hedging techniques.

Detecting declining corporate earnings. Fintech can aggregate alternative data for a company and, through ML techniques, determine whether declining earnings are on the horizon. Advance notice of declining earnings can help investment managers avoid falling stock prices.

Analyzing real-time trading patterns. By analyzing real-time market data, fintech can identify near-term trading patterns, which can be invaluable to investment managers seeking to avoid losses.

Portfolio scenario analysis and back-testing. Investment managers will use scenario analysis and stress-testing to determine how their portfolios will behave during hypothetical or historic events, especially with respect to liquidity considerations. Computations for these types of analyses can be very complex. AI and ML techniques can facilitate this process and improve the usefulness of results.

Assessing alternative data quality. ML techniques can be applied to filter alternative data to avoid potential errors, questionable data, and outliers that need to be identified and removed from the data set before being integrated with traditional data for use in risk management programs.

Algorithmic Trading

Algorithmic trading involves computerized buying and selling based on prespecified rules and guidelines for lowering costs, improving execution speed, and providing anonymity for investment managers. Large institutional orders often use these techniques to break trades into smaller pieces and execute them over different exchanges to improve liquidity and execution price. A major benefit of trading algorithms is that they update and revise execution strategies based on changing market conditions throughout the day, which allows them to determine the most efficient way to price a trade (e.g., limit or market orders) and the best exchange on which to execute it.

Given smaller average trade sizes and the fragmentation of global financial markets into electronic exchanges, alternative trading systems, and dark pools (i.e., private trading forums), algorithmic trading is considered an essential tool for investment managers.

High-frequency trading (HFT) is a form of algorithmic trading that uses real-time, granular market data to execute trades in fractions of a second through ultra-high-speed networks when certain conditions are met. The main goal of HFT is to profit from intraday security mispricings when they occur.

LOS 43d: Describe financial applications of distributed ledger technology. Vol 4, pp 469–473

Distributed ledger technology (DLT) is a new form of financial recordkeeping that allows entities to share database information through networks. A DLT network consists of a digital ledger and a consensus mechanism that involves networked computers (or nodes) validating transactions and agreeing on updates to create unchangeable records that are easily accessible to participants on a near-real-time basis. To provide security for networks and database integrity, DLTs use cryptography (or algorithms) to encrypt data so that it is unusable to any unauthorized parties.

The goals of DLT networks are to create a quick way to exchange and track financial assets on a peer-to-peer basis and provide greater accuracy, transparency, and security of recordkeeping relative to traditional market exchange methods. DLTs also offer the benefit of eliminating third parties (i.e., exchanges) in transactions to lower trading costs. For a visual representation of how of DLT networks are structured, see Figure 2-2.

Figure 2-2: DLT Network Structure

Source: https://blockgeeks.com/guides/what-is-hyperledger/.

Blockchains

Blockchains are digital ledgers where information is sequentially recorded in "blocks" that are "chained" together using cryptography. This means transactions are grouped together into blocks that are linked to previous blocks through a secure link (or "hash"). Any new transactions must be validated through the consensus mechanism before being added to the chain of historic transactions, which involves network computers (or "miners") solving cryptographic problems. The process of using blockchains requires a significant amount of computing power and, therefore, relies on the use of networked computers (nodes). The use of blockchains and the associated computing power requirements makes it extremely difficult and expensive for a single party to alter the historic transaction records, thereby providing another layer of security.

DLT Network Types

In **permissioned** networks, members might have restrictions on their activities and level of access to the ledger, such as adding transactions, viewing transactions, and seeing limited details of transactions.

In a **permissionless** (or open) DLT network, all users can see every blockchain transaction and have the ability to perform all network functions. The primary benefit of this type of network is that all transactions are validated through the consensus mechanism and no central authority is required. Thus, the integrity of records is ensured because no single computer failure can affect historic records, as every computer node has a copy of the database.

Cryptocurrencies

Beyond making investment transactions, permissionless DLT networks are also used for cryptocurrencies such as Bitcoin. Cryptocurrencies lack any physical form, can be issued by individuals, companies, and other organizations, and generally use permissionless DLT networks to verify and record all transactions. These currencies can be used as an alternative store of value relative to traditional fiat currencies and are traded globally based on prevailing market rates. Many cryptocurrencies have self-imposed limits on the amount of currency issued to maintain their value. However, because cryptocurrencies are not backed or regulated by central banks and have no clear underlying fundamental value, they can experience wild fluctuations in value.

Cryptocurrencies can also be used as a lower-cost, faster, and unregulated way for companies to raise capital relative to traditional initial public offerings (IPOs). Instead of issuing equity shares (i.e., an IPO), companies conduct an initial coin offering (ICO), where crypto tokens are sold in exchange for fiat currency or even other cryptocurrencies. These crypto tokens can be used in the future to purchase products and services provided by the issuing company.

Tokenization

Transactions for ownership rights to physical assets such as real estate, luxury goods, and commodities can require a great deal of effort to verify ownership and identification, conduct transfers, and keep historic records. Through the use of a blockchain DLT network, tokenization can use a single electronic record to streamline this process and reduce costs relative to traditional methods that are labor intensive and involve multiple decentralized parties that use paper-based records.

Post-Trade Clearing and Settlement

The traditional process of confirming, clearing, and settling trades requires multiple interactions among counterparties and financial intermediaries. DLT can eliminate the need for third parties by providing near-real-time verification, reconciliation, and settlement of trades. The use of DLT networks benefits investors by shortening settlement times, which provides greater liquidity and decreases exposure to counterparty risks and collateral requirements.

Compliance

Meeting regulatory reporting and transparency requirements is generally a manual, labor-intensive process that requires firms to maintain and process large amounts of data. Automated DLT networks can create operational efficiencies in compliance by providing near-real-time transaction data, better post-trade reconciliation, and greater transparency, accessibility, and auditability of data for regulators. The use of DLT networks improves the flow of information and transparency among firms, exchanges, and custodians. Permissioned networks provide strong security and privacy measures through the use of cryptography and can reduce the costs associated with verifying the identity of clients and business partners for know-your-customer rules and anti-money-laundering regulations.

READING 44: MARKET ORGANIZATION AND STRUCTURE

LESSON 1: THE FUNCTIONS OF THE FINANCIAL SYSTEM, ASSETS, CONTRACTS, FINANCIAL INTERMEDIARIES AND POSITIONS

LOS 44a: Explain the main functions of the financial system. Vol 5, pp 6–14

A financial system consists of markets and financial intermediaries that facilitate the transfer of financial assets, real assets, and financial risks in various forms from one entity to another. There are three main functions of a financial system.

1. To help people achieve their purposes in using the financial system.
2. To facilitate the discovery of the rate of return where aggregate savings equal aggregate borrowings.
3. Allocating capital to its most efficient uses.

1. Helping people achieve their purposes in using the financial system

- The financial system helps in the saving process by creating investment vehicles (e.g., bank deposits, notes, stocks, etc.) that investors can buy or sell in the market without incurring heavy transaction costs.
- The financial system facilitates borrowing by aggregating funds from savers. A well-functioning financial system reduces transaction costs (e.g., the costs of arranging, monitoring, and recovering loans) and makes the borrowing process more efficient.
- Institutions in the financial system help companies in raising equity capital. Further, they value the securities that companies sell and ensure that financial information is accurate and properly disclosed. Transparency and liquidity in markets encourage investor participation.
- The financial system helps to manage various risks (e.g., default risk, exchange rate risk, interest rate risk, and other risks) by offering contracts to hedge those risks. Further, investment banks and exchanges ensure that these instruments trade in liquid markets.
- The financial system facilitates the exchange of assets by creating liquidity in spot markets (markets where assets are traded for immediate delivery). Liquidity reduces transaction costs for traders.
- The financial system facilitates information-based trading by creating liquid markets with low transaction costs. Further, accounting standards and regulatory requirements reduce the cost of information for investors.

2. Determining rates of return

Savers try to move money from the present to the future, while borrowers try to move money from the future to the present. The higher the expected return on saving, the more savers will forgo current consumption and move money to the future. On the other hand, the higher the cost of borrowing, the lower the amount of money borrowers would want to move from the future to the present. The rate at which the aggregate demand for funds (borrowing) equals the aggregate supply of funds (saving) is called the equilibrium interest rate, and determining this rate is one of the most important functions of the financial system.

> The required rates of return for securities vary by their risk characteristics, terms, and liquidity.

3. Allocating capital efficiently

Allocative efficiency is reached when the scarce capital in an economy is allocated to the most productive uses. A financial system seeks to ensure that only the best projects obtain the funds available from savers. Investors are wary of making losses, so they try to carefully study the prospects of various investments available to them in order to make well-informed decisions regarding where to invest.

LOS 44b: Describe classifications of assets and markets. Vol 5, pp 14–16

> Different classifications of assets are described in the next LOS.

Assets may be classified as financial or physical assets:

- Financial assets include securities, currencies, and contracts.
- Physical assets include commodities and real assets.

Markets may be classified on the basis of:

- The timing of delivery.
    - Markets for immediate delivery are referred to as spot markets.
    - Markets where delivery occurs at some point in the future include forward, futures, and options markets.
- Who the seller is.
    - Markets in which securities are sold by issuers (where funds flow from the purchaser to the issuer) are known as primary markets.
    - Markets in which securities are sold by investors (where funds flow between traders) are called secondary markets.
- The maturity of instruments that are traded.
    - Markets that trade debt instruments maturing in one year or less are referred to as money markets.
    - Markets that trade instruments of longer maturities are referred to as capital markets.
- The types of securities:
    - Publicly traded debt, equities, and shares in pooled investment vehicles that hold these securities are referred to as traditional investment markets.
    - Hedge funds, private equity, commodities, real estate securities and properties, and securitized debt are part of alternative investment markets.

LOS 44c: Describe the major types of securities, currencies, contracts, commodities, and real assets that trade in organized markets, including their distinguishing characteristics and major subtypes. Vol 5, pp 16–28

Securities

Securities include bonds, notes, commercial paper, mortgages, common stock, preferred stock, warrants, mutual fund shares, unit trusts, and depository receipts. They may be classified as:

- **Public securities** that trade in public markets (e.g., exchanges). Issuers of public securities are usually required to comply with strict rules and regulatory standards.

- **Private securities** that can typically only be purchased by qualified investors. Private securities are relatively illiquid.

Fixed Income Securities

Fixed income instruments are promises to repay borrowed money. Payments (which include interest and principal amounts) may be pre-specified or may vary according to a fixed formula based on a reference rate. Fixed income instruments may be classified as:

- *Notes*: Fixed income securities with maturities of 10 years or less.
- *Bonds*: Fixed income securities with maturities greater than 10 years.
- *Bills*: These are issued by governments and have maturities of one year or less.
- *Certificates of deposit:* These are issued by banks and usually mature within a year.
- *Commercial paper*: These are issued by corporations and usually mature within a year.
- *Repurchase agreements*: These are short-term lending instruments.
- *Money market instruments*: These are traded in the money market and have maturities of one year or less.

Equities

Equity owners have ownership rights in a company. Equity securities include:

- *Common shares:* Holders of common shares can participate in the company's decision-making process. They are entitled to receive dividends declared by the company, and if the company goes bankrupt they have a claim on the company's assets after all other claims have been satisfied.
- *Preferred shares:* Preferred shareholders have a higher priority in claims on dividends and on the company's assets in case of liquidation. They are entitled to receive fixed dividends on a regular basis.
- *Warrants:* Holders of warrants have the right to purchase an entity's common stock at a prespecified price at or before the warrants' expiration date.

Pooled Investments

Pooled investment vehicles (e.g., mutual funds, depositories, and hedge funds) issue securities that represent shared ownership in the assets held by them. People invest in these vehicles to benefit from their investment management expertise and to diversify their portfolios.

- *Asset-backed securities:* Companies often use pools of loans or receivables (e.g., auto loans and leases, consumer loans, credit cards, etc.) as underlying assets to issue securities known as asset-backed securities. These securities then transfer any interest and principal payments from the underlying assets to their holders on a monthly basis.

Currencies

These are monies issued by national monetary authorities and primarily trade in the foreign currency market. Retail currency trades occur through ATM machines, credit cards, and debit cards when transactions are executed in currencies different from the currency held in customers' accounts.

Contracts

Contracts are agreements between two or more parties to do something in the future. A contract's value depends on the value of its underlying, which may be a commodity, a security, an index, an interest rate, or even another contract.

Contracts may be settled in cash or may require physical delivery, and may be classified on the basis of:

- The nature of the underlying asset:
  - If the underlying asset is a physical asset, the contract is referred to as a physical contract.
  - If the underlying asset is a financial asset, the contract is referred to as a financial contract.
- The timing of delivery:
  - If the contract requires immediate delivery (i.e., in three days or less), it is referred to as a spot contract and trades in the spot market.
  - If the contract requires delivery to be made in the future (i.e., after three days or more), it may be a forward, futures, swap, or an options contract.

Forward Contracts

A forward is a contract between two parties, where one (the long position) has the obligation to buy, and the other (the short position) has an obligation to sell an underlying asset at a fixed price (established at the inception of the contract) at a future date. Market participants usually enter a forward contract to hedge a preexisting risk.

Futures Contracts

Futures contracts are similar to forward contracts in that they may also be deliverable or cash-settled, but there are also significant differences between the two. Unlike forward contracts:

- Futures contracts are standardized and trade on organized exchanges.
- A clearinghouse is the counterparty to all futures contracts.

Swap Contracts

A swap is an agreement between two parties to exchange a series of cash flows at periodic settlement dates over a certain period of time. A swap may also be looked upon as a series of forward contracts.

Option Contracts

Option contracts give their holders the right to buy or sell a security at a predetermined price (exercise price) some time in the future.

- **Call options** give their holders the right to purchase the underlying asset at some future date at the option's exercise price. Holders are likely to exercise their call options when the price of the underlying asset is greater than the exercise price.
- **Put options** give their holders the right to sell the underlying asset at some future date at the option's exercise price. Holders are likely to exercise their put options when the price of the underlying asset is lower than the exercise price.

Options that can only be exercised at their expiration dates are known as European options, while options that can be exercised anytime until or at their expiration dates are known as American options.

Other Contracts

People often enter into insurance contracts to protect themselves from unexpected losses. Insurance contracts include credit default swaps (CDSs) that promise to pay their holders the amount of principal in case a company defaults on its bonds.

Commodities

Commodities include precious metals, energy products, industrial metals, agricultural products, and carbon credits.

Commodities may trade in the spot market (for immediate delivery) or in the forward or futures market (for delivery in the future). The primary traders in commodities spot markets are producers and processors of industrial metals and agricultural products, as they have the ability to store the physical products and take or make delivery. Further, as part of their normal business operations, they obtain information that gives them an advantage as information-motivated traders.

Investment managers and other information-motivated traders participate in commodity futures markets to hedge risks and/or to speculate on future prices. These traders usually deal in futures markets, as they do not have the capacity to handle the physical products. Further, the fact that futures markets are relatively more liquid enables them to close or exit their positions easily.

Real Assets

Real assets include tangible properties such as real estate, airplanes, machinery, and lumber stands. These assets are normally held by operating companies (e.g., real estate developers and airplane leasing companies). However, institutional investors are increasingly adding them to their portfolios either directly (through direct ownership of the asset), or indirectly (through investments in securities of companies that invest in these assets). Real assets are attractive because:

- They may have low correlations with other assets in the investor's portfolio, thus providing diversification benefits.
- They offer income and tax benefits to investors.

However, real asset valuation is very difficult due to the heterogeneous nature of each investment. Further, real assets tend to be relatively illiquid and entail high management costs.

Indirect investments in real estate can be made by purchasing shares in real estate investment trusts (REITs) and master limited partnerships (MLPs). These entities pool funds from investors and invest in different types of real estate. Because these securities are relatively more homogeneous and divisible than the underlying real assets, they trade in relatively liquid markets.

LOS 44d: Describe types of financial intermediaries and services that they provide. Vol 5, pp 28–38

Financial intermediaries allow buyers and sellers of assets and contracts to transfer risk and capital between them, often without any knowledge of each other. Financial intermediaries include the following:

Brokers, Exchanges, and Alternative Trading Systems

Brokers are agents who fulfill orders for their clients. They reduce costs of trading for their clients by finding counterparties for their trades.

- *Block brokers* provide brokerage services to large traders. It is difficult to fulfill large orders, as there are not many potential counterparties for large trades. In order to induce counterparties to trade, large buy orders generally execute at a premium, while large sell orders generally trade at a discount to market prices. Large trades, if known to the public before being executed, may have a significant impact on market price and therefore must be managed carefully.
- *Investment banks* provide a variety of services to companies, including:
  - Arranging initial and seasoned security offerings.
  - Issuing securities to finance their business.
  - Identifying and acquiring other companies.

Exchanges provide a platform where traders can carry out their trades. Over time, the distinction between exchanges and brokers has become rather vague, as electronic order matching systems are increasingly being used by both to arrange trades for clients.

Alternative Trading Systems (ATSs) (also known as electronic communications networks [ECNs] and multilateral trading facilities [MTFs]) are trading venues just like exchanges. However, they differ from exchanges in that they do not exercise regulatory authority over their members except with respect to the conduct of their trading in their trading networks. Many ATSs are known as "dark pools" because they do not display orders sent to them.

Dealers

Unlike brokers, dealers fulfill orders for their clients by actually taking positions as counterparties for their trades. After executing a trade, they hope to close their positions by taking the opposite side of the original transaction with another client. Essentially, they indirectly connect two traders who arrive in the market at different points in time. By acting as counterparties to trades, dealers create liquidity in the market. They profit when their average purchase price is less than their average selling price.

Dealers may also often act as brokers and vice-versa, so practitioners often use the term **broker-dealer** to refer to brokers and dealers. Sometimes, however, there may be a conflict of interest with respect to how broker-dealers fill orders. As brokers, they must strive to find the best possible price for their clients, but as dealers they aim to maximize their own profits. Therefore, customers often specify how they want their orders to be filled (whether they want it filled by the broker or traded with another trader) when dealing with a broker-dealer.

Dealers with whom the central bank trades when conducting monetary policy are referred to as **primary dealers**. The central bank buys from and sells securities to these dealers who then trade with other market participants.

Securitizers

Securitization is the process of buying assets, placing them in a pool, and issuing securities that represent ownership of the assets in the pool. Entities that undertake this process are known as securitizers. They create and sell securitized instruments and act as financial intermediaries by connecting borrowers and lenders.

Depository Institutions and Other Financial Corporations

Depository institutions include commercial banks, savings and loan banks, credit unions, and other institutions that gather funds from depositors and lend them to borrowers. These institutions pay interest to depositors and provide transaction services (check writing and check cashing, etc.) to them. Borrowers go to these institutions in the hope of borrowing funds from them.

Brokers also act as financial intermediaries when they lend funds deposited by their clients to other clients who wish to buy securities on margin. Such brokers are known as **prime brokers**.

Insurance Companies

Insurance companies create and sell contracts that protect buyers of these contracts from risks that they seek protection from. Basically, insurance companies provide a payment to the owner of the insurance policy if the risk that she is concerned with materializes and results in a loss. Examples of insurance contracts include auto, fire, theft, and life insurance contracts.

Insurance companies are financial intermediaries, as they connect the buyers of insurance contracts with investors, creditors, and reinsurers who are willing to bear the insured risks. Insurance buyers benefit as they are able to transfer risks to entities that are willing to assume them, while owners, creditors, and reinsurers of the insurance company (who assume these risks) benefit from being able to sell their tolerance to risk without having to manage the contracts. Managing insurance contracts requires the insurance company to manage fraud, moral hazard, and adverse selection.

- Fraud occurs when people deliberately report fake losses.
- Moral hazard occurs when people are less careful about avoiding losses, as they are covered by insurance.
- Adverse selection occurs as only those who are most at risk usually buy insurance.

Arbitrageurs

The law of one price states that two securities that generate identical cash flows in the future, regardless of future events, should have the same price today. Arbitrageurs are constantly on the lookout for violations of this law. They trade on mispricings until they are eliminated and asset prices converge to their "correct levels."

Arbitrageurs, who buy and sell the same security in two different markets (at different prices), act as financial intermediaries, as they effectively connect sellers in one market with buyers in another market. They also bring liquidity to markets.

Settlement and Custodial Services

Clearinghouses arrange for the final settlement of trades. They also serve as guarantors of performance in futures markets and as escrow agents in other markets. Further, they ensure that their members have adequate capital to settle trades, and also place limits on the aggregate net order quantities (buy minus sell) of their members. All of these functions performed by the clearinghouse help limit counterparty risk.

Banks and broker-dealers may offer custodial services for holding securities on behalf of their clients. This helps prevent the loss of securities through fraud or oversight.

LOS 44e: Compare positions an investor can take in an asset. Vol 5, pp 38–41

A position in an asset refers to the quantity of the asset that an entity owns or owes.

- A person with a long position owns an asset or a contract. She benefits when there is an increase in the price of the asset or contract.
- A person with a short position has sold an asset that she does not own, or has written or sold a contract. She benefits when there is a decrease in the price of the asset or contract.

Short positions are usually taken by information-motivated traders who believe that an asset or a contract will decrease in value. However, they may also be taken by hedgers who seek to eliminate/reduce a preexisting risk. For example, a person holding gold inventories faces the risk of a fall in the price of gold. In order to protect herself from the risk of a fall in gold prices, she will take a short position on gold futures contracts. If the price of gold falls, she would incur a loss on her inventory of gold, which would be offset by a profit on her short futures position.

Positions on Forwards and Futures

The long position in a forward or a futures contract is the side that is obligated to take physical delivery of the asset or its cash equivalent at contract expiration. She will benefit from an increase in the price of the underlying asset.

The short position in a forward or a futures contract is the side that is obligated to make physical delivery of the asset or its cash equivalent at contract expiration. She will benefit from a decrease in the price of the underlying asset.

Positions on Options

The long position on an options contract is the party that holds the right to exercise the option. The short side refers to the writer of the option, who must satisfy any obligations arising from the contract.

- The long position on a call option will benefit when the underlying rises in value.
- The short position on a call option will benefit when the underlying falls in value.
- The long position on a put option will benefit when the underlying falls in value.
- The short position on a put option will benefit when the underlying rises in value.

Swap Contracts

The two parties in a swap contract simply agree to exchange contractually determined cash flows. There is no real buyer or seller, which makes it difficult to determine the long and short side of the contract. Usually, the party that benefits from an increase in the quoted price is referred to as the long.

Currency Contracts

A party that purchases one currency simultaneously sells another currency (the other currency in the price quote or exchange rate). Therefore, whenever we mention a long or a short position in a currency contract, we must mention the other currency as well. For example, we may state that a party is long on the dollar against the yen.

Short Positions

Short positions in contracts are created by selling contracts that the short seller does not own. The short seller is basically the issuer of the contract. For example, a company creates a short position on bonds (a contract between the company and bondholders or lenders) when it issues bonds in exchange for cash.

Short positions in securities are created by selling securities that the short seller does not own. In order to sell the securities, the short seller borrows the securities from long holders to deliver them to buyers. To unwind the position, the short seller then repurchases the security (hopefully at a lower price) from the market and returns it to the long holder.

The maximum profit for the holder of a long position on an asset is unlimited, while her losses are limited to the price she purchased the asset for. In contrast, the maximum profit for a short seller of an asset is limited to her selling price, while her losses are unlimited.

LOS 44f: Calculate and interpret the leverage ratio, the rate of return on a margin transaction, and the security price at which the investor would receive a margin call. Vol 5, pp 41–44

Levered Positions

Many markets allow investors to borrow funds from brokers to purchase securities. The investor borrows a portion of the price of the stock, contributes the rest of the funds herself, and puts up the stock as collateral. The borrowed money is known as the margin loan and the interest rate paid on it is the call money rate.

Traders who purchase securities on margin face minimum margin requirements. The initial margin requirement refers to the proportion of the total cost of the asset that an investor must invest with her own equity. This requirement may be determined by the government, the exchange, or the clearinghouse.

When traders borrow money to purchase securities, they are said to be leveraging their positions. The leverage ratio is the ratio of the value of the position to the value of the equity investment in it. The maximum leverage ratio for a position financed by a margin loan equals one divided by the minimum margin requirement.

Leverage enhances a trader's returns, but also magnifies losses, as illustrated in Example 1-1.

Example 1-1: Computing Total Return to a Leveraged Stock Purchase

Susan purchases 100 shares of Alpha Corp on margin for $30 per share. She sells her shares after one year at $24 per share. The following information is also available:

Dividend received on the stock = $0.30 per share
Commission paid = $0.10 per share
Leverage ratio = 2.0
Call money rate = 6%

1. What is the total return on this investment?
2. Why is the loss greater than the 20% decrease in the market price?

Solutions:

1. Total purchase price = 100 × 30 = $3,000

   Using her leverage ratio, we can calculate her equity investment as follows:

   Equity investment = 1 / 2.0 = 50%

   Therefore, she borrowed $1,500 ($3,000 × 50%).

   Commission paid on purchase transaction = 100 × 0.1 = $10

   Therefore, her total initial investment = $1,500 + 10 = $1,510

   Equity remaining after the sale is computed as follows:

Initial investment	$1,510
Purchase commission	−10
Trading gains/losses	−600
[(24 × 100) − 3,000]	
Margin interest paid	−90
(1,500 × 0.06)	
Dividends received	30
(0.3 × 100)	
Sales commission paid	−10
Remaining equity	$830

   or

Proceeds on sale	2,400
(24 × 100)	
Payoff loan	−1,500
Margin interest paid	−90
Dividends received	30
Sales commission paid	−10
Remaining equity	$830

   Therefore, total return = (830 − 1,510) / 1,510] = −45.03%

> 2. The realized loss is greater than the 20% decrease in the market price primarily because of leverage and also because of interest paid on borrowed funds. Based on leverage alone (i.e., ignoring the other cash flows), the expected return on equity would be −40% (= 2.0 × −20%).

In addition to the initial margin requirement, traders who invest on margin must also adhere to maintenance margin requirements. After the purchase of a stock, an increase or decrease in the price translates into a change in the value of the collateral backing the margin loan. If the proportion of the value of the security financed by the investor's own equity (after adjusting for the price change) falls below the maintenance margin, the investor will receive a margin call, and she would have to deposit enough funds into her account to at least meet the maintenance margin level. If she fails to do so, her broker can sell the stock to pay off the margin loan. See Example 1-2.

The price at which an investor who goes long on a stock receives a margin call is calculated as:

$$P_0 \times \frac{(1 - \text{Initial margin})}{(1 - \text{Maintenance margin})}$$

Example 1-2: Margin Calls

Determine the share price at which an investor will receive a margin call given that the share price at the time of purchase was $60, the initial margin requirement is 50%, maintenance margin is 25%, and the investor has purchased 200 shares.

Solution:

$$\text{Trigger price} = \frac{\$60(1 - 0.5)}{1 - 0.25} = \$40$$

The investor will receive a margin call when the stock price falls to $40.

Traders who sell securities short are also subject to margin requirements, as they have borrowed securities to take their positions.

LESSON 2: ORDERS, PRIMARY AND SECONDARY SECURITY MARKETS, AND MARKET STRUCTURES

LOS 44g: Compare execution, validity, and clearing instructions. Vol 5, pp 44–50

LOS 44h: Compare market orders with limit orders. Vol 5, pp 44–46

The prices at which dealers and other proprietary traders are willing to buy securities are called bid prices and those at which they are willing to sell are called ask (or offer) prices. The quantities that market participants are willing to trade at the bid and ask prices are called bid sizes and ask sizes respectively.

The highest bid in the market is the highest price that a dealer is willing to pay for the security and is known as the best bid. On the other hand, the lowest ask price is the best offer. The difference between the best bid and the best offer is the market bid-ask spread. Liquid markets with low transaction costs generally have small bid-ask spreads.

Execution Instructions

Execution instructions indicate how an order should be filled. They include:

- Market orders, which instruct brokers or the exchange to fill an order immediately at the best available price. Market orders generally execute immediately as long as there are traders willing to take the other side of the trade. However, they may be expensive to execute, especially when the order size is large relative to the normal trading activity in the market.
- Limit orders, which instruct the broker or the exchange to fill an order at a specified price or better. These specified prices (maximum price for a limit buy order and minimum price for a limit sell order) are referred to as limit prices. Limit orders prevent trades from executing at unacceptable prices. However, this also means that they may not execute at all if the limit price on a buy order is too low or the limit price on a sell order is too high.
  - A limit buy order is aggressively priced when the limit price is high relative to the market "bid" and "ask" prices.
  - A limit buy order placed above the best offer is likely to be at least partially executed immediately and is called a marketable limit order.
  - A limit buy order placed above the best bid but below the best offer is said to have created a new market by establishing the new best bid.
  - A limit buy order placed at the best bid is said to make market. This order will have to wait for all buy orders (that were placed earlier) at that price to execute first.
  - A limit buy order placed below the best bid is referred to as behind the market and will not execute unless market prices drop. These orders are known as standing limit orders.

Although aggressively priced orders execute sooner, the prices at which they trade are inferior.

Some execution instructions include limitations on order size. For example, all-or-nothing orders (AON) can only trade if their entire sizes can be traded. Traders can also specify minimum fill sizes.

Exposure Instructions

Exposure instructions specify whether, how, and to whom orders may be exposed.

Hidden orders are exposed only to the brokers or exchanges that receive them. Other traders can discover hidden size only after submitting orders that will trade with that size. However, hidden orders may not execute at all, as other traders do not know about them. Therefore, traders may sometimes indicate a specific display size (which is lower than the actual order size) with their orders to signal to other traders that someone is willing to trade at the displayed price. As most of the order size is hidden, these orders are also referred to as iceberg orders.

Validity Instructions

Validity instructions indicate when an order may be filled. They include:

- Day orders, which are only valid for the day on which they are submitted. These orders expire if not filled at the close of business.
- Good-till-canceled orders, which are valid until canceled by the broker.
- Immediate or cancel orders, which may only be filled, completely or in part, immediately and are otherwise canceled. These are also known as fill or kill orders.
- Good-on-close orders, which only execute at the close of trading and are also called market-on-close orders.
- Stop orders (often referred to as stop-loss orders), which are placed by investors to protect themselves from adverse price movements. A stop-loss buy order is placed by short sellers above the market price. If the price of the asset moves against the short seller's expectations, the stop-buy order will ensure that her losses do not exceed a particular limit. For example, if Veronica goes short on a stock that is currently priced at $50, she might place a stop-buy order at $55. If the stock were to move up to $55, her stop-loss buy order would execute and limit her loss to $5. On the other hand, a trader who is bullish on the market would place a stop-sell order below the current market price. If prices were to move down contrary to her expectations, the stop-sell order would limit her losses.

Clearing Instructions

Clearing instructions indicate how the final settlement of trades should be arranged. They include details of the entities responsible for clearing and settling the trade. Further, security sale orders must also indicate whether the sale is a long sale or a short sale.

Primary Markets

Primary markets are markets where issuers first sell their securities to investors. When a security is issued to the public for the first time, it is referred to as an initial public offering (IPO). On the other hand, when additional units of a previously issued security are sold, it is referred to as a seasoned offering (or a secondary offering) and the issue is called a seasoned issue.

Public Offerings

Companies generally issue securities to the public through an investment bank. The investment bank performs the following functions:

- Through a process called book building, it lines up subscribers who wish to purchase the security.
- It provides investment information about the issuer to its clients and to the public.

The issuer's arrangement with the investment bank may take one of the following forms:

- In an underwriting offer, the investment bank guarantees the sale of the issue at an offering price negotiated with the issuer. If the issuer is not fully subscribed, the investment bank commits to purchasing the leftover securities at the offer price.
- In a best-efforts offering, the investment bank merely acts as a broker. It tries its best to sell the securities at the negotiated price, but does not promise to purchase unsold securities.

Underwritten offerings lead to a conflict of interest for investment banks regarding pricing. As an agent the investment bank must strive to obtain the best (highest) possible price for issuers. However, since the investment bank is obligated to purchase leftover securities in case the issue is not fully subscribed, it would prefer the issue to be priced lower.

First-time issuers usually accept relatively low offer prices because they do not want to leave their issue undersubscribed as it sends out a negative signal about the company. For seasoned issues, it is easier to determine the price as the securities are already being traded in the secondary market.

Private Placements

In a private placement, securities are not offered to the public. Companies sell securities directly to a group of qualified investors, usually through an investment bank. Qualified investors are generally those who understand associated risks and have sufficient wealth to withstand significant losses. Private placements are typically cheaper than public offerings, as they do not require as much public disclosure. However, since privately placed securities do not trade on organized secondary markets, investors require a higher rate of return from them.

Other Primary Market Transactions
- Companies that issue securities via a shelf registration make all the public disclosures that are required in a regular offering, but they do not need to issue all the shares at once. They can sell them directly in the secondary market over time, which offers them flexibility, as they can raise capital when they need it.
- Companies that issue securities through dividend reinvestment plans (DRPs) allow shareholders to reinvest their dividends by purchasing shares of the company. These shares may be newly issued or purchased from the open market.
- Companies sometimes offer rights to existing shareholders to purchase additional shares of the company in proportion to their current holdings at a fixed price.

Secondary Markets

The secondary market is that part of the financial market where previously issued securities and financial instruments are traded. Secondary markets play a very important role in that they provide liquidity to investors who purchased their securities in the primary market. Investors will hesitate to participate in the primary market if they cannot subsequently sell their holdings in the secondary market.

Secondary markets are also important for seasoned security issuers, as the prices of their new offerings are derived from the prices of currently outstanding securities that trade on the secondary market.

LOS 44j: Describe how securities, contracts, and currencies are traded in quote-driven, order-driven, and brokered markets. Vol 5, pp 53–58

Trading Sessions

In a call market, all bid and ask prices for an asset are gathered to determine one price where the quantity offered for sale is close to the quantity demanded. All transactions take place at this single price. Call markets are popular in smaller markets; however, they are also used on larger exchanges to determine the opening price of a trading session.

In a continuous market, transactions can take place whenever the market is open. Prices are set either through an auction process or by dealer bid-ask quotes. Most global stock exchanges are continuous markets.

The advantage of a call market is that it makes it easier for buyers and sellers to find each other by gathering all traders at the same place at the same time. In a continuous market, if a buyer and seller (or their orders) are not present at the same time, they cannot trade. The advantage of a continuous market is that a willing buyer and seller can trade anytime the market is open. In a call market they would only be able to trade when the market is called.

Execution Mechanisms

A pure auction market (order-driven market) is one where participants submit their bid and ask prices to a central location. Matching bids and offers are paired together and orders are executed. Order-driven matching mechanisms are characterized by two sets of rules:

- Order matching rules match buy orders to sell orders. They rank buy and sell orders based on:
  - Price precedence: Highest priced buy orders and lowest priced sell orders are ranked first.
  - Display precedence: Displayed quantities have precedence over undisplayed quantities at the same price.
  - Time precedence: Orders that arrive first have precedence over orders that arrive later with the same price and with the same display status.
- Trade pricing rules determine the prices at which matched trades take place. Prices may be determined based on the any of the following:
  - Under a uniform pricing rule, the same price is used for all trades. This rule is used by call markets where the market chooses the price that maximizes total quantity traded.
  - Under a discriminatory pricing rule, the limit price of the order or quote that arrive first (the standing order) determines the trade price. Continuous trading markets use this rule.
  - A derivative pricing rule uses the midpoint of the best bid and ask quotes from another market. Crossing networks (which may themselves be organized as call or continuous trading markets) use this pricing rule.

> Crossing networks are trading systems that match buyers and sellers who are willing to trade at prices obtained from other markets.

A dealer market (quote-driven market or price-driven market) consists of individual dealers who are assigned specific securities. These dealers create liquidity by purchasing and selling against their own inventory of securities. Competition between dealers ensures that competitive prices are available.

In a brokered market, brokers arrange trades among their clients. Brokers organize markets for unique items (e.g., real estate properties and fine art masterpieces) that interest only a limited number of people.

Market Information Systems

Markets may be structured based on the type and quantity of information they disseminate to the public.

- Pre-trade transparent markets publish real-time data about quotes and orders.
- Post-trade transparent markets publish data about trade prices soon after trades occur.

LESSON 3: WELL-FUNCTIONING FINANCIAL SYSTEMS AND MARKET REGULATION

LOS 44k: Describe characteristics of a well-functioning financial system. Vol 5, pp 58–60

As mentioned previously, a well-functioning financial system helps:

- Investors to save for the future.
- Entities to borrow funds.
- Hedgers to manage various risks.
- The exchange of assets by creating liquidity in spot markets.

A financial system helps to achieve these goals by establishing financial markets and financial intermediaries. A financial market is a platform that brings together buyers and sellers to facilitate transfers of assets. A well-functioning securities market has the following features:

- **Timely and accurate disclosures** so that market participants can make well-informed decisions.
- **Liquidity** so that costs of trading are minimized.
- **Complete markets** that allow people to solve their financial problems.
- **External or informational efficiency**, where prices respond to changes in fundamental values.

> If all the assets or contracts needed to achieve these four objectives are available to trade, the financial system is said to have complete markets.
>
> If the costs of trading are low, the financial market is said to be operationally efficient.
>
> If assets and contracts are properly priced (given all available relevant information) the financial market is said to be informationally efficient.

Financial intermediaries are also an integral part of the financial system. They:

- Match buyers and sellers by organizing trading venues, such as exchanges, brokerages, alternative trading systems, and so on.
- Provide liquidity.
- Lower borrowing costs by securitizing assets.
- Manage banks that match investors and borrowers by taking deposits and making loans.
- Manage insurance companies that pool uncorrelated risks.
- Provide investment advisory services to investors at a low cost.
- Organize clearinghouses that ensure the settlement of trades.
- Organize depositories that ensure safety of assets.

A well-functioning financial system leads to informationally efficient prices. Market participants analyze securities and push up (push down) prices of undervalued (overvalued) securities. However, this depends on the cost of obtaining fundamental information and market liquidity.

- Accounting standards help to lower the cost of obtaining relevant information by requiring companies to make timely financial disclosures.
- Liquid markets enable traders to act on that information and make investment decisions.

As a result of efficient markets, capital is allocated to its most productive use in society (i.e., allocative efficiency is reached).

LOS 44l: Describe the objectives of market regulation. Vol 5, pp 60–63

The following problems could arise in financial markets if they were left unregulated:

- Fraud and theft.
- Insider trading.
- Increase in the cost of information.
- Increase in the number of defaults.

In light of these problems, it is imperative that financial markets are regulated. Regulation of the financial system has the following objectives:

- To control fraud or deception of market participants.
- To control agency problems by setting minimum standards of competence for agents and by defining and enforcing minimum standards of practice.
- To promote fairness by creating a level playing field for market participants.
- To set mutually beneficial standards for financial reporting.
- To prevent undercapitalized financial firms from exploiting their investors by making excessively risky investments.
- To ensure that long-term liabilities are funded. For example, regulation seeks to ensure that insurance companies and pension funds have sufficient capital to honor their long-term commitments.

Regulation may be provided by governments or industry groups (self-regulating organizations or SROs).

READING 45: SECURITY MARKET INDICES

LESSON 1: INDEX DEFINITION, CALCULATIONS, CONSTRUCTION, AND MANAGEMENT

LOS 45a: Describe a security market index. Vol 5, pp 78–79

A **security market index** consists of individual securities (also called constituent securities) that represent a given security market, market segment, or asset class. Each security market index may have two versions depending on how returns are calculated:

- A price return index only reflects the prices of constituent securities.
- A total return index not only reflects prices, but also assumes reinvestment of all income received since inception.

The values of both versions of an index are the same at inception. However, as time passes, the total return index will be greater in value than the price return index by an increasing amount.

LOS 45b: Calculate and interpret the value, price return, and total return of an index. Vol 5, pp 79–82

The value of a price return index is calculated as follows:

$$V_{PRI} = \frac{\sum_{i=1}^{N} n_i P_i}{D}$$

where:
V_{PRI} = Value of the price return index
n_i = Number of units of constituent security i held in the index portfolio
N = Number of constituent securities in the index
P_i = Unit price of constituent security i
D = Value of the divisor

The divisor is initially chosen as a value that gives the index a convenient initial value (e.g., 1,000). However, over time the divisor must be adjusted to ensure that changes in the index only reflect changes in prices of constituent securities. For example, if some constituent securities are replaced by others in the index, the divisor must be adjusted so that the value of the index remains unchanged.

Index return calculations may measure price return or total return:

- Price return measures only the percentage change in price.
- Total return measures the percentage change in price plus interest, dividends, and other distributions.

Calculation of Single Period Returns

Price Return

The price return of an index can be calculated as:

$$PR_I = \frac{V_{PRI1} - V_{PRI0}}{V_{PRI0}}$$

where:
PR_I = Price return of the index portfolio (as a decimal number)
V_{PRI1} = Value of the price return index at the end of the period
V_{PRI0} = Value of the price return index at the beginning of the period

The price return of each constituent security is calculated as:

$$PR_i = \frac{P_{i1} - P_{i0}}{P_{i0}}$$

where:
PR_i = Price return of constituent security i (as a decimal number)
P_{i1} = Price of the constituent security i at the end of the period
P_{i0} = Price of the constituent security i at the beginning of the period

The price return of the index equals the weighted average price return of the constituent securities. It is calculated as:

$$PR_I = w_1 PR_1 + w_2 PR_2 + ... + w_N PR_N$$

where:
PR_I = Price return of the index portfolio (as a decimal number)
PR_i = Price return of constituent security i (as a decimal number)
w_i = Weight of security i in the index portfolio
N = Number of securities in the index

Total Return

The total return of an index can be calculated as:

$$TR_I = \frac{V_{PRI1} - V_{PRI0} + Inc_I}{V_{PRI0}}$$

where:
TR_I = Total return of the index portfolio (as a decimal number)
V_{PRI1} = Value of the total return index at the end of the period
V_{PRI0} = Value of the total return index at the beginning of the period
Inc_I = Total income from all securities in the index held over the period

The total return of each constituent security is calculated as:

$$TR_i = \frac{P_{1i} - P_{0i} + Inc_i}{P_{0i}}$$

where:
TR_i = Total return of constituent security i (as a decimal number)
P_{1i} = Price of constituent security i at the end of the period
P_{0i} = Price of constituent security i at the beginning of the period
Inc_i = Total income from security i over the period

The total return of the index equals the weighted average total return of the constituent securities. It is calculated as:

$$TR_I = w_1 TR_1 + w_2 TR_2 + ... + w_N TR_N$$

where:
TR_I = Total return of the index portfolio (as a decimal number)
TR_i = Total return of constituent security i (as a decimal number)
w_i = Weight of security i in the index portfolio
N = Number of securities in the index

Calculation of Index Returns over Multiple Time Periods

Given a series of price returns for an index, the value of a price return index can be calculated as (see Example 1-1):

$$V_{PRIT} = V_{PRI0}(1 + PR_{I1})(1 + PR_{I2}) \dots (1 + PR_{IT})$$

where:
V_{PRI0} = Value of the price return index at inception
V_{PRIT} = Value of the price return index at time t
PR_{IT} = Price return (as a decimal number) on the index over the period

Similarly, the value of a total return index may be calculated as:

$$V_{TRIT} = V_{TRI0}(1 + TR_{I1})(1 + TR_{I2}) \dots (1 + TR_{IT})$$

where:
V_{TRI0} = Value of the index at inception
V_{TRIT} = Value of the index at time t
TR_{IT} = Total return (as a decimal number) on the index over the period

Example 1-1: Price Return and Total Return Indices

An analyst obtained the following information regarding an equity market index created at the beginning of 2008:

	2008	2009
Price return	7.5%	8.3%
Total return	12.6%	13.4%

Given that the index value at inception is 1,000, calculate the values of price return and total return indices at the end of 2008 and 2009.

Solution:

Price return index

Value at the end of 2008 = 1,000 × 1.075 = 1,075

Value at the end of 2009 = 1,000 × 1.075 × 1.083 = 1,164.225

Total return index

Value at the end of 2008 = 1,000 × 1.126 = 1,126

Value at the end of 2009 = 1,000 × 1.126 × 1.134 = 1,276.884

LOS 45c: Describe the choices and issues in index construction and management. Vol 5, pg 82

Constructing and managing a security market index involves:

- Target market selection.
- Security selection.
- Index weighting.
- Rebalancing.
- Reconstitution.

Target Market and Security Selection

When constructing a security market index, the first decision that must be made relates to which market, market segment, or asset class the index should represent. The target market may be based on:

- Asset class (e.g., equities, fixed income, or real estate)
- Geographic region (e.g., Japan, South Africa, or Europe)
- The exchange on which the securities are traded (e.g., New York, London, or Tokyo)
- Other characteristics (e.g., economic sector, company size, and investment style)

An index may consist of all the securities in the target market or just a representative sample of the target market. Some indices (e.g., S&P 500) fix the number of securities to be included in the index, while others (e.g., TOPIX) allow the number of securities to vary to reflect changes in the target market or to maintain a certain percentage of the target market.

LOS 45d: Compare the different weighting methods used in index construction. Vol 5, pp 82–91

LOS 45e: Calculate and analyze the value and return of an index given its weighting method. Vol 5, pp 82–91

Price Weighting

In a price-weighted index the weight of each constituent security is determined by dividing its price by the sum of the prices of all constituent securities:

$$w_i^P = \frac{P_i}{\sum\limits_{i=1}^{N} P_i}$$

The value of a price-weighted index is computed by dividing the sum of the security prices by the divisor. See Example 1-2. At inception, the divisor is typically set to the number of securities in the index.

Example 1-2: Price-Weighted Index

A price-weighted equity index consists of one share each of five securities. The prices of these securities at the end of 2008 and 2009 are given below:

Securities	Price at the End of 2008 ($)	Price at the End of 2009 ($)
A	30	34
B	22	28
C	35	31
D	50	54
E	48	44

1. Calculate the value of the index at the beginning of 2009.
2. Calculate the weights of each security at the beginning of 2009.
3. Calculate the price return of the index for 2009.

Solutions:

1. Value of the index at the beginning of 2009:

$$= \frac{(30 \times 1) + (22 \times 1) + (35 \times 1) + (50 \times 1) + (48 \times 1)}{5} = 37$$

2. Weight of security A = 30/185 = 16.22%
   Weight of security B = 22/185 = 11.89%
   Weight of security C = 35/185 = 18.92%
   Weight of security D = 50/185 = 27.03%
   Weight of security E = 48/185 = 25.95%

3. Value of the index at the end of 2009:

$$= \frac{(34 \times 1) + (28 \times 1) + (31 \times 1) + (54 \times 1) + (44 \times 1)}{5} = 38.2$$

Price return of the index for 2009 = (38.2 − 37) / 37 = 3.24%

In the examples relating to various weighting methods, we have concentrated on determining only the price return on the index to keep it simple. Total return index calculations are similar, the only difference being that total returns for each constituent security are used instead of price returns.

The advantage of a price-weighted index is its simplicity. One of the issues with a price-weighted index is that a stock split or stock dividend by one of the constituent securities changes the weights of all securities in the index. To prevent stock splits and stock dividends from changing the value of the index, the divisor of a price-weighted index must be adjusted. This is illustrated in Example 1-3.

Example 1-3: Calculation of Index Divisor After a Stock Split

A price-weighted market index includes four stocks: A, B, C, and D. Stock B issues a four-for-one stock split. The table below lists the prices of the stocks before and after the split.

Stock	Before Split	After Stock Split by Stock B
A	40	40
B	80	20
C	70	70
D	50	50
	240	**180**
		$180 \div x = 60$
	Index = $240 \div 4 = 60$	$x = 3$

If the divisor is not adjusted for the stock split, the index will fall from 60 to 45 (180/4) even though there has been no change in prices other than to adjust for the split. To reflect the fact that stock values really have not changed, the index divisor must be adjusted. This new divisor, x, is calculated as (40 + 20 + 70 + 50) / 60 = 3.

Price-weighted indices suffer from a *downward* bias. Companies that split their stock are typically those that have witnessed substantial increases in their stock prices. As their stock prices fall to adjust for the split, their weight in the index also falls.

Equal Weighting

In an equal-weighted index, each constituent security is given an identical weight in the index at inception. The weights are calculated as:

$$w_i^E = \frac{1}{N}$$

where:
w_i = Fraction of the portfolio that is allocated to security i or weight of security i
N = Number of securities in the index

The number of shares of each security included in the index is calculated as the value allotted to each constituent security divided by the price of the security. Unlike a price-weighted index, where the weights are arbitrarily determined by market prices, the weights in an equal-weighted index are effectively determined by the index provider (in choosing the particular weighting mechanism). See Example 1-4.

Example 1-4: Equal-Weighted Index

An equal-weighted equity index with an initial value of 10,000 consists of five securities whose prices at the end of 2008 and 2009 are given below:

Securities	Price at the End of 2008 ($)	Price at the End of 2009 ($)
A	30	34
B	22	28
C	35	31
D	50	54
E	48	44

1. Calculate the number of shares of each security included in the equal-weighted index.
2. Calculate the index value at the end of 2009.
3. Calculate the price return of the index for 2009.

Solutions:

Since the index consists of five securities, each security will be assigned a weight of 20% in the index. As the total value of the index is 10,000, the value assigned to each security will be 2,000.

1. Number of shares of Stock A = 2,000/30 = 66
   Number of shares of Stock B = 2,000/22 = 90
   Number of shares of Stock C = 2,000/35 = 57
   Number of shares of Stock D = 2,000/50 = 40
   Number of shares of Stock E = 2,000/48 = 41

   The number of shares of each security in this example has been rounded off for simplicity.

2. The value of the index position in each security at the end of 2009 is calculated as:

   Security A: 66 × 34 = 2,244
   Security B: 90 × 28 = 2,520
   Security C: 57 × 31 = 1,767
   Security D: 40 × 54 = 2,160
   Security E: 41 × 44 = 1,804

   Therefore, the total value of the index at the end of 2009 is calculated as:

   2,244 + 2,520 + 1,767 + 2,160 + 1,804 = 10,495

3. The price return of the index for 2009 = (10,495 / 10,000) − 1 = 4.95%

Equal-weighted indices are also preferred because of their simplicity. However, they have a few disadvantages:

- Assigning an equal weight to all securities underrepresents (overrepresents) those securities that constitute a relatively large (small) fraction of the target market.
- The index does not remain equally weighted once the prices of the constituent securities change. Frequent adjustments must be made to maintain equal weighting.

Market-Capitalization Weighting

A market-capitalization-weighted (value weighted) index is based on the total market value (current stock price times the total number of shares outstanding) of all stocks in the index. The proportion of each constituent security is determined by dividing its market capitalization by the total market capitalization of all the securities in the index:

$$w_i^M = \frac{Q_i P_i}{\sum_{j=1}^{N} Q_j P_j}$$

where:
w_i = Fraction of the portfolio that is allocated to security i or weight of security i
Q_i = Number of shares outstanding of security i
P_i = Share price of security i
N = Number of securities in the index

The initial market value is assigned a base number (e.g., 100) and a new market value is computed periodically. The change in the index is measured by comparing the new market value to the base market value. See Example 1-5.

Example 1-5: Market-Capitalization-Weighted Index

A market-capitalization-weighted equity index consists of five securities whose prices and number of shares outstanding are given below:

Securities	Price at the End of 2008 ($)	Price at the End of 2009 ($)	Shares Outstanding
A	30	34	4,000
B	22	28	6,000
C	35	31	2,000
D	50	54	2,500
E	48	44	3,000

1. Calculate the weight of each security in the index at the beginning of 2009.
2. Calculate the value of the divisor that gives an index value of 1,000 at the beginning of 2009.
3. Calculate the price return of the index for 2009.

Solutions:

1. Total market capitalization at the beginning of 2009:

   $$= (30 \times 4,000) + (22 \times 6,000) + (35 \times 2,000) + (50 \times 2,500) + (48 \times 3,000) = 591,000$$

   The weights of each of the 5 securities are calculated below:

   Security A = (30 × 4,000) / 591,000 = 20.30%
   Security B = (22 × 6,000) / 591,000 = 22.34%
   Security C = (35 × 2,000) / 591,000 = 11.84%
   Security D = (50 × 2,500) / 591,000 = 21.15%
   Security E = (48 × 3,000) / 591,000 = 24.37%

2. Value of the divisor = 591,000 / 1,000 = 591

3. Total market capitalization at the end of 2009:

   $$= (34 \times 4,000) + (28 \times 6,000) + (31 \times 2,000) + (54 \times 2,500) + (44 \times 3,000) = 633,000$$

   Price return of the index for 2009 = (633,000/591) / 1,000 − 1 = 7.11%

Value-weighted indices automatically adjust for stock splits and stock dividends.

Float-Adjusted Market-Capitalization Weighting

In a float-adjusted market-capitalization-weighted index, the proportion of each constituent security is determined by adjusting its market capitalization for its market float.

Market float generally refers to the number of shares of the constituent security that are available to the investing public. Shares held by controlling shareholders, other corporations, and governments are subtracted from the total number of outstanding shares to determine the market float. See Example 1-6.

The float-adjusted market-capitalization weight of each constituent security is calculated as:

$$w_i^M = \frac{f_i Q_i P_i}{\displaystyle\sum_{j=1}^{N} f_j Q_j P_j}$$

where:

f_i = Fraction of shares outstanding in the market float
w_i = Fraction of the portfolio that is allocated to security i or weight of security i
Q_i = Number of shares outstanding of security i
P_i = Share price of security i
N = Number of securities in the index

Example 1-6: Float-Adjusted Market-Capitalization-Weighted Indices

A float-adjusted market-capitalization-weighted equity index consists of five securities. Further information is provided in the table below:

Securities	Price at the End of 2008 ($)	Price at the End of 2009 ($)	Shares Outstanding	Percentage of Shares in Market Float
A	30	34	4,000	40
B	22	28	6,000	70
C	35	31	2,000	80
D	50	54	2,500	50
E	48	44	3,000	60

1. Calculate the number of shares of each security that will be included in the index.
2. Calculate the total float-adjusted market-capitalization at the beginning of 2009.
3. Calculate the price return of the index for 2009.

Solutions:

1. The number of shares of each security to be included in the index is calculated as:

   Security A = 4,000 × 40% = 1,600
   Security B = 6,000 × 70% = 4,200
   Security C = 2,000 × 80% = 1,600
   Security D = 2,500 × 50% = 1,250
   Security E = 3,000 × 60% = 1,800

2. The total float-adjusted market-capitalization at the beginning of 2009 is calculated as:

   $(30 \times 1,600) + (22 \times 4,200) + (35 \times 1,600) + (50 \times 1,250) + (48 \times 1,800) = 345,300$

3. The total float-adjusted market-capitalization at the end of 2009 is calculated as:

$$(34 \times 1,600) + (28 \times 4,200) + (31 \times 1,600) + (54 \times 1,250) + (44 \times 1,800) = 368,300$$

Price return of the index for 2009 = (368,300 / 345,300) − 1 = 6.66%

The primary advantage of market capitalization weighting (and float-adjusted market capitalization weighting) is that securities are held in proportion to their value in the target market. A disadvantage is that stocks with larger market values have a larger impact on the index. Stocks that have seen their prices rise (fall) will see their relative weight in the index increase (decline). The effect of market value weighting is therefore similar to that of a momentum trading strategy.

Fundamental Weighting

Instead of using prices of constituent securities, a fundamental-weighted index uses other measures of a company's size (that are independent of the stock price) such as book value, cash flow, revenues, and earnings to determine weights of securities in the index. Some fundamental indices use a single measure to weight the constituent securities, while others combine weights from several measures to form a composite value that is used for weighting. See Example 1-7.

The fundamental weight on security i can be calculated as:

$$w_i^F = \frac{F_i}{\sum_{j=1}^{N} F_j}$$

where:

F_i = A given fundamental size measure of company i

Earnings yield equals earnings per share for the most recent 12-month period divided by the current market price per share. The earnings yield (which is the inverse of the P/E ratio) shows the percentage of each dollar invested in the stock that was earned by the company.

The earnings yield is used by many investment managers to determine optimal asset allocations.

Example 1-7: Fundamental Weighting

Consider two stocks, A and B, which are the only securities in an index. Market capitalization and earnings information for the stocks is given below:

	Stock A	Stock B	Total
Market capitalization ($)	1.4 billion	600 million	2 billion
Earnings ($)	40 million	40 million	80 million

The earnings yield of Stock A is 2.86% (0.04b/1.4b) and that of Stock B is 6.67% (40m/600m).

The weights assigned to the two stocks in a market-capitalization-weighted and fundamental-weighted index (based on earnings) are given next:

	Stock A	Stock B
Market-capitalization weighted	1.4/(1.4 + 0.6) = 70%	0.6 /(1.4 + 0.6) = 30%
Fundamental weighted	40/(40 + 40) = 50%	40/(40 + 40) = 50%

Notice that compared to a value-weighted index, a fundamental-weighted index assigns a higher weight to Stock B (50% versus 30%) and a lower weight to Stock A (50% versus 70%). Stocks with a higher earnings yield than that of the overall market weighted portfolio will be more heavily weighted under fundamental weighting compared to market value weighting. Fundamental weighting, therefore, results in a "value tilt."

In contrast to market-capitalization-weighted indices, in which the weight of a stock in the index moves in the same direction as its price, fundamental-weighted indices have a "contrarian" effect in that the portfolio weights move away from securities whose prices have risen (as higher prices result in a lower earnings yield).

LOS 45f: Describe rebalancing and reconstitution of an index.
Vol 5, pp 91–93

Rebalancing

We have seen that the weights assigned to constituent securities at inception of an index change as their prices change. In order to keep the weights of constituent securities consistent with the index's weighting method, security weights must be adjusted or rebalanced.

- In equal-weighted indices, the weights of securities that have witnessed price appreciation increase over time, and weights of securities that have underperformed decrease over time. Rebalancing an equal-weighted index would require reducing the weight of securities that have outperformed and increasing the weight of securities that have underperformed.
- Price-weighted indices do not need to be rebalanced, as the weight of each constituent security is determined by its price.
- Market-capitalization-weighted indices rebalance themselves to reflect changes in the market-capitalization of constituent securities. They only need to be rebalanced to reflect mergers, acquisitions, liquidations, and so on.

Reconstitution

This refers to the process of changing the constituent securities in an index. Constituent securities need to be examined on a regular basis to evaluate whether they still meet the criteria for inclusion in the index. If they no longer meet the criteria, they must be replaced with securities that do meet the criteria. Index reconstitution is performed in order to:

- Reflect changes in the target market as a result of bankruptcies, de-listings, mergers, and so on.
- Reflect the judgment of the selection committee.

Reconstitution creates turnover within the index (especially for market value weighted indices), as once the revised list of constituent securities is determined, the weights of all constituent securities must be recalculated. Further, the frequency of reconstitution is a major issue for widely used indices and their constituent securities. Even before a scheduled reconstitution is undertaken by the index provider, investors speculate on which securities will be added to or removed from the index. If investors bet on a particular security being added to a popular index (by purchasing significant quantities of that particular security), the stock can see a dramatic increase in its price before it is actually added to the index.

LESSON 2: USES OF MARKET INDICES AND TYPES OF INDICES

LOS 45g: Describe uses of security market indices. Vol 5, pp 93–95

- Indices are good indicators of the collective opinion of market participants and are used to gauge market sentiment. However, indices typically only include a sample of stocks and therefore do not reflect the behavior of investors who trade in other stocks.
- They are used as proxies for measuring and modeling returns, systematic risk, and risk-adjusted performance. For example, when applying the CAPM, the S&P 500 is used as a proxy for the market portfolio in the United States.
- By exhibiting the risk and return profiles of select groups of securities, indices act as proxies for asset classes in asset allocation models. They provide the historical data used to model the risks and returns of different asset classes.
- In the field of performance evaluation, indices are used as benchmarks for actively managed portfolios. For example, the performance of a portfolio consisting of global small-capitalization stocks might be compared to the performance of the FTSE Global Small Cap Index, which includes 4,600 small-capitalization stocks across 48 countries.
- Security market indices serve as the basis for the creation of numerous investment products. For example, they led to the development of index portfolios, which subsequently led to the introduction of exchange-traded funds (ETFs). ETFs in turn led to the development of new indices to serve the other needs of investors.

LOS 45h: Describe types of equity indices. Vol 5, pp 95–97

Equity indices include the following:

Broad market indices: A broad equity market index contains securities representing more than 90% of the selected market. For example, the Russell 3000 consists of the largest 3,000 stocks (by market capitalization), and represents 99% of the U.S. equity market.

Multi-market indices: Multi-market indices consist of security market indices from different countries and may represent multiple national markets, geographic regions, economic development groups, or even the entire world. A number of index providers, including MSCI-Barra, publish multi-market indices. Index providers weight constituent securities in each country by market capitalization and determine the weight of each country in the overall index based on relative GDPs, effectively creating fundamental weighting in these indices.

Sector indices: Sector indices only include securities representing a particular economic sector (e.g., finance, health care, technology, etc.) where the economic sector may be classified on a national, regional, or global basis. These play an important role in evaluating a portfolio manager's performance and determining whether she is better at stock selection or sector allocation. Further, they serve as model portfolios for sector-specific ETFs and other investment portfolios.

Style indices: Financial firms like Dow Jones and Standard & Poor's have developed different indices based on specific investment strategies used by portfolio managers. These indices include those based on size (e.g., small-cap versus large-cap equities) and others based on style (e.g., growth versus value stocks). Stocks may need to be reclassified over time based on changing valuation ratios or market capitalizations. Therefore, style indices generally have much higher turnover than broad market indices.

LOS 45i: Describe types of fixed-income indices. Vol 5, pp 98–101

Creating bond-market indices presents the following challenges:

- There is a broader universe of bonds than of stocks.
- The universe of bonds is constantly changing as a result of new issues, calls, and maturities.
- The price volatility of a bond (as measured by duration) is constantly changing. Duration changes with a bond's maturity and market yields.
- Current and continuous transaction prices are not available for bonds.

Types of Fixed-Income Indices

Fixed-income securities can be classified along the following dimensions:

- Type of issuer (government, government agency, corporation).
- Type of financing (general obligation, collateralized).
- Currency of payments.
- Maturity.
- Credit quality (investment grade, high yield, credit agency ratings).
- Absence or presence of inflation protection.

Fixed-income indices can be categorized as follows:

- Aggregate or broad market indices.
- Market sector indices.
- Style indices.
- Economic sector indices.
- Specialized indices such as high-yield, inflation-linked, and emerging market indices.

Due to the wide variety of instruments, fixed-income indices may be subdivided based on a variety of dimensions. For example, indices categorizing securities as investment-grade and high-yield may be subdivided by maturity and credit rating.

LOS 45j: Describe indices representing alternative investments.
Vol 5, pp 101–104

Investments in asset classes other than equities and fixed-income have gained popularity as investors have looked to diversify their portfolios. Several indices have been created to represent the performance of these asset classes.

Commodity indices: Commodity indices consist of futures contracts on one or more commodities and have the following characteristics:

- They do not have an obvious weighting method so index providers create their own weighting methods. Commodities may either be weighted equally, or on the basis of price, or may have fixed weights as determined by a committee. The returns of different commodity indices that contain the same commodities may differ due to differences in weighting methods.
- Different weighting methods lead to different exposures to specific commodities, which result in very different risk and return profiles of commodity indices. Equity and fixed-income indices that target the same markets share similar risk and return profiles.
- The performance of commodity indices may differ from that of the underlying commodities because indices consist of futures contracts on commodities rather than the actual commodities. Aside from being affected by changes in prices of the underlying commodities, index returns are also affected by the risk-free rate, changes in futures prices, and roll yield.

Real estate investment trust indices: Real estate indices represent the market for real estate and real estate securities. They can be categorized as:

- Appraisal indices
- Repeat sales indices
- Real estate investment trust (REIT) indices

REIT indices consist of shares of publicly traded REITs (public or private organizations that combine individual investors' funds and provide them access to real estate investments). Shares issued by REITs trade on various exchanges around the world and are priced continuously.

Hedge fund indices: Hedge fund indices are designed to represent the performance of hedge funds (private investment vehicles that typically use leverage and long and short investment strategies) on a very broad, global level or the strategy level. Hedge fund indices have the following characteristics:

- They rely on voluntary disclosures from funds, as it is not mandatory for hedge funds to disclose performance to any party other than investors.

- If they do decide to disclose performance, hedge funds have a choice regarding which index or indices they report their performance to. Therefore, rather than index providers determining the constituents, the constituents determine the index. Further, different hedge fund indices may reflect very different performance for the hedge fund industry over the same period of time based on the hedge funds represented in those indices.
- Poorly performing hedge funds may stop reporting their performance to hedge fund indices or may cease to exist altogether. This leads to survivorship bias and an upward bias in hedge fund performance as represented by these indices.

LOS 45k: Compare types of security market indices. Vol 5, pp 103–104

Table 2-1: Representative Indices Worldwide[1]

As indicated in this reading, the choice of indices to meet the needs of investors is extensive. Investors using security market indices must be careful in their selection of the index or indices most appropriate for their needs. The following table illustrates the variety of indices reflecting different asset classes, markets, and weighting methods.

Index	Representing	Number of Securities	Weighting Method	Comments
Dow Jones Industrial Average	U.S. blue-chip companies	30	Price	The oldest and most widely-known U.S. equity index. *Wall Street Journal* editors choose 30 stocks from among large, mature, blue-chip companies.
Nikkei Stock Average	Japanese blue-chip companies	225	Modified price	Known as the Nikkei 225 and originally formulated by Dow Jones & Co. Because of extreme variations in price levels of component securities, some high price shares are weighted as a fraction of share price. Index contains some illiquid stocks.
TOPIX	All companies listed on the Tokyo Stock Exchange First Section	Varies	Float-adjusted market cap	Represents about 93 percent of the market value of all Japanese companies. Contains a large number of very small, illiquid stocks, making exact replication difficult.
MSCI All Country World Index	Stocks of 23 developed and 22 emerging markets	Varies	Free-float-adjusted market cap	Composed of companies representative of the market structure of developed and emerging market countries in the Americas, Europe/Middle East, and Asia/Pacific regions. Price return and total return versions available in both USD and local currencies.

---

1 - Representative Indices Worldwide, Volume 5, CFA Program Curriculum 2019

Table 2-1: Representative Indices Worldwide (*continued*)

Index	Representing	Number of Securities	Weighting Method	Comments
S&P Developed Ex-U.S. BMI Energy Sector Index	Energy sector of developed global markets outside the United States	Varies	Float-adjusted market cap	Serves as a model portfolio for the SPDR® S&P Energy Sector Exchange-Traded Fund (ETF).
Barclays Capital Global Aggregate Bond Index	Investment-grade bonds in the North American, European, and Asian markets	Varies	Market cap	Formerly known as Lehman Brothers Global Aggregate Bond Index
Markit iBoxx Euro High-Yield Bond Indices	Sub-investment-grade euro-denominated corporate bonds	Varies	Market cap and variations	Rebalanced monthly. Represents tradable part of market. Price and total return versions available with such analytical values as yield, duration, modified duration, and convexity. Provides platform for research and structured products.
FTSE EPRA/ NAREIT Global Real Estate Index	Real estate securities in the North American, European, and Asian markets	335	Float-adjusted market cap	The stock of REITs that constitute the index trade on public stock exchanges and may be constituents of equity market indices.
HFRX Global Hedge Fund Index	Overall composition of the HFR database	Varies	Asset weighting	Comprise all eligible hedge fund strategies. Examples include convertible arbitrage, distressed securities, market neutral, event driven, macro, and relative value arbitrage. Constituent strategies are asset weighted on the basis of asset distribution within the hedge fund industry.
HFRX Equal Weighted Strategies EUR Index	Overall composition of the HFR database	Varies	Equal weighting	Denominated in euros and is constructed from the same strategies as the HFRX Global Hedge Fund Index.
Morningstar Style Indices	U.S. stocks classified by market cap and value/ growth orientation	Varies	Float-adjusted market cap	The nine indices defined by combinations of market cap (large, mid, and small) and value/growth orientation (value, core, growth) have mutually exclusive constituents and are exhaustive with respect to the Morningstar U.S. Market Index. Each is a model portfolio for one of the iShares Morningstar ETFs.

READING 46: MARKET EFFICIENCY

LESSON 1: THE CONCEPT OF MARKET EFFICIENCY AND FORMS OF MARKET EFFICIENCY

LOS 46a: Describe market efficiency and related concepts, including their importance to investment practitioners. Vol 5, pp 117–119

An informationally efficient market (an efficient market) is one where security prices adjust rapidly to reflect any new information. It is a market where asset prices reflect all past and present information.

Investment managers and analysts are interested in market efficiency because it dictates how many profitable trading opportunities may abound in the market.

- In an efficient market, it is difficult to find inaccurately priced securities. Therefore, superior risk-adjusted returns cannot be attained in an efficient market, and it would be wise to pursue a passive investment strategy, which entails lower costs.
- In an inefficient market, securities may be mispriced and trading in these securities can offer positive risk-adjusted returns. In such a market, an active investment strategy may outperform a passive strategy on a risk-adjusted basis.

In an efficient market, the time frame required for security prices to reflect any new information is very short. For example, in the foreign exchange market and developed equity markets, prices reflect new information in less than a minute. In a relatively inefficient market, the time frame of the price adjustment is long enough to allow many traders to earn profits with little risk.

Finally, in an efficient market, prices only adjust to new or unexpected information (surprises). Investors absorb the new information and revise their expectations regarding the security's risk and return accordingly. They then take positions on the asset in light of their new forecasts. If the expected return is adequate compensation for the security's perceived risk, investors will purchase the asset, and if the expected return does not offer sufficient compensation for the asset's perceived risk, they will liquidate positions in the asset or even short it.

LOS 46b: Distinguish between market value and intrinsic value. Vol 5, pp 119–120

The market value or market price of the asset is the price at which the asset can currently be bought or sold. It is determined by the interaction of demand and supply for the security in the market. Intrinsic value or fundamental value is the value of the asset that reflects all its investment characteristics accurately. Intrinsic values are estimated in light of all the available information regarding the asset; they are not known for certain.

In an efficient market, investors widely believe that the market price reflects a security's intrinsic value. On the other hand, in an inefficient market, investors may try to develop their own estimates of intrinsic value in order to profit from any mispricing (difference between the market price and intrinsic value).

The challenge for investors lies in estimating an asset's intrinsic value. Estimates of intrinsic value are derived by forecasting the amount and timing of the security's future cash flows, and then discounting them at an appropriate discount rate (which reflects the riskiness of these cash flows). As new, relevant information continues to flow to investors, estimates of intrinsic value and market prices keep changing.

LOS 46c: Explain factors that affect a market's efficiency. Vol 5, pp 120–124

Markets cannot strictly be classified as efficient or inefficient. Market efficiency should be viewed as falling on a continuum between these two extremes. A relatively efficient market reflects new information in market prices more quickly and more accurately than a relatively inefficient market.

Factors Contributing to and Impeding a Market's Efficiency

Market participants: Generally speaking, the greater the number of active market participants (investors and financial analysts) that analyze an asset or security, the greater the degree of efficiency in the market. Restrictions that prevent investors from trading in a market or in a particular security impede market efficiency.

Information availability and financial disclosure: The availability of accurate and timely information regarding trading activities and traded companies contributes to market efficiency. For a market to be considered efficient, investors should have access to the information necessary to value securities that trade in the market. Further, all investors should have fair and equal opportunity to act on this information.

Limits to trading: The activities of arbitrageurs, who seek opportunities to trade on mispricings in the market to earn arbitrage (riskless) profits, contribute to market efficiency. Arbitrageurs purchase securities that they believe are undervalued (bidding their prices up to their intrinsic values) and short securities that they believe are overvalued (bringing their prices down to their intrinsic values). Limitations on arbitrage trading (e.g., difficulty in executing trades immediately and high costs of trading) reduce market efficiency.

Transaction costs and information-acquisition costs: Investors should consider transaction costs and information-acquisition costs in evaluating the efficiency of a market.

Two securities that should trade for the exact same price in an efficient market may trade at different prices if the costs of trading on the mispricing (to make a profit) for the lowest-cost traders are greater than the potential profit. In such cases, these prices are still "efficient" within the bounds of arbitrage. The bounds of arbitrage are relatively narrow in highly liquid markets (e.g., U.S. T-bills), but wider in relatively illiquid markets.

Further, there are always costs associated with gathering and analyzing information. Net of information-acquisition costs and the return offered on a security should be commensurate with the security's level of risk. If superior returns can be earned after deducting information-acquisition costs, the market is relatively inefficient.

LOS 46d: Contrast weak-form, semi-strong form, and strong-form market efficiency. Vol 5, pp 124–129

Weak-Form Efficient Market Hypothesis

Weak-form EMH assumes that current stock prices reflect *all security market information*, including historical trends in prices, returns, volumes, and other market-generated information such as block trades and trading by specialists. Under this hypothesis, because current stock market prices have essentially factored in all historical data, future returns on a stock should be independent of past returns or patterns.

Proponents of weak-form EMH assert that abnormal risk-adjusted returns cannot be earned by using trading rules and technical analysis, which make investing decisions based on historical security market data.

On the whole, various tests for weak-form EMH have backed the theory that current market prices reflect all available security market information and have led to the conclusion that the markets tend to be weak-form efficient. However, there is evidence that in countries with developing markets (e.g., China, Bangladesh, and Turkey) opportunities to profit from technical analysis do exist.

> Abnormal returns are returns in excess of those implied by the SML for a stock with a given level of risk.

Semi-Strong Form Efficient Market Hypothesis

Semi-strong form EMH assumes that current security prices fully reflect *all security market information* and other public information. It encompasses weak-form EMH and also includes nonmarket public information such as dividend announcements, various financial ratios, and economic and political news in the set of information that is already factored into market values.

Proponents of the hypothesis assert that investors cannot earn abnormal risk-adjusted returns if their investment decisions are based on important material information after it has been made public. They stress that security prices rapidly adjust to reflect all public information.

Overall, semi-strong form EMH has received considerable support from studies in developed markets. In these markets, it has been found that abnormal risk-adjusted returns cannot be earned based on public information because security prices adjust for the information very quickly. However, there is some evidence that developing countries may not have semi-strong form efficient markets.

Strong-Form Efficient Market Hypothesis

Strong-form EMH contends that stock prices reflect *all public and private information*. It implies that no group of investors has sole access to any information that is relevant in price formation. Basically, there is no information out there that has not already been accounted for in current market prices.

Strong-form EMH encompasses weak-form and semi-strong form EMH and assumes perfect markets where information is cost free and available to all. Under strong-form EMH, no one can consistently achieve abnormal risk-adjusted returns, not even company insiders.

Studies have found that securities markets are not strong-form efficient. Abnormal risk-adjusted returns can be earned if material nonpublic information is used.

See Table 1-1 for a summary.

Table 1-1: Summary of Assertions of Various Forms of EMH

Form of EMH	Prices Fully Reflect	Types of Investors Who Cannot Earn Abnormal Returns Consistently
Weak form	All market (public) information.	Technical traders.
Semi-strong form	All market and nonmarket public information.	Technical traders and fundamental investors.
Strong form	All public and private information.	All investors.

Markets that are semi-strong form efficient must be weak-form efficient as well since public information includes market information. Similarly, markets that are strong-form efficient must also be semi-strong form efficient and weak-form efficient.

However, markets that are weak-form efficient may or may not be semi-strong form and strong-form efficient. Similarly, markets that are semi-strong form efficient may or may not be strong-form efficient.

LOS 46e: Explain the implications of each form of market efficiency for fundamental analysis, technical analysis, and the choice between active and passive portfolio management. Vol 5, pp 128–129

Implications of Efficient Market Hypothesis

- Securities markets are weak-form efficient. Therefore, past trends in prices cannot be used to earn superior risk-adjusted returns.
- Securities markets are also semi-strong form efficient. Therefore, investors who analyze information should consider what information is already factored into a security's price, and how any new information may affect its value.
- Securities markets are not strong-form efficient. This is because insider trading is illegal.

Efficient Markets and Technical Analysis

Technical analysts utilize charts to identify price patterns, which are used to make investment decisions. If the market is weak-form efficient, prices already reflect all available security market public information, and technical trading systems that depend only on past trading and price data cannot hold much value. Since tests have predominantly confirmed weak-form efficiency of markets, technical trading rules should not generate abnormal risk-adjusted profits after accounting for risks and transaction costs.

Efficient Markets and Fundamental Analysis

Fundamental analysts are concerned with the company that underlies the stock. They evaluate a company's past performance and examine its financial statements. They compute many performance ratios that aid them in assessing the validity of the stock's current price. They believe that a company's stock price can differ from its true intrinsic value, and investors who recognize the discrepancy can profit from it.

Fundamental analysis is necessary in a well-functioning securities market, as it helps market participants understand the implications of any new information. Further, fundamental analysis can help generate abnormal risk-adjusted returns if an analyst is superior to her peers in valuing securities.

Efficient Markets and Portfolio Management

If markets are weak-form and semi-strong form efficient, active management is not likely to earn superior risk-adjusted returns on a consistent basis. Therefore, passive portfolio management would outperform active management. Studies have shown that on a risk-adjusted basis, mutual funds perform as well as the market before considering fees and expenses, but underperform the market after considering these costs.

The implication here is that the role of the portfolio manager is not necessarily to beat the market, but to manage the portfolio in light of the investor's risk and return objectives.

LESSON 2: MARKET PRICING ANOMALIES AND BEHAVIORAL FINANCE

LOS 46f: Describe market anomalies. Vol 5, pp 129–136

There is considerable evidence to suggest that markets are generally efficient. However, research has also highlighted a number of potential inefficiencies or anomalies that result in securities being mispriced. An anomaly occurs when a change in the price of an asset cannot be explained by the release of new information into the market.

- If markets are efficient, trading strategies designed to exploit market anomalies will not generate superior risk-adjusted returns on a consistent basis.
- An exception to the notion of market efficiency (an anomaly) would occur if a mispricing can be used to earn superior risk-adjusted returns consistently.

Observed anomalies can be placed into three categories.

1. Time-Series Anomalies

Calendar Anomalies

January effect: Studies have shown that since the 1980s, investors have earned significantly higher returns in the equity market during January compared to other months of the year. Tax reasons and "window-dressing" by portfolio managers have been held out as reasons to explain the January effect. However, recent evidence has suggested that the January effect is not persistent and does not produce superior returns on a risk-adjusted basis. Therefore, it is not a pricing anomaly. See Table NaN for other calendar anomalies.

Table 2-1: Other Calendar-Based Anomalies[1]

Anomaly	Observation
Turn-of-the-month effect	Returns tend to be higher on the last trading day of the month and the first three trading days of the next month.
Day-of-the-week effect	The average Monday return is negative and lower than the average returns for the other four days, which are all positive.
Weekend effect	Returns on weekends tend to be lower than returns on weekdays.
Holiday effect	Returns on stocks in the day prior to market holidays tend to be higher than other days.

1 - Exhibit 4, Volume 5, CFA Program Curriculum 2019.

Momentum and Overreaction Anomalies

Certain short-term share price patterns arise as a result of investors overreacting to the release of new information. Investors tend to inflate stock prices of companies that have released good news and depress stock prices for those that have released bad news. Studies have shown that "losers" (stocks that have witnessed a recent price decline due to the release of bad news) have outperformed the market in subsequent periods, while winners have underperformed in subsequent periods.

However, other studies have also shown that securities that have outperformed in the short term continue to generate high returns in subsequent periods (carrying on price momentum).

The overreaction and momentum anomalies go against the assertions of weak-form efficiency in markets.

2. Cross-Sectional Anomalies

Size Effect

Studies conducted in the past showed that shares of smaller companies outperformed shares of larger companies on a risk-adjusted basis. However, recent studies have failed to reach the same conclusion.

Value Effect

Studies have found that low P/E stocks have experienced higher risk-adjusted returns than high P/E stocks. These results go against semi-strong form market efficiency. However, when the Fama and French three-factor model is used instead of the CAPM to predict stock returns, the value stock anomaly disappears.

3. Other Anomalies

Closed-End Investment Fund Discounts

Several studies have shown that closed-end funds tend to trade at a discount (sometimes exceeding 50%) to their per-share NAVs. Theoretically, investors could purchase all the shares in the fund, liquidate the fund, and make a profit by selling the constituent securities at their market prices. However, after accounting for management fees, unrealized capital gains taxes, liquidity, and transaction costs, any profit potential is eliminated.

Earnings Surprises

Several studies have shown that although earnings surprises are quickly reflected in stock prices most of the time, this is not always the case. Investors may be able to earn abnormal returns using publicly available earnings information by purchasing stocks of companies that have announced positive earnings surprises. However, recent evidence has suggested that abnormal returns observed after earnings surprises do not control for transaction costs and risk.

Initial Public Offerings (IPOs)

Evidence suggests that investors who are able to acquire the shares of a company in an IPO at the offer price may be able to earn abnormal profits. However, this has not always proven to be the case. Further, over the long run, performance of IPOs has generally been below average.

Predictability of Returns Based on Prior Information

Considerable research has suggested that equity returns are based on factors such as interest rates, inflation rates, stock volatility, and so on. However, the fact that equity returns are related to economic fundamentals is not evidence of market inefficiency.

Implications for Investment Strategies

Although there is some evidence to support the existence of valid anomalies, it is difficult to consistently earn abnormal returns by trading on them. On average, markets are efficient. Further, it is possible that identified anomalies may not be violations of market efficiency, but the result of the statistical methodologies used to detect them.

LOS 46g: Describe behavioral finance and its potential relevance to understanding market anomalies. Vol 5, pp 136–139

Behavioral Finance

Behavioral finance looks at investor behavior to explain why individuals make the decisions that they do, whether these decisions are rational or irrational. It is based on the premise that individuals do not always make "efficient" investment decisions, nor do they always act rationally due to the presence of behavioral biases. The existence of these biases has been offered as a possible explanation for a number of pricing anomalies.

Most asset-pricing models assume that markets are rational and that the intrinsic value of a security reflects this rationality. Note that market efficiency and asset-pricing models do not require that each individual is rational; instead the market overall must be rational. If certain individuals do not behave in a rational manner, other investors respond to this by executing trades that profit themselves, thereby moving the market toward efficiency.

Behavioral Biases

Loss Aversion

In most financial models, the assumption is that investors are risk averse; that is, investors dislike risk, and they require higher expected returns as compensation for exposure to additional risk. Behavioral finance asserts that investors exhibit loss aversion (i.e., they dislike losses more than they like comparable gains), which results in a strong preference for avoiding losses as opposed to achieving gains. Advocates of this bias argue that loss aversion is more important to investors than risk aversion, which is why the overreaction anomaly is observed. While loss aversion can explain the overreaction anomaly, studies have shown that underreactions are just as common as overreactions, which counters the assertions of this bias.

Herding

Herding is a behavioral bias that explains both underreactions and overreactions in financial markets. Herding occurs when investors ignore their own analysis, and instead make investment decisions in line with the direction of the market.

Overconfidence

Overconfidence bias asserts that investors have an inflated view of their ability to process new information appropriately. Overconfident investors are inaccurate when it comes to valuing securities given new information, and therefore stocks will be mispriced if an adequate number of such investors are in the market. Further, if mispricings are persistent and predictable, it may be possible for investors to earn abnormal profits.

Evidence has suggested that overconfidence has led to mispricing in most major markets around the world, but the bias has been observed predominantly in higher-growth companies, whose prices are slow to factor in any new information.

Another aspect of this bias is that overconfident investors tend to maintain portfolios that are less than optimally diversified because they tend to overestimate their stock-picking abilities.

Information Cascades

An information cascade is a concept that is similar but not identical to herding. Herding refers to clustered trading that may or may not be based on information. An information cascade refers to the transfer of information from market participants who are the first to take investment action upon the release of new information, and whose decisions influence the decisions of others. For example, earnings announcements are difficult to interpret without access to complete financial statements and "noisy" because it is uncertain what current earnings indicate regarding future profitability. In the immediate aftermath of the announcement, if the stock price moves in a particular direction, uninformed traders assume that trades conducted by more informed traders are behind the change in stock price, and are therefore tempted to trade in the same direction themselves, creating an information cascade.

Information cascades can be rational. If informed traders act first and uninformed traders follow their lead, there will be an improvement in market efficiency as the cascade is helping the market correctly incorporate relevant information. Information cascades can also result in serial correlation in stock returns and to overreactions to information. Studies have shown that information cascades tend to be greater for stocks when reliable and relevant information about the underlying company is not easily available. They can actually improve the quality of information available to investors.

Other Behavioral Biases

- Representativeness, where investors assess probabilities of future outcomes as being similar to what they are in the current state.
- Mental accounting, where investors keep track of gains and losses from different investments in separate mental accounts.
- Conservatism, where investors are slow to react to changes, and continue to maintain their initial views.
- Narrow framing, where investors focus on issues in isolation.

All investors exhibit behavioral biases to different degrees. An understanding of these biases can help investors to recognize factors that affect their decision making, and, once they understand their own shortcomings, to make improved decisions going forward. The implications of behavioral finance on market efficiency are unclear. On one hand, if all investors must be rational for markets to be efficient, then the existence of behavioral biases suggests that markets cannot be efficient. On the other hand, if market efficiency means that investors cannot consistently earn superior risk-adjusted returns, then the evidence suggests that markets indeed tend to be efficient.

READING 47: OVERVIEW OF EQUITY SECURITIES

LESSON 1: OVERVIEW OF EQUITY SECURITIES

Equities in Global Financial Markets.

In order to evaluate the importance of equity securities in global financial markets, we must look at the total market capitalization and trading volumes of global equity markets and the prevalence of equity ownership across various geographic regions.

- In 2008, on a global level, the equity market capitalization to GDP ratio was close to 100% (more than twice the long run average of 50%). This shows that investors attach a significant value to publicly traded equities relative to the aggregate market value of goods and services produced globally every year (global GDP).
- Studies have shown that during 1900 to 2011, government bonds and bills earned annualized real returns of less than 2%, which is in line with the inflation rate. On the other hand, equity markets earned real returns in excess of 4% per year in most markets. Equity securities entail higher risk than government bonds and bills, but they earn higher returns to compensate for the higher risk. Note that equity securities also tend to be more volatile over time.
- In most developed countries, equity ownership as a percentage of the population was between 20% and 50%. This illustrates how heavily weighted equity securities are in most investor portfolios.

LOS 47a: Describe characteristics of types of equity securities.
Vol 5, pp 155–161

LOS 47b: Describe differences in voting rights and other ownership characteristics among different equity classes. **Vol 5, pp 155–161**

A company may issue debt or equity securities to finance its operations. Issuing debt creates a liability for the company, as it is contractually obligated to make regular payments to its creditors. Investors who purchase debt securities are primarily interested in interest income.

On the other hand, issuing equity does not give rise to a liability. Shareholders have a residual claim on the company's assets after all liabilities have been paid. Investors who purchase equity securities are interested in capital appreciation as well as dividend income and therefore focus on the long-term performance of the company.

A company may issue the following types of equity securities:

Common Shares

Investors in common shares have an ownership interest in the company. They share the operating performance of the company, participate in the governance process through voting rights, and have a residual claim on the company's net assets in case of liquidation.

Voting rights enable common shareholders to have their say in major corporate decisions, including the election of the board of directors, and whether to merge with or acquire another company. In elections for the board of directors, companies may use statutory voting, where each share represents one vote, or cumulative voting, where total voting rights are based on the number of shares owned multiplied by the number of board directors being elected. Shareholders may apply all of their votes to a single candidate or spread them across the candidates in any proportion. Cumulative voting provides better representation of minority shareholders on the board.

Companies may issue different classes of common shares, each with different ownership and voting rights. Further, these different classes of shares might be entitled to different claims on the company's net assets in case of liquidation.

Common shares may also be callable or putable.

- **Callable** common shares give the issuing company the right, but not the obligation, to buy back shares from investors at a later date at the call price (which is specified when the shares are originally issued). Companies are likely to buy back shares when their market price is higher than the call price. This is beneficial for the company as it is able to:
  - Buy shares at a lower price and resell them at the higher market price.
  - Save on dividend payments and preserve its capital.

Callable common shares are also beneficial for the investors as they get a guaranteed return on their investments when the shares are called.

- **Putable** common shares give investors the right, but not the obligation, to sell their shares back to the issuing company at the put price (which is specified when the shares are originally issued). Investors are likely to exercise this right when the market price of shares is lower than the put price. Putable common shares limit investor losses. As far as the company is concerned, they make it easier to raise capital, as the put feature makes the shares more appealing to investors.

Preference Shares

Preference shares (also known as preferred stock) have the following characteristics:

- They do not give holders the right to participate in the operating performance of the company and they do not carry voting rights unless explicitly allowed for at issuance.
- They receive dividends before ordinary shareholders. Further, preferred dividends are fixed and are usually higher than dividends on common shares. However, the company is still not contractually obligated to make regular payments to holders of preferred stock.
- In case of liquidation, they have a higher priority in claims on the company's net assets than common shares. However, they still have a lower priority than bondholders.
- They can be perpetual (i.e., have no fixed maturity date), can pay dividends indefinitely, and can be callable or putable.

Preference shares can be classified into the following categories:

- **Cumulative:** Unpaid dividends on cumulative preference shares accrue over time and must be paid in full before dividends on common shares can be paid.
- **Noncumulative:** Unpaid dividends for one or more periods are forfeited permanently and are not accrued over time to be paid at a later date.
- **Participating:** These are entitled to preferred dividends plus additional dividends if the company's profits exceed a pre-specified level. Further, investors in participating preferred shares might be entitled to an additional distribution of the company's assets upon liquidation above the par value of the preference shares. Participating preference shares are more common in smaller, riskier companies in which investors are concerned about the company's possible future liquidation.
- **Nonparticipating:** These are only entitled to a fixed preferred dividend and the par value of shares in the event of liquidation.
- **Convertible:** These are convertible into a specified number of common shares based on a conversion ratio that is determined at issuance. They have the following advantages:
    - They allow investors to earn a higher dividend than if they had invested in the company's common shares.
    - They offer investors the opportunity to share the profits of the company.
    - They allow investors to benefit from a rise in the price of common shares through the conversion option.
    - Their price is less volatile than the underlying common shares because their dividend payments are known and more stable.

  Convertible preference shares are becoming increasingly common in venture capital and private equity transactions.

LOS 47c: Distinguish between public and private equity securities.
Vol 5, pp 162–164

Equity securities can also be issued and traded in private equity markets. Such securities are issued primarily to institutional investors via nonpublic offerings, such as private placements, and have the following characteristics:

- There is no active secondary market for them as they are not listed on public exchanges. Therefore, they do not have market-determined quoted prices.
- They are highly illiquid, and require negotiations between investors in order to be traded.
- The issuing companies are not required by regulatory authorities to publish financial statements and other important information regarding the company, which makes it difficult to determine fair values.

Types of Private Equity Investments
- **Venture capital:** Venture capital funds invest in companies that are still in the early stages of development and require additional capital for expansion. These investments are usually made through limited partnerships, where managing partners actively participate in the management of the investee. These investments require a horizon of several years, as the securities are not traded publicly. Eventual exit is a very important consideration in such investments and available exit routes include buyouts and initial public offerings (IPOs).

- **Leveraged buyout (LBO):** An LBO occurs when a group of investors uses debt financing to purchase all of the outstanding common shares of a publicly traded company. The company is then taken "private" and its shares cease to be traded publicly. Typically, companies with undervalued assets and/or assets that can generate high levels of cash flow are subjects of LBOs. Companies that are bought out in this manner are usually restructured and later taken public again by issuing new shares to the public in the primary market.
- **Private investment in public equity (PIPEs):** Sometimes private investors may invest in a public company that is in need of additional capital quickly in return for a significant ownership position (typically at a discount to the publicly quoted market price). Companies may require funds quickly to avail significant investment opportunities or to deal with high levels of debt.

Advantages of Private Companies

- The longer investment horizons allow investors to focus on long-term value creation and to address any underlying operational issues facing the company. As a result, private equity firms are increasingly issuing convertible preference shares to attract investors with their greater total return potential. Publicly traded companies feel pressured to focus on short-term performance (e.g., to meet market expectations regarding earnings, growth, etc.).
- Certain costs that public companies must bear, such as those incurred to meet regulatory and stock exchange filing requirements, are avoided by private companies.

Advantages of Public Companies

- Public equity markets are much larger than private equity networks. Therefore, they provide more opportunities to companies for raising capital cheaply.
- Publicly traded companies are encouraged to be open about their policies, which ensures that they act in shareholder interest.

LOS 47d: Describe methods for investing in nondomestic equity securities. Vol 5, pp 164–169

Technological advancements have led to the growth and integration of global capital markets. The ability to exchange information quickly through electronic networks has helped both companies and investors in the following ways:

- Companies are able to issue shares in international markets, making it easier and cheaper for them to raise capital and to expand their shareholder base beyond their local markets.
- Investors are able to invest in companies that are located abroad, which has enabled them to diversify their portfolios.

Studies have shown that reduced barriers to foreign ownership have led to improved equity market performance over the long term. As a result, more and more countries are becoming increasingly open to foreign investment. The following trends have emerged over the past two decades:

- An increasing number of companies have issued shares in markets outside of their home country.
- The number of companies whose shares are traded in markets outside of their home country has increased.
- An increasing number of companies are dual-listed (i.e., their shares are simultaneously issued and traded in two or more markets).

Listing a company on an international exchange has the following benefits:

- It improves awareness about the company's products and services.
- It enhances the liquidity of the company's shares.
- It increases corporate transparency due to the additional market exposure and the need to meet a greater number of filing requirements.

Methods for Investing in Nondomestic Equity Securities

Direct Investing

The most obvious way to invest in equity securities of foreign companies is to buy and sell securities directly in foreign markets. However, direct investing has the following implications:

- All transactions are in the company's, not the investor's domestic currency. Therefore, investors are also exposed to exchange rate risk.
- Investors must be familiar with the trading, clearing, and settlement regulations and procedures of the foreign market.
- Investing directly may lead to less transparency (due to the unavailability of audited financial statements on a regular basis) and increased volatility (due to limited liquidity).

Depository Receipts

A depository receipt (DR) is a security that trades like an ordinary share on a local exchange and represents an economic interest in a foreign company. It is created when a foreign company deposits its shares with a bank (the depository) in the country on whose exchange the shares will trade. The bank then issues a specific number of receipts representing the deposited shares based on a pre-determined ratio. Hence, one DR might represent one share, a number of shares, or a fractional share of the underlying stock.

The structure of the DR causes its price to be affected by the same factors that influence the price of the underlying shares, such as company fundamentals, market conditions, analysts' expectations, and so on. However, there might be short-term differences in the prices of the DR and the underlying stock giving rise to quick arbitrage opportunities.

A DR can be sponsored or unsponsored.

- A sponsored DR is when the foreign company that deposits its shares with the depository has a direct involvement in the issuance of receipts. Investors in sponsored DRs have the same rights as those enjoyed by direct owners of the company's common shares.
- In an unsponsored DR, the foreign company that deposits its shares with the depository has no involvement in the issuance of receipts. Therefore, it is the depository, not the investors, that enjoys rights as a direct owner of the company's common shares.

There are two types of depository receipts:

- *Global Depository Receipts (GDRs)*: GDRs are issued by the depository bank outside of the company's home country and outside of the United States. Their main advantage is that they are not subject to foreign ownership and capital flow restrictions that may be imposed by the issuing company's home country, as they are sold outside of the home country.
- *American Depository Receipts (ADRs)*: ADRs are denominated in U. S. dollars and trade like a common share on U. S. exchanges. They are basically GDRs that can be publicly traded in the United States. There are four primary types of ADRs, whose characteristics are listed in Table 1-1.

Table 1-1 Types of ADRs[1]

	Level I (Unlisted)	Level II (Listed)	Level III (Listed)	Rule 144A (Unlisted)
Objectives	Develop and broaden U.S. investor base with existing shares	Develop and broaden U.S. investor base with existing shares	Develop and broaden U.S. investor base with existing/ new shares	Access qualified institutional buyers (QIBs)
Raising capital on U.S. markets?	No	No	Yes, through public offerings	Yes, through private placements to QIBs
SEC registration	Form F-6	Form F-6	Forms F-1 and F-6	None
Trading	Over the counter (OTC)	NYSE, Nasdaq, or AMEX	NYSE, Nasdaq, or AMEX	Private offerings, resales, and trading through automated linkages such as PORTAL
Listing fees	Low	High	High	Low
Size and earnings requirements	None	Yes	Yes	None

---

1 - Exhibit 16, Volume 5, CFA Program Curriculum 2019.

Global Registered Shares (GRS)

A GRS is an ordinary share that is quoted and traded in different currencies on different stock exchanges around the world. GRSs offer more flexibility than DRs as the shares represent actual ownership in the issuing company, they can be traded anywhere, and currency conversions are not required to trade them.

Basket of Listed Depository Receipts (BLDR)

This is an exchange-traded fund (ETF) that represents a portfolio of DRs. Like all other ETFs, it trades throughout the day and can be bought, sold, or sold short just like an individual share. Further, it can be purchased on margin and used in hedging and arbitrage strategies.

LOS 47e: Compare the risk and return characteristics of different types of equity securities. Vol 5, pp 169–171

Return Characteristics of Equity Securities

The two main sources of an equity security's total return are:

1. Capital gains from price appreciation.
2. Dividend income.

$$\text{Total Return, } R_t = (P_t - P_{t-1} + D_t)/P_{t-1}$$

where:
P_{t-1} = Purchase price at time t – 1
P_t = Selling price at time t
D_t = Dividends paid by the company during the period

The total return on nondividend paying stocks only consists of capital gains. Companies that are in the early stages of their life cycle generally do not pay any dividends, as they try to reinvest their profits to avail growth opportunities. On the other hand, companies that are in the mature stage may not have as many profitable growth opportunities to avail, so they distribute profits to investors in the form of dividends or through share repurchases.

Investors in depository receipts and foreign shares also incur foreign exchange gains (or losses). These arise due to changes in the exchange rate between the investor's domestic currency and the foreign currency over the investment horizon. Appreciation of the foreign currency (depreciation of the domestic currency) leads to foreign exchange gains, while depreciation of the foreign currency (appreciation of the domestic currency) leads to foreign exchange losses.

Another source of return arises from the compounding effects of reinvested dividends. Reinvested dividends are cash dividends that an investor uses to purchase additional shares in the company. Studies have shown that the compounding effects of reinvested dividends have significantly influenced long-run returns on equity securities.

Risks of Equity Securities

The risk of an equity security refers to the uncertainty associated with its expected future cash flows or expected total return.

- Preference shares are less risky than common shares because:
  - Dividends on preference shares are known and fixed, reducing the uncertainty about future cash flows.
  - Preferred shareholders receive dividends and other distributions before common shareholders.
  - The amount that preference shareholders stand to receive if the company is liquidated is known and fixed as the par (or face) value of the shares. However, there is no guarantee that investors will receive this amount.
- Common shares are more risky because:
  - A relatively large proportion of their total return comes from capital gains and future dividends, which are unknown.
  - The amount that they receive if the company is liquidated depends on what is left over after all creditors and preferred shareholders have been paid off.
- Putable common shares are less risky than callable or noncallable common shares.
  - The option to sell the shares back to the issuer at a pre-determined price establishes the minimum expected return and reduces the uncertainty associated with future cash flows.
- Callable common and preference shares are more risky than their noncallable counterparts.
  - The option held by the issuer to buy back the shares at a pre-determined price limits the investors' potential total return.
- Cumulative preference shares are less risky than noncumulative preference shares as they accrue unpaid dividends.

LOS 47f: Explain the role of equity securities in the financing of a company's assets. Vol 5, pp 171–172

LOS 47g: Distinguish between the market value and book value of equity securities. Vol 5, pg 176

Equity Securities and Company Value

A company may issue equity securities to raise capital, to acquire another company, provide stock option-based incentives to employees, acquire long-lived assets, invest in expansion projects, enter new markets, improve capital adequacy ratios, or to ensure that debt covenants are met.

The primary aim of management is to increase the book value and market value of the company. Book value (shareholders' equity on the company's balance sheet) is calculated as total assets less total liabilities. It reflects the historical operating and financing decisions made by the company. Management can directly influence book value (e.g., by retaining net income).

However, management can only indirectly influence a company's market value as it is primarily determined by investors' expectations about the amount, timing, and uncertainty of the company's future cash flows. A company may increase its book value by retaining net income, but it will only have a positive effect on the company's market value if investors expect the company to invest its retained earnings in profitable growth opportunities. If investors believe that the company has a significant number of cash flow generating investment opportunities coming through, the market value of the company's equity will exceed its book value.

A useful ratio to evaluate investor's expectations about a company is the price-to-book ratio (also known as the market-to-book) ratio.

- If a company has a price-to-book ratio that is greater than industry average, it suggests that investors believe that the company has more significant future growth opportunities than its industry peers.
- It may not be appropriate to compare price-to-book ratios of companies in different industries because the ratio also reflects investors' growth outlook for the industry itself. Companies in high growth industries (e.g., technology) will have a higher average price-to-book ratio than companies in mature industries (e.g., manufacturing heavy equipment).

An important measure used by investors to evaluate the effectiveness of management in increasing the company's book value is accounting return on equity.

LOS 47h: Compare a company's cost of equity, its (accounting) return on equity, and investors' required rates of return. Vol 5, pp 171–177

Accounting Return on Equity

The accounting return on equity (ROE) measures the rate of return earned by a company on its equity capital. It indicates how efficient a firm is in generating profits from every dollar of net assets. The ROE is computed as net income available to ordinary shareholders (after preference dividends have been paid) divided by the average total book value of equity.

$$ROE_t = \frac{NI_t}{\text{Average BVE}_t} = \frac{NI_t}{(BVE_t + BVE_{t-1})/2}$$

When using the ROE, analysts should bear in mind that net income and book value are directly affected by the management's choice of accounting methods (e.g., depreciation method and inventory cost flow assumption). These differences can make it difficult to compare the ROE across firms and to evaluate the ROE for the same firm over time (if accounting methods have changed).

> In companies where book values are relatively stable, the beginning book value may be used in the denominator instead of the average book value. It is more appropriate to use average values for companies that experience more volatile year-end book values.

An increase in ROE might not always be a positive sign for the company.

- The increase in ROE may be the result of net income decreasing at a slower rate than shareholders' equity. A declining net income is a source of concern for investors.
- The increase in ROE may be the result of debt issuance proceeds being used to repurchase shares. This would increase the company's financial leverage (risk).

Therefore, investors should examine the sources of change in ROE. This can be done through DuPont decomposition, which has been discussed in an earlier reading.

Book values and ROE do help analysts evaluate companies, but they cannot be used as the primary means to determine a company's intrinsic value. Intrinsic value refers to the present value of the company's expected future cash flows, and can only be estimated as it is impossible to accurately predict the amount and timing of a company's future cash flows. Astute investors aim to profit from differences between market prices and intrinsic values.

The Cost of Equity and Investors' Required Rates of Return

A company may raise capital by issuing debt or equity, both of which have associated costs.

- A company's cost of debt is easy to estimate, as it is reflected in the interest payments that the company is contractually obligated to make to debt holders.
- Estimating cost of equity is difficult because the company is not contractually obligated to make any payments to common shareholders.

Investors' minimum required rates of return refer to the return they require for providing funds to the company.

- For investors who provide debt capital to the company, their minimum required rate of return is the periodic interest rate they charge the company for using their funds. Further, all providers of debt capital receive the same interest rate. Therefore, the company's cost of debt and investors' minimum required rate of return on debt are the same.
- For investors who provide equity capital to the company, the future cash flows that they expect to receive are uncertain (in both timing and amount), so their minimum required rate of return must be estimated. Further, each investor may have different expectations regarding future cash flows. Therefore, the company's cost of equity may be different from investors' minimum required rate of return on equity.

You should think about the cost of equity as the minimum expected rate of return that a company must offer investors to purchase its shares in the primary market and to maintain its share price in the secondary market. If the required rate of return is not maintained, the price of the security in the secondary market will adjust to reflect the minimum rate of return required by investors.

- If investors require a higher return than the company's cost of equity, they will sell the company's shares and invest elsewhere, which would bring down the company's stock price. This decline in the stock price will lead to an increase in the company's cost of equity and bring it in line with the (higher) required rate of return.

Please note:

- The company's cost of equity can be estimated using the dividend discount model (DDM) and capital asset pricing model (CAPM), which are discussed in other readings.
- The costs of debt and equity are used to estimate a company's weighted average cost of capital (WACC), which represents the minimum required rate of return that the company must earn on its average investment. This measure is frequently used in capital budgeting process and has been discussed in an earlier reading in the Corporate Finance section.

READING 48: INTRODUCTION TO INDUSTRY AND COMPANY ANALYSIS

LESSON 1: INTRODUCTION TO INDUSTRY AND COMPANY ANALYSIS

LOS 48a: Explain uses of industry analysis and the relation of industry analysis to company analysis. Vol 5, pp 188–189

Industry analysis has the following uses:

To understand a company's business and business environment. This is used in fundamental analysis, stock selection, and valuation as it provides insights into a company's growth opportunities, competitive dynamics, business risks, and credit risk.

To identify active equity investment opportunities. An analysis of industry fundamentals helps an analyst in forecasting the industry's growth and profitability. Analysts then decide the weights of different industries in their portfolios. Studies have shown that the industry factor is at least as important as the country factor in predicting stock returns. Industry analysis is also very important for industry and sector rotation strategies.

To attribute portfolio performance. Portfolio managers are evaluated on the relative performance of their sector and industry allocations. Industry classification plays an important role in performance attribution.

LOS 48b: Compare methods by which companies can be grouped, current industry classification systems, and classify a company, given a description of its activities and the classification system. Vol 5, pp 189–197

Industry classification divides companies into groups that have similar attributes. There are three major approaches to industry classification.

Products and/or Services Supplied

This classification scheme groups companies that make similar products and/or services. Companies are placed in industries based on their principal business activity (i.e., the source from which the company derives most of its revenues and/or earnings). Industries that are related to each other are grouped together to form a sector.

Business-Cycle Sensitivities

This approach groups companies based on their relative sensitivity to business cycles.

A cyclical company is one whose performance is positively correlated with the performance of the overall economy. Cyclical companies perform very well when the economy is booming, but perform relatively poorly during recessions. Cyclical companies typically have high operating leverage, which may be accompanied by high financial risk. Examples of cyclical industries include autos, industrials, and technology.

A non-cyclical company is one whose performance is relatively independent of the business cycle. Demand for products made by non-cyclical companies remains relatively stable. Examples of non-cyclical industries include health care and utilities.

LOS 48c: Explain the factors that affect the sensitivity of a company to the business cycle and the uses and limitations of industry and company descriptors such as "growth," "defensive," and "cyclical." Vol 5, pp 189–197

Analysts also often classify industries as defensive or growth industries. Defensive or stable industries are those whose profits are least affected by fluctuations in overall economic activity. Growth industries are industries whose specific demand dynamics override economic factors in determining their performance. These industries generate growth irrespective of overall economic conditions, though their growth rates may decline in recessions.

Limitations of these classifications

- The classification of companies as cyclical or non-cyclical is somewhat arbitrary. Economic downturns affect all companies, so cyclical and non-cyclical industries are better understood on a relative basis.
- At a given point in time, different countries and regions may be undergoing different stages of the business cycle. Comparing companies in the same industry that are currently operating in very different economic conditions may help identify investment opportunities, but establishing industry benchmark values with the data would be misleading.

Statistical Similarities

Statistical approaches group companies on the basis of correlations of historical returns. For example, cluster analysis separates companies into groups such that companies within a group have a high correlation of returns, but correlations between groups are low. This approach has the following limitations:

- The composition of industry groups may vary significantly over time and across geographical regions.
- There is no guarantee that past correlations will continue to hold going forward.
- A relationship may arise by chance.
- A relationship that is actually economically significant may be excluded.

Industry Classification Systems

Industry classification systems help analysts in studying industry trends and valuing companies. They enable analysts to make global comparisons of companies in the same industry.

Commercial Industry Classification Systems

Major index providers around the world classify companies in their equity indices into industry groupings. These systems have multiple levels of classification. They include:

- *Global Industry Classification Standard (GICS)*, which classifies industries according to their principal business activity.
- *Russell Global Sectors (RGS)*, which classifies industries on the basis of goods and/or services produced.
- *Industry Classification Benchmark (ICB)*, which groups companies on the basis of primary revenue sources.

Table 1-1 lists the types of companies in each representative sector.

Table 1-1: Description of Representative Sectors

Broad Industry Classifications	Includes
Basic materials and processing	Companies that produce building materials Companies that produce chemicals Companies that produce paper and forest products Companies that produce containers and packaging Metal, mineral, and mining companies
Consumer discretionary (Demand for products and services offered by these companies exhibits a relatively high level of economic sensitivity)	Automotive, apparel, hotel, and restaurant businesses
Consumer staples (Demand for products and services offered by these companies exhibits a relatively low level of economic sensitivity)	Manufacturers of food, beverage, tobacco, and personal care products
Energy	Energy exploration, refining, and production companies Companies that supply equipment to energy companies
Financial services	Banking companies Insurance companies Real estate companies Asset management companies Brokerage companies
Health care	Manufacturers of pharmaceutical and biotech products Manufacturers of medical devices Manufacturers of health care equipment Manufacturers of medical supplies Providers of health care services
Industrial/producer durables	Manufacturers of heavy machinery and equipment Aerospace and defense companies Transportation services Commercial services and supplies

(continued)

Table 1-1 *(continued)*

Broad Industry Classifications	Includes
Technology	Companies involved in the manufacture and sale of computers, software, semiconductors, and communications equipment Internet services Electronic entertainment Technology consulting
Telecommunications	Companies that provide fixed-line and wireless communication services
Utilities	Electric, gas, and water utilities Telecommunication companies are also sometimes included in this category

Governmental Industry Classification Systems

Various government agencies organize statistical data according to the type of industrial or economic activity to facilitate comparisons over time and across countries that use the same system. Governmental industry classification systems include:

- *International Standard Industrial Classification of All Economic Activities (ISIC),* which classifies entities on the basis of their primary business activity. This system is currently being used by the UN and its specialized agencies, the International Monetary Fund, the World Bank, and other international bodies.
- *Statistical Classification of Economic Activities in the European Community (NACE),* which uses a basis similar to that of ISIC.
- *Australian and New Zealand Standard Industrial Classification (ANZSIC)*
- *North American Industry Classification System (NAICS)*

Strengths and Weaknesses of Current Systems

Commercial classification systems generally have an advantage over government systems for the following reasons:

- Most government systems do not disclose information about specific businesses or companies, so an analyst does not have access to the constituents of a particular category.
- Commercial classification systems are reviewed and updated more frequently than government classification systems.
- Government classification systems do not distinguish between small and large businesses, between for-profit and not-for-profit organizations, or between public and private companies. Commercial classification systems make distinctions between small and large companies automatically by virtue of the companies' association with a particular equity index. Further, commercial classification systems only include for-profit and publicly traded organizations.

LOS 48d: Explain how a company's industry classification can be used to identify a potential "peer group" for equity valuation. Vol 5, pp 198–202

The narrowest classification group assigned to a company by current classification systems generally cannot be assumed to be its peer group. A peer group is a group of companies engaged in similar business activities whose economics and valuations are influenced by closely related factors. Comparing a company to a well-defined peer group is very useful in evaluating company performance and in relative valuation.

Commercial classification systems do provide a starting point in the construction of a peer group, as they provide a list of companies operating in the same industry. Analysts can then filter this list to come up with a set of companies whose businesses are truly comparable with that of the company being studied.

Steps in constructing a preliminary list of peer companies
- Examine commercial classification systems to identify companies operating in the same industry.
- Review the subject company's annual report to identify any mention of competitors.
- Review competitors' annual reports to identify other potential comparable companies.
- Review industry trade publications to identify comparable companies.
- Confirm that comparable companies have primary business activities that are similar to those of the subject company.

Steps in constructing a preliminary list of peer companies
- What proportion of revenue and operating profit is derived from business activities similar to those of the subject company? Generally speaking, a higher percentage results in a more meaningful comparison.
- Does a potential peer company face a demand environment similar to that of the subject company? A comparison of growth rates, margins, and valuations may be of limited value when comparing companies that are exposed to different stages of the business cycle.
- Does a potential company have a finance subsidiary? Some companies operate a finance division to facilitate the sale of their products. To make a meaningful comparison of companies, the analyst should make adjustments to the financial statements to eliminate the impact of finance subsidiaries on relevant financial ratios.

Companies with limited lines of business may easily be classified into a single peer group. However, companies with multiple divisions may be included in more than one category. Analysts should look to ensure that comparable companies have primary business activities and performance drivers similar to those of the subject company.

LOS 48e: Describe the elements that need to be covered in a thorough industry analysis. Vol 5, pp 202–203

Investment managers and analysts examine an industry's performance in relation to other industries to identify industries with superior returns. They also evaluate industries over time to determine how consistent and stable their returns are.

Figure 1-1: A Framework for Industry Analysis[1]

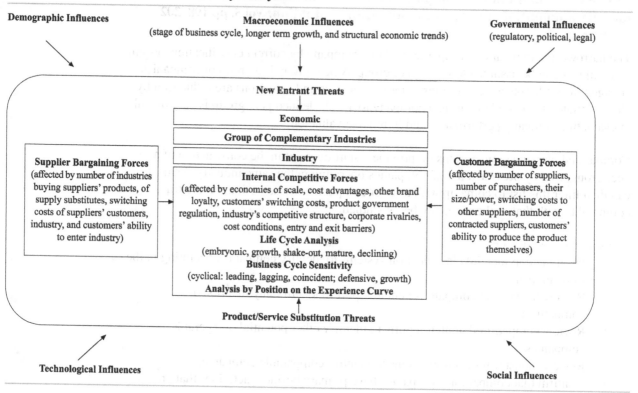

Figure 1-1 illustrates the macroeconomic, demographic, governmental, social, and technological factors that affect an industry at the macro level, and how an industry is affected by competitive forces, life-cycle issues, business-cycle considerations, and its position on the experience curve.

LOS 48f: Describe the principles of strategic analysis of an industry.
Vol 5, pp 204–206

When analyzing an industry, analysts need to understand the environment in which a company operates. Analysis of the industry with a view to examining the implications of the industrial environment on corporate strategy is known as **strategic analysis**.

Porter's Five Forces Framework

The starting point of strategic analysis is Michael Porter's "five forces" framework, which describes the following determinants of the intensity of competition in an industry.

1. Threat of substitute products: If customers find products to substitute for those produced by the company, demand for the company's products will decline.
2. Bargaining power of customers: This refers to the leverage enjoyed by customers in their dealings with the company. If the company has a small number of customers, they can be tough negotiators when it comes to determining prices.

3. Bargaining power of suppliers: This refers to the leverage enjoyed by suppliers in their dealings with the company. Suppliers of scarce or limited parts often have significant pricing power.
4. Threat of new entrants: This depends on the strength of barriers to entry into an industry. Low barriers to entry imply a higher degree of competition within an industry.
5. Intensity of rivalry: This is dependent on the industry's competitive structure. Industries that exhibit the following characteristics experience relatively more intense rivalries:
   - There are many small competitors.
   - Fixed costs are relatively high.
   - The companies produce similar products.
   - There are high exit barriers.

Note that the last two forces merit further investigation because almost all companies have competitors and must be wary of new entrants to their industries. When studying these forces, analysts should bear in mind that:

- Higher/stronger barriers to entry reduce competition.
- Greater concentration (where a small number of firms control a large part of the market) implies lower competition, while market fragmentation (where a large number of firms each have a relatively small share in the market) implies higher competition.
- Unused capacity in an industry, especially over an extended period, results in intense price competition.
- Stable market shares for industry firms imply less competition.
- Greater price sensitivity in customer purchasing decisions results in greater competition.
- More mature industries tend to exhibit slower growth.

LOS 48g: Explain the effects of barriers to entry, industry concentration, industry capacity, and market share stability on pricing power and price competition. Vol 5, pp 206–213

Barriers to Entry

Generally speaking:

- Low barriers to entry mean that new competitors can easily enter the industry, which makes the industry highly competitive. Companies in relatively competitive industries typically have little pricing power.
- High barriers to entry mean that existing companies are able to enjoy economic profits for a long period of time. These companies have greater pricing power.

However, bear in mind that these characteristics of high and low barrier industries are not always observed. For instance, companies might have little pricing power in industries with high barriers to entry because of fierce competition among existing companies (e.g., autos and aircraft manufacturing). Further, it is important to note that:

- Barriers to entry should not be confused with barriers to success. Entering some industries may be easy, but that does not necessarily mean that new entrants will be successful.
- Barriers to entry can change over time.

Industry Concentration

Generally speaking:

- If an industry is relatively concentrated (i.e., a few large firms dominate the industry), there is less price competition. This is because:
  - It is relatively easy for a few firms to coordinate their activities.
  - Larger firms have more to lose from destructive price behavior.
  - The fortunes of large firms are more tied to those of the industry as a whole, so they are more likely to be wary of the long-run impact of a price war on industry economics.
- If an industry is relatively fragmented (i.e., there is a large number of small firms in the industry), there is relatively high price competition. This is because of the following reasons:
  - Firms are unable to monitor their competitors' actions, which makes coordination difficult.
  - Each firm has only a small share of the market, so a small market share gain (through aggressive pricing) can make a large difference to each firm.
  - Each firm is small relative to the overall market so it tends to think of itself individualistically, rather than as a member of a larger group.

Bear in mind that there are important exceptions to the rules just defined. For example, Boeing and Airbus dominate the aircraft manufacturing industry, but competition between the two remains fierce.

Industry Capacity

Generally speaking:

- Limited capacity gives companies more pricing power as demand exceeds supply.
- Excess capacity results in weak pricing power as excess supply chases demand.

In evaluating the future competitive environment in an industry, analysts should examine current capacity levels as well as how capacity levels are expected to change in the future. Further, it is important to keep in mind that:

- If new capacity is physical (e.g., manufacturing facilities), it will take longer for the new capacity to come on line, so tight supply conditions may linger for an extended period. Usually however, once physical capacity is added, supply may overshoot, outstrip demand, and result in weak pricing power for an extended period.
- If new capacity requires financial and human capital, companies can respond to tight supply conditions fairly quickly.

Market Share Stability

Generally speaking:

- Stable market shares indicate less competitive industries.
- Unstable market shares often indicate highly competitive industries with little pricing power.

Market shares are affected by the following factors:

- Barriers to entry: Other things remaining the same, high barriers to entry prevent new firms from entering the industry, resulting in stable market shares of existing companies.

- New products: Other things remaining the same, frequent introductions of new products in the market lead to significant variation in market shares of existing firms. Market shares change quickly if switching costs are low and there is a relatively high benefit from switching.
- Product differentiation: Other things remaining the same, firms that are able to effectively differentiate their products from those of competitors are able to increase their share in the market.

LOS 48h: Describe industry life-cycle models, classify an industry as to life-cycle phase, and describe limitations of the life-cycle concept in forecasting industry performance. Vol 5, pp 213–218

Industry life-cycle analysis is an important part of strategic analysis of an industry. The sequential stages that an industry goes through are illustrated in Figure 1-2.

Figure 1-2: An Industry Life-Cycle Model[2]

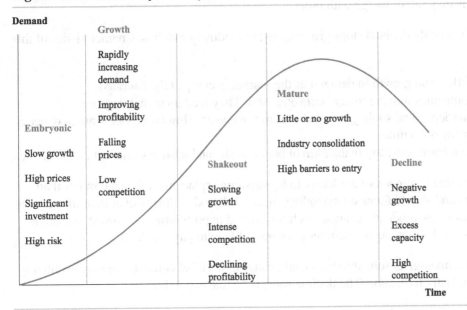

The different stages in an industry's life cycle are:

Embryonic: Industries in this stage are just beginning to develop. They are characterized by:

- Slow growth as customers are still unfamiliar with the product.
- High prices as volumes are too low to achieve significant economies of scale.
- Significant initial investment.
- High risk of failure.

Companies focus on raising product awareness and developing distribution channels during this stage.

Growth: Once the new product starts gaining acceptance in the market, the industry experiences rapid growth. The growth stage is characterized by:

- New customers entering the market, which increases demand.
- Improved profitability as sales grow rapidly.

---

2 - Exhibit 6, Volume 5, CFA Program Curriculum 2019.

- Lower prices as economies of scale are achieved.
- Relatively low competition among companies in the industry as the overall market size is growing rapidly. Firms do not need to wrestle market share away from competitors to grow.
- High threat of new competitors entering the market due to low barriers to entry.

During this stage, companies focus on building customer loyalty and reinvest heavily in the business.

Shakeout: The period of rapid growth is followed by a period of slower growth. The shakeout stage is characterized by:

- Slower demand growth as fewer new customers are left to enter the industry.
- Intense competition as growth becomes dependent on market share growth.
- Excess industry capacity, which leads to price reductions and declining profitability.

During this stage, companies focus on reducing their costs and building brand loyalty. Some firms may fail or merge with others.

Mature: Eventually demand stops growing and the industry matures. Characteristics of this stage are:

- Little or no growth in demand as the market is completely saturated.
- Companies moving toward consolidation. They recognize that they are interdependent so they stay away from price wars. However, price wars may occur during downturns.
- High barriers to entry in the form of brand loyalty and relatively efficient cost structures.

During this stage, companies are likely to be pursuing replacement demand rather than new buyers and should focus on extending successful product lines rather than introducing revolutionary new products. Companies have limited opportunities to reinvest and often have strong cash flows. As a result, they are more likely to pay dividends.

Decline: Technological substitution, social changes, or global competition may eventually cause an industry to decline. The decline stage is characterized by:

- Negative growth.
- Excess capacity due to diminishing demand.
- Price competition due to excess capacity.
- Weaker firms leaving the industry.

Limitations of Industry Life-Cycle Analysis

- The following factors may change the shape of the industry life cycle, cause some stages to be longer or shorter than expected, or even result in certain stages being skipped altogether.
    - Technological changes: An industry may go from growth to decline if a revolutionary product or distribution channel is introduced in the market.
    - Regulatory changes: Deregulation may suddenly increase competition in an industry.
    - Social changes: For example, the casual dining industry has prospered over the past few decades as a result of an increase in the number of dual-income families.
    - Demographics: For example, an aging population is likely to benefit the health care industry.

- Industry life-cycle analysis is most useful in analyzing industries during periods of relative stability. It is not as useful in analyzing industries experiencing rapid change.
- Not all companies in an industry display similar performance. For example, Nokia has consistently been able to earn above average returns in a fiercely competitive industry.

Price Competition

Generally speaking:

- Industries in which price is the most significant consideration in customers' purchase decisions tend to be highly competitive. A slight increase in price may cause customers to switch to substitute products if they are widely available.
- Price is not as important if companies in an industry are able to effectively differentiate their products in terms of quality and performance. Customers may not focus on price as much if product reliability is more important to them.

LOS 48i: Compare characteristics of representative industries from the various economic sectors. Vol 5, pp 219–221

For an industry comparison, see Table 1-2.

Table 1-2: Elements of a Strategic Analysis for Three Industries[3]

	Branded Pharmaceuticals	Oil Services	Confections/Candy
Major companies	Pfizer, Novartis, Merck, GlaxoSmithKline	Schlumberger, Baker Hughes, Halliburton	Cadbury, Hershey, Mars/Wrigley, Nestle
Barriers to entry/success	*Very High*: Substantial financial and intellectual capital required to compete effectively. A potential new entrant would need to create a sizable R&D operation, a global distribution network, and large-scale manufacturing capacity.	*Medium*: Technological expertise is required, but high level of innovation allows niche companies to enter the industry and compete in specific areas.	*Very High*: Low finance or technological hurdles, but new players would lack the established brands that drive consumer purchase decisions.
Impact of industry capacity	*NA*: Pharmaceutical pricing is primarily determined by patent protection and regulatory issues, including government approval of drugs and of manufacturing facilities. Manufacturing capacity is of little importance.	*Medium/High*: Demand can fluctuate quickly depending on commodity prices, and industry players often find themselves with too few (or too many) employees on the payroll.	*NA*: Pricing is driven primarily by brand strength. Manufacturing capacity has little effect.

(continued)

---

3 - Exhibit 7, Volume 5, CFA Program Curriculum 2019.

Table 1-2 *(continued)*

	Branded Pharmaceuticals	Oil Services	Confections/Candy
Level of concentration	*Concentrated*: A small number of companies control the bulk of the global markets for the branded drugs. The recent mergers have increased level of concentration.	*Fragmented*: Although only a small number of companies provide a full range of services, many smaller players compete effectively in specific areas. Service arms of national oil companies may control significant market share in their own countries, and some product lines are concentrated in the mature U.S. market.	*Very Concentrated*: Top four companies have a large proportion of global market share. Recent mergers have increased level of concentration.
Industry stability	*Stable*: The branded pharmaceutical market is dominated by major companies and consolidation via mega mergers. Market shares shift quickly, however, as new drugs are approved and gain acceptance or lose patent protection.	*Unstable*: Market shares may shift frequently depending on technology offerings and demand levels.	*Very Stable*: Market shares change glacially.
Life cycle	*Mature*: Overall demand does not change greatly from year to year.	*Mature*: Demand does not fluctuate with energy prices, but normalized revenue growth is only mid-single digits.	*Very Mature*: Growth is driven by population trends and pricing.
Price competition	*Low/Medium*: In the United States, price is a minimal factor because of consumer and provider driven, deregulated health care system. Price is a larger part of the decision process in single payer systems, where efficacy hurdles are higher.	*High*: Price is a major factor in purchaser decisions. Some companies have modest pricing power because of a wide range of services or best-in-class technology, but primary consumers (major oil companies) can usually substitute with in-house services if prices are too high. Also innovation tends to diffuse quickly throughout the industry.	*Low*: A lack of private level competition keeps pricing stable among established players, and brand/familiarity plays a much larger role in consumer purchase decisions than price.

Table 1-2 *(continued)*

	Branded Pharmaceuticals	Oil Services	Confections/Candy
Demographic influences	*Positive*: Populations of developed markets are aging, which slightly increases demand.	*NA*	*NA*
Government and regulatory influences	*Very High*: All drugs must be approved for sale by national safety regulators. Patent regimes may differ among countries. Also, health care is heavily regulated in most countries.	*Medium:* Regulatory framework can affect energy demand at the margin. Also, government plays an important role in allocating exploration opportunities to E&P companies, which can indirectly affect the amount of work flowing down to service companies.	*Low:* Industry is not regulated, but childhood obesity concerns in developed markets are a low-level potential threat. Also, high-growth emerging markets may block entry of established players into their markets, possibly limiting growth.
Social influences	*NA*	*NA*	*NA*
Technological influences	*Medium/High*: Biologic (large molecule) drugs are pushing new therapeutic boundaries, and many large pharmaceutical companies have a relatively small presence in biotech.	*Medium/High*: Industry is reasonably innovative, and players must reinvest in R&D to remain competitive. Temporary competitive advantages are possible via commercialization of new processes or exploitation of new accumulated expertise.	*Very Low*: Innovation does not play a major role in the industry.
Growth vs. Defensive vs. Cyclical	*Defensive*: Demand for most health care services does not fluctuate with the economic cycle, but demand is not strong enough to be considered "growth."	*Cyclical*: Demand is highly variable and depends on oil prices, exploration budget, and the economic cycle.	*Defensive*: Demand for candy and gum is extremely stable.

Note: "NA" in this table stands for "not applicable."

LOS 48j: Describe macroeconomic, technological, demographic, governmental, and social influences on industry growth, profitability, and risk. Vol 5, pp 221–228

Macroeconomic Influences

An industry's prospects are affected by overall economic activity. Gross domestic product (GDP), interest rates, availability of credit, and inflation all have an impact on the company's revenues, costs, and profits.

Technological Influences

Advancements in technology lead to new products being developed, which may replace older products. Further, these developments can sometimes change the way other industries that use these products conduct their operations.

Demographic Influences

Demography (population size, age distribution, and gender distribution) has important influences on economic growth and on the types of goods and services consumed. For example, an aging population has a negative effect on the economy as the size of the workforce declines. However, the health care industry benefits in the form of a larger customer base.

Governmental Influences

Government regulations have an impact on all sectors of the economy. Governments might exert their influence on an industry directly through taxes or subsidies, or indirectly by establishing regulatory bodies to govern the actions of an industry.

Social Influences

These influences refer to changes in how people work, spend their money, enjoy their leisure time, and conduct other aspects of their lives. Tobacco consumption has been on the decline as a result of increased social awareness regarding the harmful effects of smoking, and the perception that smoking in public is socially incorrect.

LOS 48k: Describe the elements that should be covered in a thorough company analysis. Vol 5, pp 228–232

Company analysis includes an analysis of the company's financial position, products and/or services, and competitive strategy. Porter identified two main competitive strategies:

Cost Leadership

Companies pursuing this strategy strive to cut down their costs to become the lowest-cost producers in an industry so that they can gain market share by charging lower prices. Pricing may be defensive (to protect market positions when competition is low) or aggressive (to increase market share when competition is intense).

Product/Service Differentiation

Companies pursuing this strategy strive to differentiate their products from those of competitors in terms of quality, type, or means of distribution. These companies are then able to charge a premium price for their products. This strategy is successful only if the price premium is greater than the cost of differentiation and the source of differentiation appeals to customers and is sustainable over time.

Elements That Should Be Considered in a Company Analysis

A thorough company analysis should:

- Provide an overview of the company.
- Explain relevant industry characteristics.
- Analyze the demand for the company's products and services.
- Analyze the supply of products and services, including an analysis of costs.
- Explain the company's pricing environment.
- Present and interpret relevant financial ratios, including comparisons over time and comparisons with competitors. See Exhibit 1-1.

Exhibit 1-1: A Checklist for Company Analysis[4]

Corporate Profile
- Identity of company's major products and services, current position in industry, and history
- Composition of sales
- Product life-cycle stages/experience curve effects
- Research and development activities
- Past and planned capital expenditures
- Board structure, composition, electoral system, anti-takeover provisions, and other corporate governance issues
- Management strengths, weaknesses, compensation, turnover, and corporate culture
- Benefits, retirement plans, and their influence on shareholder value
- Labor relations
- Insider ownership levels and changes
- Legal actions and the company's state of preparedness
- Other special strengths or weaknesses

(continued)

---

4 - Exhibit 8, Volume 5, CFA Program Curriculum 2019.

Exhibit 1-1 *(continued)*

Industry Characteristics
- Stage in its life-cycle
- Business-cycle sensitivity or economic characteristics
- Typical product life-cycles in the industry (short and marked by technological obsolescence or long, such as pharmaceuticals protected by patents)
- Brand loyalty, customer switching costs, and intensity of competition
- Entry and exit barriers
- Industry supplier considerations (concentration of sources, ability to switch suppliers or enter supplier's business)
- Number of companies in the business and whether it is, as determined by market shares, fragmented or concentrated
- Opportunity to differentiate product/service and related product/service, price, cost, and quality advantages/disadvantages
- Technologies used
- Government regulations
- State and history of labor relations
- Other industry problems/opportunities

Analysis of Demand for Products/Services
- Sources of demand
- Product differentiation
- Past records, sensitivities, and correlations with social, demographic, economic, and other variables
- Outlook—short, medium, and long term, including new product and business opportunities

Analysis of Supply of Products/Services
- Sources (concentration, competition, and substitutes)
- Industry capacity outlook—short, medium, and long term
- Company's capacity and cost structure
- Import/export considerations
- Proprietary products or trademarks

Analysis of Pricing
- Past relationships among demand, supply, and prices
- Significance of raw materials and labor costs and the outlook for their cost and availability
- Outlook for selling prices, demand, and profitability based on current and anticipated future trends

Exhibit 1-1 (*continued*)

Financial Ratios and Measures
(In multi-year spreadsheets with historical and forecast data)

- Activity Ratios, measuring how efficiently a company performs such functions as the collection of receivables and inventory management:
    - Days of sales outstanding (DSO)
    - Days of inventory on hand (DOH)
    - Days of payables outstanding (DPO)
- Liquidity Ratios, measuring a company's ability to meet its short-term obligations:
    - Current ratio
    - Quick ratio
    - Cash ratio
    - Cash conversion cycle (DOH + DSO − DPO)
- Solvency Ratios, measuring a company's ability to meet its obligations (in the following, "net debt" is the amount of interestbearing liabilities after subtracting cash and cash equivalents):
    - Net debt to EBITDA (earnings before interest, taxes, depreciation, and amortization)
    - Net debt to capital
    - Debt to assets
    - Debt to capital (at book and market values)
    - Financial leverage ratios (Average total assets/Average total equity)
    - Cash flow to debt
    - Interest coverage ratio
    - Off-balance sheet liabilities and contingent liabilities
    - Non-arm's-length financial dealings
- Profitability Ratios, measuring a company's ability to generate profitable sales from its resources (assets):
    - Gross profit margin
    - Operating profit margin
    - Pretax profit margin
    - Net profit margin
    - Return on investment capital or ROIC (Net operating profits after tax/ Average invested capital)
    - Return on assets or ROA (Net income/Average total assets)
    - Return on equity or ROE (Net income/Average total equity)

(continued)

Exhibit 1-1 *(continued)*

- Financial Statistics and Related Considerations, quantities, and facts about a company's finances that an analyst should understand:
  - Growth rate of net sales
  - Growth rate of profit
  - EBITDA
  - Net income
  - Operating cash flow
  - EPS
  - Operating cash flow per share
  - Operating cash flow in relation to maintenance and total capital expenditures
  - Expected rate of return on retained cash flow
  - Debt maturities and ability of company to refinance and/or repay debt
  - Dividend payout ratio (Common dividends/Net income available to common shareholders)
  - Off-balance-sheet liabilities and contingent liabilities
  - Non-arm's-length financial dealings

Spreadsheet Modeling

Spreadsheet modeling is an important tool available to analysts to evaluate the historical performance of companies and to forecast future performance. It is widely used to quantify the effects of changes in certain swing factors on the company's performance. However, such models can be quite complex and analysts should bear in mind that any conclusions drawn from the model are dependent on the assumptions that were made in developing it.

READING 49: EQUITY VALUATION: CONCEPTS AND BASIC TOOLS

LESSON 1: INTRODUCTION

LOS 49a: Evaluate whether a security, given its current market price and a value estimate, is overvalued, fairly valued, or undervalued by the market.
Vol 5, pp 244–246

The aim of equity analysis is to identify mispriced securities. Securities are mispriced or incorrectly priced by the market when their market prices are different from their intrinsic values. Intrinsic or fundamental value refers to a security's true value and is estimated by analysts using a variety of models/techniques.

- If the estimate for a security's intrinsic value is lower than the market price, the security is overvalued by market.
- If the estimate for a security's intrinsic value is greater than the market price, the security is undervalued by the market.
- If the estimate for a security's intrinsic value equals the market price, the security is fairly valued.

In practice however, the analysis is not so straightforward. There are several uncertainties regarding the intrinsic value estimate with respect to the appropriateness of the valuation method used and its underlying assumptions. The final conclusion also depends on the analyst's level of confidence in her estimate of intrinsic value. If she finds that her estimates of intrinsic value tend to fall short of market consensus and current market prices, she might want to revisit her valuation models and assumptions before acting on a conclusion of overvaluation.

LOS 49b: Describe major categories of equity valuation models.
Vol 5, pp 246–248

There are three major categories of equity valuation models:

- Present value models (also known as discounted cash flow models)
- Multiplier models
- Asset-based valuation models

Each of these categories is discussed in detail in the remaining LOS of this reading.

LESSON 2: PRESENT VALUE MODELS

LOS 49c: Explain the rationale for using present value models to value equity and describe the dividend discount and free-cash-flow-to-equity models. Vol 5, pp 248–250

LOS 49e: Calculate and interpret the intrinsic value of an equity security based on the Gordon (constant) growth dividend discount model or a two-stage dividend discount model, as appropriate. Vol 5, pp 256–261

LOS 49f: Identify characteristics of companies for which the constant growth or a multistage dividend discount model is appropriate. Vol 5, pp 261–264

LOS 49k: Explain advantages and disadvantages of each category of valuation model. Vol 5, pp 248–264

Present Value Models

Dividends: Background for the Dividend Discount Model

Generally speaking, there are two sources of return from investing in a stock: (1) cash dividends received during the holding period and (2) the change in the stock price over the holding period.

A **cash dividend** is a cash distribution made to a company's shareholders. Cash dividends are typically paid out regularly at known intervals, and these are known as **regular cash dividends**. In contrast, an **extra dividend** or a **special dividend** refers to a dividend payment by a company that does not usually pay dividends, or a dividend payment on top of the company's regular dividend. Companies in cyclical industries and companies undergoing corporate and/or financial restructuring are among those that usually pay extra dividends.

A company is not obliged to pay dividends. The company's board of directors must authorize the dividends, and in some jurisdictions they must also be approved by shareholders. Dividend discount models address discounting expected cash dividends.

A **stock dividend** or a **bonus issue** occurs when a company issues additional commons hares in the company (instead of cash) to shareholders. It basically divides the market value of shareholders' equity into smaller pieces without affecting (1) the total value of the pie or (2) shareholders' proportional ownership in the company. Thus, stock dividends are not relevant for valuation.

Stock splits and **reverse stock splits** are similar to stock dividends in that they have no economic effect on the company or shareholders. A stock results in an increase in the number of shares outstanding and a consequent decrease in share price. For example, if a company announces a three for one stock split, it means that each investor will get an additional two shares (to make a total of three) for each share originally held.

A reverse stock split increases the share price and reduces the number of shares outstanding. A reverse stock split involves a reduction in the number of shares outstanding with a corresponding increase in share price.

Share repurchases (unlike stock dividends and stock splits) are an alternative to cash dividends. A share repurchase occurs when a company buys back its own shares. Shares that are repurchased by the company are known as treasury shares and once repurchased are notconsidered for dividends, voting, or calculating earnings per share. All other things remaining the same, share repurchases can be viewed as equivalent to cash dividends in terms of their impact of shareholder wealth.

Arguments for Share Repurchases

- Share repurchasessend out a signal to the market that management believes that the company's stock is undervalued, or that management will support the stock price.
- They offer the company flexibility in its cash distributions. A share repurchase does not set the expectation of continued distributions in the future as cash dividends might.
- There is a tax advantage to distributing cash through repurchases in markets where capital gains are taxed at a lower rate than dividends.
- They can be used to limit the increase in the number of shares outstanding when a significant number of employee stock options have been exercised.

Dividend Payment Chronology

Declaration date is the date on which a company announces a particular dividend. The company also announces the holder of record date and the payment date on the declaration date.

Ex-dividend date or **ex-date** is the first day that the share trades without the dividend. Any investor who holds the stock on the ex-dividend date or who purchased it the day before the ex-dividend date is entitled to receive the dividend. On the ex-dividend date, the share price is adjusted for the amount of the dividend. For example, if a stock that has announced a $2 per share dividend closes at $100 on the trading day before the ex-dividend date, it will open at $98 on the ex-dividend date.

Holder-of-record date, also known as the **owner-of-record date, shareholder-of-record date, record date, date of record**, or **date of book closure**, is the date at which a shareholder listed in the company's records will be entitled to receive the upcoming dividend. The length of the period between the holder of record date and the ex-dividend date depends on the trade settlement cycle of the particular exchange.

Payment date or **payable date** is the date on which the company actually mails out or transfers the dividend payment to shareholders.

Investors save money (defer consumption) in return for future benefits. Similarly, they make investments because they expect a return over the investment horizon. The value of an investment therefore must equal the present value of its expected future cash flows. The simplest present value model for equity valuation is the dividend discount model (DDM):

The **dividend discount model (DDM)** values a share of common stock as the present value of its expected future cash flows (dividends).

$$\text{Value} = \frac{D_1}{(1+k_e)^1} + \frac{D_2}{(1+k_e)^2} + \ldots + \frac{D_\infty}{(1+k_e)^\infty}$$

$$\text{Value} = \sum_{t=1}^{n} \frac{D_t}{(1+k_e)^t}$$

Important:

- When an investor sells a share of common stock, the value that the purchaser will pay equals the present value of the future stream of cash flows (i.e., the remaining dividend stream). Therefore, the value of the stock at any point in time is still determined by its expected future dividends. When this value is discounted to the present, we are back at the original dividend discount model.

- If a company pays no dividends currently, it does not mean that its stock will be worthless. There is an expectation that after a certain period of time the firm will start making dividend payments. Currently, the company is reinvesting all its earnings in its business with the expectation that its earnings and dividends will be larger and will grow faster in the future. If the company does not make positive earnings going forward, there will still be an expectation of a liquidating dividend. The amount of this dividend will be discounted at the required rate of return to compute the stock's current price.

- The required rate of return on equity (k_e) is usually estimated using the capital asset pricing model (CAPM). Another approach for calculating the required return on equity simply adds a risk premium to the before-tax cost of debt of the company.

Examples of DDM in Valuing Common Stock

One-year holding period: If our holding period is just one year, the value that we will place on the stock today is the present value of the dividends that we will receive over the year plus the present value of the price that we expect to sell the stock for at the end of the holding period. See Example 2-1.

$$\text{Value} = \frac{\text{Dividend to be received}}{(1+k_e)^1} + \frac{\text{Year-end price}}{(1+k_e)^1}$$

Example 2-1: One Period DDM

An analyst gathered the following information about a company:

- Current dividend per share (D_0) of common stock = $4.00.
- Expected growth rate for the year (g) = 20%.
- Risk-free rate of return = 6%.
- Expected return on the market portfolio = 11%.
- Beta of the company's common stock = 1.2.

Given that the stock will sell for $15.40 at the end of the year and that it will make only one dividend payment over the holding period (at the end of the year), calculate the value of the company's common stock.

Solution:

The next dividend is calculated by multiplying the current dividend by 1 plus the projected growth rate.

$$D_1 = D_0(1+g)$$
$$= 4(1+0.2)$$
$$= \$4.80$$

The assumption here is that the stock only pays a dividend at the end of the year.

The required return on equity is estimated using the CAPM:

$$k_e = R_F + \beta(R_M - R_F)$$
$$= 0.06 + 1.2(0.11 - 0.06)$$
$$= 12.0\%$$

Finally, we compute the present value of the expected future dividend and the expected future selling price:

$$V = \frac{\$4.80}{(1+0.12)} + \frac{\$15.40}{(1+0.12)}$$
$$= \$4.29 + \$13.75$$
$$= \$18.04$$

The stock is worth $18.04 based on the analyst's expectations of dividend growth, beta, market risk premium, and future selling price. This may or may not be the price that the stock is currently trading at. If the price calculated by the analyst (intrinsic value) of the stock based on her assumptions is *greater* than the current market price, the analyst should *buy* the stock because she expects its return to be *higher* than the required return for the stock given its beta (systematic risk).

Multiple-Year Holding Period DDM

We apply the same discounting principles for valuing common stock over multiple holding periods. In order to estimate the intrinsic value of the stock, we first estimate the dividends that will be received every year that the stock is held and the price that the stock will sell for at the end of the holding period. Then we simply discount these expected cash flows at the cost of equity (required return). See Example 2-2.

$$V = \frac{D_1}{(1+k_e)^1} + \frac{D_2}{(1+k_e)^2} + \ldots + \frac{D_n + P_n}{(1+k_e)^n}$$

where:
P_n = Price at the end of n years.

If we assume that dividends are growing at a constant rate every year, then:

$$D_1 = D_0(1+g); \quad D_2 = D_0(1+g)^2 \text{ and } D_n = D_0(1+g)^n$$

Example 2-2: DDM for Multiple Holding Periods

Assume that a stock currently pays a dividend of $1.00, has an expected growth rate of 6%, and a required rate of return of 14.1%. Calculate the value of stock today if we expect to sell it for $15.30 in 2 years.

Solution:

$$PV(D_1) = \frac{\$1.06}{1.141} = \$0.93$$

$$PV(D_2) = \frac{\$1.06(1.06)}{(1.141)^2} = \$0.86$$

PV of expected dividends over the holding period = $0.93 + $0.86 = $1.79

PV of the expected future selling price at the end of holding period = $\frac{\$15.30}{(1.141)^2} = \$11.75$

Value of stock = $1.79 + $11.75 = $13.54

The value of the stock based on the investor's expectations equals $13.54.

Infinite Period DDM (Gordon Growth Model)

The infinite period dividend discount model assumes that a company will continue to pay dividends for an infinite number of periods. It also assumes that the dividend stream will grow at a constant rate (g_c) over the infinite period. In this case, the intrinsic value of the stock is calculated as:

$$PV_0 = \frac{D_0(1+g_c)^1}{(1+k_e)^1} + \frac{D_0(1+g_c)^2}{(1+k_e)^2} + \frac{D_0(1+g_c)^3}{(1+k_e)^3} + \ldots + \frac{D_0(1+g_c)^\infty}{(1+k_e)^\infty}$$

This equation simplifies to:

$$PV = \frac{D_0(1+g_c)^1}{(k_e - g_c)^1} = \frac{D_1}{k_e - g_c}$$

The long-term (constant) growth rate is usually calculated as:

$$g_c = RR \times ROE$$

The Gordon growth model is highly appropriate for valuing dividend-paying stocks that are relatively immune to the business cycle and are relatively mature (e.g., utilities). It is also useful for valuing companies that have historically been raising their dividend at a stable rate.

Applying the DDM is relatively difficult if the company is not currently paying out a dividend. A company may not pay out a dividend because:

- It has a lot of lucrative investment opportunities available and it wants to retain profits to reinvest them in the business.
- It does not have sufficient excess cash flow to pay out a dividend.

Even though the Gordon growth model can be used for valuing such companies, the forecasts used are generally quite uncertain. Therefore, analysts use one of the other valuation models to value such companies and may use the DDM model as a supplement. The DDM can be extended to numerous stages. See Example 2-3. For example:

- A three-stage DDM is used to value fairly young companies that are just entering the growth phase. Their development falls into three stages—growth (with very high growth rates), transition (with decent growth rates), and maturity (with a lower growth into perpetuity).
- A two-stage DDM can be used to value a company currently undergoing moderate growth, but whose growth rate is expected to improve (rise) to its long-term growth rate.

Example 2-3: Applying the Gordon Growth Model

An analyst obtained the following information regarding Global Transporters Inc.:

Current share price = $28
Recent dividend per share = $1.95
Earnings per share = $4.25
Return on equity = 25%
Required rate of return = 20%

1. Use the Gordon growth model to estimate Global's intrinsic value.
2. How much does the dividend growth assumption add to the intrinsic value estimate?
3. Based on the intrinsic value estimate, is the company's share undervalued, fairly valued, or overvalued?
4. Calculate the intrinsic value if the growth rate estimate is lowered to 12%.
5. Calculate the intrinsic value if the growth rate estimate is lowered to 12% and the required rate of return estimate is increased to 22%.

Solutions:

1. Dividend payout ratio = 1.95 / 4.25 = 45.88%

   Therefore, earnings retention rate = 100% − 45.88% = 54.12%

   Dividend growth rate = Retention rate × ROE = 0.5412 × 0.25 = 13.53%

   Intrinsic value = $\dfrac{1.95 \times (1 + 0.1353)}{(0.2 - 0.1353)}$ = $34.21

2. Effect of the dividend growth assumption = 34.21 − (1.95 / 0.2) = $24.46

3. Global's current market price ($28) is lower than its intrinsic value ($34.21). Therefore, its stock is undervalued.

4. Intrinsic value = $\dfrac{1.95 \times (1 + 0.12)}{(0.2 - 0.12)}$ = $27.30

5. Intrinsic value = $\dfrac{1.95 \times (1 + 0.12)}{(0.22 - 0.12)}$ = $21.84

> If the growth rate were zero, the stock would be valued as a perpetuity and its intrinsic value would equal:
>
> $1.95/0.2 = $9.75

The relation between k_e and g_c is critical:

- As the difference between k_e and g_c *increases,* the intrinsic value of the stock *falls.*
- As the difference *narrows,* the intrinsic value of the stock *rises.*
- Small changes in either k_e or g_c can cause *large* changes in the value of the stock.

For the infinite-period DDM model to work, the following assumptions must hold:

- Dividends grow at a rate, g_c, which is not expected to change.
- k_e must be greater than g_c; otherwise, the model breaks down because of the denominator being negative.

Notice that the DDM formula on the previous page can be rearranged to make the required return, k_e, the subject:

$$k_e = \frac{D_1}{PV_0} + g_c$$

This expression for the cost of equity tells us that the return on an equity investment has two components:

- The dividend yield (D_1/P_0).
- Growth over time (g_c).

Valuation of Common Stock with Temporary Supernormal Growth

Growth companies are firms that are able to earn returns on investment that are consistently above their required rates of return. In order to take advantage of such opportunities, these companies tend to retain a very high proportion of their earnings and reinvest them in the business. These high retention rates translate into high growth rates (recall that a firm's sustainable growth rate equals its retention rate times its ROE). The assumptions of the infinite-period DDM do not hold for these growth companies because:

- They do not have constant dividend growth rates. The growth rate of dividends can be impressively high, but only for a temporary period. Eventually, competition catches up with these firms and their growth rate slows down.
- During periods when they experience extremely high growth rates, their growth rate can exceed the cost of equity (k_e).

The correct valuation model to value such "supernormal growth" companies is the **multistage dividend discount model** that combines the multi-period and infinite-period dividend discount models.

$$\text{Value} = \frac{D_1}{(1+k_e)^1} + \frac{D_2}{(1+k_e)^2} + \ldots + \frac{D_n}{(1+k_e)^n} + \frac{P_n}{(1+k_e)^n}$$

where:

$$P_n = \frac{D_{n+1}}{k_e - g_c}$$

D_n = Last dividend of the supernormal growth period
D_{n+1} = First dividend of the constant growth period

The following steps must be followed to value stocks of companies that experience temporary supernormal growth:

- Estimate the amount and duration of dividends during the supernormal growth phase.
- Forecast the normal, constant growth rate in dividends (g_c) that will occur once the supernormal growth period ends.
- Project the first dividend after the commencement of normal growth.
- Calculate the price of the stock at the end of the supernormal growth period using the infinite-period DDM. The first dividend after commencement of normal growth will be the numerator.
- Determine the cost of equity, k_e.
- Calculate the present value of supernormal growth-period dividends and the terminal stock price (the stock price at the end of supernormal growth).

If a company has two or three stages of supernormal growth, we must calculate the dividend for each year during supernormal growth separately. Once the growth rate stabilizes below the required rate of return, we can compute the terminal value of the firm by using the constant growth DDM. This method should become clear after going through Example 2-4.

Example 2-4: Valuation with Temporary Supernormal Growth

A company is expected to experience dividend growth rate of 20% for the next 3 years, 15% for the subsequent 2 years, and a constant growth rate of 6% thereafter. The last dividend paid out by the company was $1.50 per share and its cost of equity is 12%. Calculate the value of the company's stock.

Solution:

First we calculate the dividends for each year during the supernormal growth phase:

$$D_1 = D_0 (1 + g_1)^1 = (1.50)(1.20)^1 = \$1.80$$
$$D_2 = D_0 (1 + g_1)^2 = (1.50)(1.20)^2 = \$2.16$$
$$D_3 = D_0 (1 + g_1)^3 = (1.50)(1.20)^3 = \$2.59$$
$$D_4 = D_3 (1 + g_2)^1 = (2.59)(1.15)^1 = \$2.98$$
$$D_5 = D_3 (1 + g_2)^2 = (2.59)(1.15)^2 = \$3.43$$

After Year 5, growth falls to a constant rate of 6%. The dividend for the 6TH year will be:

$$D_6 = 3.43(1.06) = \$3.63$$

We use D_6 to calculate the value of the stock as of the beginning of the constant, infinite-growth period (end of Year 5),

$$P_5 = \frac{D_6}{k_e - g_c} = \frac{\$3.63}{(0.12 - 0.06)} = \$60.56$$

This value (P_5) represents the present value of remaining (constant growth) dividends on the stock as of the end of Year 5. It is also called the terminal value of the stock.

Finally, we add the present values of the high growth-period dividends and the terminal value of the stock at end of Year 5 to determine the intrinsic value of the stock:

$$\text{Value} = \frac{1.80}{(1+0.12)} + \frac{2.16}{(1+0.12)^2} + \frac{2.59}{(1+0.12)^3} + \frac{2.98}{(1+0.12)^4} + \frac{3.43}{(1+0.12)^5} + \frac{60.56}{(1+0.12)^5}$$

$$\text{Value} = 1.61 + 1.72 + 1.84 + 1.89 + 1.95 + 34.36 = \$43.37$$

Another variant of the supernormal growth scenario is when a company does not pay out dividends in the high growth period because it chooses to reinvest all of its earnings in the business. The company then pays out a dividend at the beginning of the constant growth period, and maintains a stable dividend payout ratio thereafter. See Example 2-5.

Example 2-5: Delayed Dividend Payment

A firm is expected to have 3 years of extraordinary growth during which no dividends will be paid. Beginning in Year 4, earnings will stabilize and grow at sustainable 5% rate indefinitely, and the firm will pay out 45% of its earnings in dividends. Given that earnings in Year 4 (E_4) are expected to be $3.45 and the required return on equity is 10%, calculate value of this stock today.

Solution:

D_4 = (dividend payout ratio)(E_4) = $(0.45)(3.45)$ = $1.5525

$$P_3 = \frac{D_4}{k_e - g_c} = \frac{\$1.5525}{(0.10 - 0.05)} = \$31.05$$

The value of this stock today equals the present value of the terminal value (P_3), which equals $31.05/1.1^3 = $23.33

The Free-Cash-Flow-to-Equity (FCFE) Model

Many analysts assert that a company's dividend-paying capacity should be reflected in its cash flow estimates instead of estimated future dividends. FCFE is a measure of dividend paying capacity and can also be used to value companies that currently do not make any dividend payments. FCFE can be calculated as:

$$FCFE = CFO - FC\ Inv + Net\ borrowing$$

Analysts may calculate the intrinsic value of the company's stock by discounting their projections of future FCFE at the required rate of return on equity.

$$V_0 = \sum_{t=1}^{\infty} \frac{FCFE_t}{(1 + k_e)^t}$$

LOS 49d: Calculate the intrinsic value of a noncallable, non-convertible preferred stock. Vol 5, pp 254–256

When preferred stock is noncallable, nonconvertible, has no maturity date, and pays dividends at a fixed rate, the value of the preferred stock can be calculated using the perpetuity formula:

$$V_0 = \frac{D_0}{r}$$

For a noncallable, nonconvertible preferred stock with maturity at time, n, the value of the stock can be calculated using the following formula:

$$V_0 = \sum_{t=1}^{n} \frac{D_t}{(1+r)^t} + \frac{F}{(1+r)^n}$$

where:
V_0 = value of preferred stock today (t = 0)
D_t = expected dividend in year t, assumed to be paid at the end of the year
r = required rate of return on the stock
F = par value of preferred stock

Preferred shares may also be callable or putable:

- A callable preferred stock grants the issuer the right to call the stock at some point prior to maturity at a price determined at inception. Such call options tend to reduce the value of the issue for investors, as they favor the issuer.
- A putable preferred stock grants the holder the right to sell the stock back to the issuer at some point prior to maturity at a price determined at inception. Put options increase the value of the issue for investors as they favor the holder. See Example 2-6.

Example 2-6: Preferred Share Valuation: Two Cases

Aramis International issued perpetual preferred shares with a par value of $20 and pays an annual dividend of $3.65. Given a required rate of return of 8%, answer the following questions:

1. Calculate the intrinsic value of the shares if they are noncallable and nonconvertible.
2. Calculate the intrinsic value of the shares if they are retracted at par value after 3 years.

Solution:

1. Intrinsic value = Dividend / Required rate of return = 3.65 / 0.08 = $45.63
2. Retractable term preferred shares specify a retraction date, at which the preferred shareholders have the option to sell back the shares to the issuer at a predetermined price. The intrinsic value in such cases is calculated as follows:

Intrinsic value = $[(3.65 / 1.08) + (3.65 / 1.08^2) + (3.65 / 1.08^3) + (20 / 1.08^3)]$
= $25.28

LESSON 3: MULTIPLIER MODELS AND ASSET-BASED VALUATION

LOS 49g: Explain the rationale for using price multiples to value equity, how the price to earnings multiple relates to fundamentals, and the use of multiples based on comparables. Vol 5, pp 265–273

Price multiples are ratios that compare the price of a stock to some sort of value. Price multiples allow an analyst to evaluate the relative worth of a company's stock. Popular multiples used in relative valuation include price-to-earnings, price-to-sales, price-to-book, and price-to-cash-flow.

A common criticism of price multiples is that they do not consider the future in that their values are calculated from trailing or current values of the divisor. For example a company's price to earnings ratio may be calculated by dividing the current market price by the company's earnings per share (EPS) over the most recent four quarters. To counter this criticism, analysts make forecasts of fundamental values (e.g., earnings) into the future and use forward-looking or leading multiples. For example, the leading P/E ratio may be calculated as the current stock price divided by expected EPS over the next four quarters.

Multiples Based on Fundamentals

A price multiple may be related to fundamentals through a dividend discount model such as the Gordon growth model. The expressions developed in such an exercise are interpreted as the justified (or based on fundamental) values for a multiple. Let's use the Gordon growth model to derive an expression for the justified P/E multiple for a stock.

Gordon growth DDM:

$$P_0 = \frac{D_1}{r - g}$$

Divide both sides of the equation by next year's earnings forecast, E_1.

$$\frac{P_0}{E_1} = \frac{D_1 / E_1}{r - g}$$

D_1/E_1 is known as the dividend payout ratio. It equals the proportion of its earnings that a company pays out as dividends.

Analysis of justified forward P/Es:

- The P/E ratio is inversely related to the required rate of return.
- The P/E ratio is positively related to the growth rate.
- The P/E ratio appears to be positively related to the dividend payout ratio. However, this relationship may not always hold because a higher dividend payout ratio implies that the company's earnings retention ratio is lower. A lower earnings retention ratio translates into a lower growth rate. This is known as the "dividend displacement" of earnings.

Justified forward P/E estimates are very sensitive to small changes in the assumptions used to compute them. Since the growth rate is calculated as ROE times the retention ratio, any changes in the dividend payout ratio also has an impact on the growth rate. Analysts usually carry out sensitivity analysis to study the impact of different assumptions on the justified ratio. See Example 3-1.

Example 3-1: Justified P/Es

Assume that a stock has an expected payout ratio of 40% and a required return on equity of 10%. With an expected growth rate of dividends of 8%, calculate the stock's justified P/E multiple.

Solution:

$$\frac{P_0}{E_1} = \frac{D_1/E_1}{k_e - g_c} = \frac{0.40}{0.1 - 0.08} = 20$$

Multiples Based on Comparables

This method compares relative values estimated using multiples to determine whether an asset is undervalued, overvalued, or fairly valued. The benchmark multiple can be any of:

- A multiple of a closely matched individual stock.
- The average or median multiple of a peer group or the firm's industry.
- The average multiple derived from trend or time-series analysis.

Sometime analysts may face difficulties in finding a benchmark or "comparable" to evaluate a company's price multiple. For example, large companies have several different lines of business. Analysts should be careful to select only those companies that have similar size, product lines, and growth prospects to the company being valued as comparables.

LOS 49h: Calculate and interpret the following multiples: price to earnings, price to an estimate of operating cash flow, price to sales, and price to book value. Vol 5, pg 265

Price to Earnings Ratio

Advantages
- Earnings are key drivers of stock value.
- The ratio is simple to calculate and widely used in the industry.
- According to empirical research, differences in P/E ratios are significantly related to long-term stock returns.

Disadvantages
- Companies that make losses have negative EPS and P/Es. Negative P/E ratios are useless as far as relative valuation is concerned.
- Earnings of some companies are very volatile, which makes the task of determining a fundamental stock value very challenging.
- Management can use different accounting assumptions to prepare their financial statements. This reduces the comparability of P/E ratios across companies.

Price to Cash Flow

See Example 3-2.

Advantages
- Cash flows are less prone to management manipulation than earnings.
- Price to cash flow is more stable than the P/E ratio.
- Using the price to cash flow ratio gets around the problem related to differences in accounting methods used by companies.
- Differences in price to cash flow ratio over time are related to differences in long term average returns on stocks.

Disadvantages
- When "EPS plus noncash charges" is used as the definition for cash flow, noncash revenue and changes in working capital items are ignored.
- Free cash flow is more appropriate for valuing a company than cash flow. However FCFE has the following drawbacks:
  - For many businesses, it is more volatile than CF.
  - It is more frequently negative than CF.

$$\text{Price to cash flow ratio} = \frac{\text{Market price of share}}{\text{Cash flow per share}}$$

Example 3-2: Calculating P/CF

ABC Company reported net income of $2.3 million for the year 2008. It recorded noncash charges of $0.4 million for the year, and has 2 million shares outstanding. The market price of the company's stock is currently $40. Compute its price to cash flow ratio.

Solution:

Cash flow = $2,300,000 + $400,000 = $2,700,000
Cash flow per share = $2,700,000 / 2,000,000 = $1.35
Price to cash flow = $40 / $1.35 = 29.63

Price to Sales

Advantages
- Sales are less prone to manipulation by management than earnings and book values.
- Sales are positive even when EPS is negative.
- The P/S ratio is usually more stable than the P/E ratio.
- Price to sales is considered an appropriate measure for valuing mature, cyclical, and loss-making companies.
- Studies have shown that differences in price to sales ratios are related to differences in long-term average returns on stocks.

Disadvantages
- Using sales reveals no information about the operating profitability of a company. Ultimately, a company derives its value from its ability to generate profits.
- Using the P/S ratio does not reflect the differences in cost structure and operating efficiency between companies.
- Revenue recognition practices may allow management to distort revenue figures.

$$\text{Price to sales ratio} = \frac{\text{Market price per share}}{\text{Net sales per share}}$$

$$\text{Price to sales ratio} = \frac{\text{Market value of equity}}{\text{Total net sales}}$$

Net sales are calculated as gross sales less returns, customer discounts, and any dealer commissions. See Example 3-3.

Example 3-3: Calculating P/S

Krivya Chemicals reported net sales of $4,650,000 for the year ended 2008. It currently has 225,000 shares outstanding and its stock price is $14.35. Calculate Krivya's P/S ratio.

Solution

Sales per share = $4,650,000/225,000 = $20.67
Price to sales ratio = $14.35 / $20.67 = 0.69.

Price to Book Value

See Example 3-4.

Advantages
- Book value usually remains positive even when the company reports negative earnings.
- Book value is typically more stable over time compared to reported earnings.
- For financial sector companies that have significant holdings of liquid assets, P/BV is more meaningful, as book values reflect recent market values.
- P/BV is useful in valuing a company that is expected to go out of business.
- Studies suggest that differences in P/BV ratios over time are related to differences in long term average returns on stocks.

Disadvantages
- Book values ignore nonphysical assets such as the quality of a company's human capital and brand image.
- P/BV can lead to misleading valuations if significantly different levels of assets are being used by the companies being studied.
- Accounting differences can impair the comparability of P/BV ratios across companies. In most cases, book values of assets are based on historical cost adjusted for accumulated depreciation. However, over time, inflation and changes in technology may result in significant differences between accounting book values and actual values of a company's assets.

$$P/BV = \frac{\text{Current market price of share}}{\text{Book value per share}}$$

$$P/BV = \frac{\text{Market value of common shareholders' equity}}{\text{Book value of common shareholders' equity}}$$

where:
Book value of common shareholders' equity =
(Total assets − Total liabilities)− Preferred stock

Example 3-4: Calculating P/BV

The following table contains the equity portion of ADF Company's balance sheet:

	December 2006
Common stock (issued 20,000 common shares)	$200,000
Preferred stock (issued 1,000 preferred shares)	$25,000
Additional paid in capital	$1,000
Retained earnings	$43,875
Total shareholders' equity	$269,875

The current market price of ADF stock is $14.35. Calculate its P/BV ratio.

Solution:

Common shareholders' equity = Total shareholders' equity − Total value of equity claims that are senior to common stock

= $269,875 − $25,000 = $244,875

Book value per share = $244,875/20,000 = $12.24

P/B = $14.35/$12.24 = $1.17

LOS 49i: Describe enterprise value multiples and their use in estimating equity value. Vol 5, pp 274–276

Enterprise value (EV) is calculated as the market value of the company's common stock, plus the market value of outstanding preferred stock if any, plus market value of debt, less cash and short term investments (cash equivalents). It can be thought of as the cost of taking over a company.

<table>
<tr><td>EBITDA refers to earnings before interest, tax, depreciation, and amortization.</td></tr>
</table>

The most widely used EV multiple is the EV/EBITDA multiple. EBITDA is used as a proxy for operating cash flow, as it excludes noncash depreciation and amortization expenses. However, it may include other noncash expenses and revenues. The company pays out interest, dividends and taxes from its EBITDA. Therefore, EBITDA measures a company's income before payments to any providers of capital are made.

- The EV/EBITDA multiple is often used when comparing two companies with different capital structures.
- Loss-making companies usually have a positive EBITDA, which allows analysts to use the EV/EBITDA multiple to value them. The P/E ratio is meaningless (negative) for a loss-making company, as its earnings are negative.

Enterprise value may be difficult to calculate for companies whose debt is not publicly traded. Analysts may then use market prices of similar debt issues that are publicly traded as a proxy for the market value of the company's debt. Using book value as a proxy of market value will only provide a rough estimate, as book values do not incorporate changes in market interest rates and changes in the company's risk (as perceived by the market). See Example 3-5.

Example 3-5: EV/Operating Income

An analyst gathered the following information regarding five companies operating in the same industry:

Company	Enterprise Value ($)	Operating Income ($)
A	12,486,354	501,460
B	34,270,688	652,775
C	1,776,018	−306,210
D	6,688,225	210,985
E	3,206,250	427,500

1. Based on the information given, calculate each company's EV/OI.
2. Which company is the most undervalued?

Solution:

1. The following table shows the EV/OI for each company:

Company	Enterprise Value ($)	Operating Income ($)	EV/OI
A	12,486,354	501,460	24.9
B	34,270,688	652,775	52.5
C	1,776,018	−306,210	−5.8
D	6,688,225	210,985	31.7
E	3,206,250	427,500	7.5

2. Company E has the lowest positive EV/OI ratio and therefore is the most undervalued or favorably priced stock. Note the negative EV/OI ratio of Company C. Negative EV/OI ratios are difficult to interpret and so the analyst must use some other means to evaluate such companies.

LOS 49j: Describe asset-based valuation models and their use in estimating equity value. Vol 5, pp 276–280

Asset-based valuation uses market values of a company's assets and liabilities to determine the value of the company as a whole.

Asset-based valuation works well for:

- Companies that do not have a significant number of intangible or "off-the-book" assets, and have a higher proportion of current assets and liabilities.
- Private companies, especially if applied together with multiplier models.
- Financial companies, natural resource companies, and companies that are being liquidated.

Asset-based valuation may not be appropriate when:

- Market values of assets and liabilities cannot be easily determined.
- The company has a significant amount of intangible assets.
- Asset values are difficult to determine (e.g., n periods of very high inflation).
- Market values of assets and liabilities significantly differ from their carrying values.